THE PUSAN PERIMETER

THE PUSAN PERIMETER

Edwin P. Hoyt

STEIN AND DAY/*Publishers*/New York

The photographs in this book are reproduced courtesy of the United States Army Signal Corps and the United States Marine Corps. The following maps are courtesy of the U.S. Marine Corps: The Pusan Perimeter, August-September 1950; Brigade Action on Southwestern Front; and Second Naktong Counteroffensive. The following maps are courtesy of the U.S. Army: The North Korean Invasion; Delaying Action, 34th Infantry; Task Force Smith at Osan; Stages of North Korean Advance; The Fall of Taejon; The Front Moves South; The Pusan Perimeter, August 4, 1950; The North Korean Attacks in the East; The North Korean Attacks on Taegu; The North Korean Naktong Offensive, U.S. 25th Division Sector; and The North Korean Naktong Offensive, U.S. 2nd Division Sector. The map Combat Action Between Chinju and Masan, courtesy of the U.S. Army, comes from the 1970 revised edition of Russell Gugeler's *Combat Actions in Korea.*

FIRST STEIN AND DAY PAPERBACK EDITION
SEPTEMBER 1985
The Pusan Perimeter was originally published in hardcover
by Stein and Day/*Publishers*.
Copyright © 1984 by Edwin P. Hoyt
All rights reserved, Stein and Day, Incorporated
Designed by Louis A. Ditizio
Printed in the United States of America
STEIN AND DAY/*Publishers*
Scarborough House
Briarcliff Manor, N.Y. 10510
ISBN 0-8128-8200-8

**This book is for Diana,
and she knows why**

Contents

Illustrations

Maps

THE PUSAN
PERIMETER

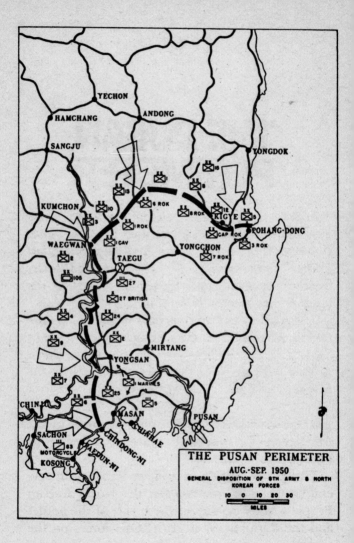

THE PUSAN PERIMETER
AUG.-SEP. 1950
GENERAL DISPOSITION OF 8TH ARMY & NORTH
KOREAN FORCES

10 0 10 20 30
MILES

1.

Surprise Attack

Sunday, June 25, 1950. Before dawn the troops were in the line and at a signal they began to move. It was raining heavily along the 38th parallel, but farther south they could expect to find better weather. At Seoul, their immediate objective, the weather was overcast but not rainy.

The artillery and mortars broke loose first on the Ongjin Peninsula on the west coast, northwest of Seoul. Less than an hour later infantry of the North Korean People's Army moved south across the border. The Korean War had begun.

THE ATTACK CAME as a complete surprise to the Americans who supposedly were the protectors of the Republic of Korea.

The spring of the year had been marked by several border conflicts between the North Korean People's Army on the northern side of the border and the Republic of Korea (ROK) forces on the south.

That spring some of the senior officers of the ROK forces had suggested that the North Koreans were gearing up for a real attack on South Korea. Such statements were always greeted by the American military advisers with cynicism because for years President Syngman Rhee had been asking for the creation of, and American financial support for, a powerful ROK Army. Rhee's pleas had become stronger when the Americans pulled their troops out of South Korea in 1949, and his constant complaints and predictions of disaster had fallen on deaf ears in Washington. Dr. Rhee was a dedicated enemy of communism, and the purveyors of conventional wisdom in Washington suggested that if South Korea were to be given a large army, Dr. Rhee would march north and perhaps start World War III. So Dr. Rhee was denied his large army. As of June 1950, the South Korean military force consisted of an Army of 94,000 men; a Coast Guard of 6,100; an Air Force of 1,800; and a National Police Force of 45,000. Of the Army, about 50,000 of the 65,000 combat troops were equipped with the modern American M-1 rifle. Their field guns consisted of 105mm howitzers and 37mm antitank guns. Only eighty-nine serviceable 105mm howitzers were on hand. The South Korean Army had no tanks, no small (41mm) mortars, no recoilless rifles. Many of the ROK Army troops were still equipped with the rifles surrendered by the Japanese at the end of World War II.

The ROK Air Force had no fighters and no

bombers. Its total air strength was sixty planes, all trainers and L-4 and L-5 liaison planes, based at Kimpo and Seoul airfields. The American military advisory group had been allocated ten old P-51 fighters, but no South Korean pilots had yet been trained to fly them.

The South Korean Navy consisted of a fairly modern 173-foot patrol boat purchased from the United States, three more patrol boats that were just then en route from Hawaii, an LST, fifteen surplus U.S. minesweepers, ten old minelayers surrendered by the Japanese, and a handful of launches and small craft suitable for nothing more vigorous than harbor patrol.

Now, on this fateful day, the ROK forces faced a North Korean military machine that consisted of 89,000 combat troops plus a constabulary and reserve that matched the South Korean National Police Force in strength and completely over-matched that force in training and capability. The North Korean People's Army had 150 Soviet T-34 tanks mounting 85mm guns, against which the South Korean 37mm antitank guns would be virtu-ally useless. The North Koreans had 122mm guns, plus 76mm self-propelled guns and 76mm guns that outmatched the 105mm howitzers of the South Koreans in range and firepower. The North Korean artillery exceeded the South Korean by three to one.

The North Korean Air Force consisted of 132 combat aircraft: 62 Ilyushin Il-10 ground support fighters; and 70 Yak-3, Yak-7B, Yak-9, and La-7 jet fighters. The North Koreans also had 22 Yak-18 twin-engined transports and eight Polikarpov Po-2 training planes. The pilots were well trained in combat techniques by Soviet flier veterans of World War II.

Only in naval strength were the South Koreans on fairly equal ground with the North Koreans. The North Korean striking force was built around a number of 60-foot aluminum torpedo boats they had secured from the Soviets. The North Korean naval crews were well trained by the Soviet Navy. Most of the rest of the North Korean craft consisted of supply ships, a few transports, and small craft. The North Korean leaders were planning a land war and gave little consideration to naval matters.

TO SAY THAT the attack came as a complete surprise is not quite correct. To put it a little differently, there was no reason why it should have come as a surprise. ROK Army intelligence had advance knowledge of a North Korean buildup along the border. But this had occurred before, and the result had been maneuvers and a border skirmish or two— no more than that. Early in June, when ROK officers had told members of the United Nations Commission on Korea that the North Koreans were planning to attack very soon, the U.N. officials had gotten the wind up enough to pose some sharp questions to U.S. Brigadier General William L. Roberts, whose small Korean Military Advisory Group was all that remained of American military power on the Korean peninsula. General Roberts' staff assured the U.N. officials that this sort of talk had been heard many times before. There had been attacks. They had been repelled by the South Korean forces. The ROK Army was quite capable of handling anything that came along, said the American advisers. Indeed, recently the problem had been to hold the South Koreans back. It was well known that President Rhee would like nothing better than to have a force strong enough to march north and "unify" Korea by overthrowing the North Korean government. Officials at the U.S. Embassy had been reporting for months that the South Koreans were as responsible for the border incidents as were the Northerners.

There also had been some problems of a different kind. A year earlier a battalion of South Korean troops had been led by their officers across the border to surrender and join the enemy. Many of those troops had not liked the idea and had come back, but from then on the loyalty of the Army could no longer be unquestioned. But matters had been improving.

There was no reason, said the American advisers, to believe that the situation that June was any different than it had been three months earlier.

THE FACT WAS, however, that the situation was very different. If the U.S. Department of State or even the American press in Moscow had been on its toes,

Washington would have known that fact on June 10.

On that day *Izvestia*, one of the most important Soviet newspapers, published a manifesto issued two days earlier in the North Korean capital, Pyongyang, which in effect declared war on South Korea.

On June 7, said the newspaper report, the Central Committee of the United Democratic Patriotic Front had announced that in August a Parliament would be elected from North and South Korea and that it would meet in Seoul on August 15, the fifth anniversary of the Japanese surrender to the Allies.

There was no way that such an election could be held under the political conditions that prevailed as of early June 1950. Korea had been divided by the Allies at the Yalta conference of 1945, with the Soviets given control of the area north of the 38th parallel and the Americans control of the area south. Theoretically, the two big powers were supposed to bring forth a united democratic government of Korea, and the Americans seem to have duped themselves at the time of Yalta into believing that was possible. But all that had happened since had made it impossible. The Soviets had immediately installed a Soviet-style "Democratic People's Republic" in North Korea. The Americans had maintained a military government far longer but had finally yielded to South Korean political pressure and arranged elections in the South, out of which old Korean patriot Dr. Syngman Rhee had emerged as the most powerful figure. Since that time the two Koreas had developed along the lines of their mentor nations, and unity was farther away than it had ever been. Certainly if the North Korean Patriotic Front was talking about national elections, everyone knew that that condition could only be met by conquest.

Two days after a National Front call to the South was rejected flatly by the Rhee government, the North Koreans were ready to move. Obviously the plan had been laid and perfected over many weeks, for on June 9 National Security Minister Choe Yong-gon, and General Kang Gon, chief of staff of the North Korean People's Army, called all the senior commanders of the Army to a meeting at the National Security Department.

The internal security was superb; not a single hint of this vital meeting got out to the South. Even the commanders were told only that they were now to engage in a "task force operation," as opposed to the divisional war games played in the past. This coming exercise would be a complete test of the readiness of the Army.

"This exercise may take a little longer than in the past," said Major General Kim Hwang-hyop, chief of operations of the general staff. "But I am sure two weeks will be more than enough to finish it up. No need for any one of you to carry heavy loads, and you have only to prepare a bag to carry maps or documents during the period of the exercise."

There was something about these orders that seemed odd and aroused the curiosity of many senior officers. The clue was next: So secret were these operations that the officers were not even to tell their wives.

There could be only one reason for such secrecy in the Korea of 1950. So the senior staff officers, without being told, were effectively notified that they were on their way south and that the high command anticipated virtually no difficulty in taking over the whole country.

Had the Americans been watching, they would have known of the rejection of the North Korean ploy by South Korea and of the casual little report in *Izvestia* two days later.

BUT AS THE Soviets and the North Koreans anticipated, the Americans were not looking. They had not been looking for three years. The Americans had no diplomatic relations with North Korea, and the American armed forces had virtually no intelligence about activity in North Korea.

Virtually no one in the American military and political establishments in Washington expected an attack on Korea, although, in fact, more than four months earlier Secretary of State Dean Acheson had virtually invited just such an attack in a speech to the National Press Club of Washington. In that address he declared that Korea was not inside the zone of primary American national security concern. In other words, the secretary had indicated that if Korea was attacked, Korea would be allowed to fall. The 1949 withdrawal of the American troops had underlined the American position, and that position had not since been changed significantly by President Harry Truman.

FROM THE VANTAGE point of more than thirty years, it may seem hard to believe that the United States, the most powerful nation in the world at that time, could have been so easily gulled into dismantling its military superiority. But that is the way of the American republic and always has been.

In effect, the military situation of the United States in June 1950 was uncomfortably close to the situation that existed on December 6, 1941. Militarily and psychologically, the Americans were totally unprepared for an attack in the Far East. The military capability of the United States had been deteriorating steadily since 1945, and for the same reason that the Americans had demobilized their military forces in 1919. That year they declared that they had won "the war to end all wars" and had "preserved the world for democracy." In 1945 the same cries were heard as soon as the Japanese surrender was official. World War II had been won. "Bring the boys home" said mothers, fathers, lovers, and the press. Congress responded, and before the end of 1945 the U.S. military machine was being disassembled.

After 1945, it took three years for the Americans to learn that the Soviets did not regard the world in the same way that the Western powers did. The end of the German and Japanese wars were to the Soviet state merely pauses in the international struggle for "socialist" power.

By 1950 the American military machine was prepared (theoretically) for a war in Europe if one should break out. Actually, the American readiness to meet any sort of attack anywhere was debatable. The U.S. Army had been cut down to ten combat divisions, all but one of them understrength. The U.S. Marine Corps had only two divisions, both of them understrength. The Navy had suffered most of all from congressional cutbacks.

On paper, the U.S. Far Eastern Command looked strong enough. It consisted of the Army 7th, 24th, 25th, and dismounted 1st Cavalry divisions. This force was called the U.S. Eighth Army, under the command of Lieutenant General Walton H. Walker.

In fact, all those divisions were understrength: two battalions to a regiment instead of three. Most of the troops were raw and insufficiently trained to engage in combat, and they were underarmed.

General George E. Stratemeyer commanded a total of 1,200 planes in the Far East Air Forces, but these were scattered from Honolulu to Tokyo, with the mission of defending the Philippines, Okinawa, Guam, Japan, and preventing the invasion of Taiwan.

Vice Admiral Turner C. Joy, commander of U.S. Naval Forces in the Far East, had available a small task force. Built around the light cruiser *Juneau*, it included a handful of destroyers and minesweepers, and a very small amphibious force, whose major enterprise was training. This force, too, was scattered halfway across the Pacific. So it was obvious that the United States was anything but ready for an attack in the Far East.

One reason for this was the bitter struggle for influence and power that had occupied the U.S. armed forces for three years. The new Air Force wanted to control everything that flew, and its managers and sycophants insisted that air power controlled the world, that a navy was hardly necessary anymore, and that an army was of only limited use. The interservice battle had come close to sinking the U.S. Navy, but it hadn't helped the Air Force or the Army much either, since Congress cut military appropriations to the bone.

Despite the fact that General Douglas MacArthur required a military machine to control Japan, the strength of the U.S. Army, Navy, and Air Force had been sapped to the point of impotence. All that saved the naval force was the U.S. national preoccupation with the safety of Chiang Kai-Shek's Nationalist forces, who had fled to Taiwan after being defeated by the Communist Chinese on the mainland. For that reason, a sort of fleet was maintained on watch in the Pacific.

ON THAT MORNING of June 25, the North Korean invasion force moved fast. The South Korean defenders along the border were totally unprepared. Theoretically four ROK divisions and one independent regiment were stationed along the border, but in fact only one regiment of each division and only one battalion of the independent regiment were in place along the 38th parallel. The rest of the troops were in reserve camps as far as thirty miles behind the border. So psychologically unprepared were the ROK forces that many of the senior officers were in Seoul on leave. So were many of the American advisers.

The North Koreans moved precisely: The attack began on the west coast, and each unit took its cue from the one to its right. The guns opened up, and by a few minutes after 4:00 A.M. they were firing along the parallel from the western to the eastern shore.

The ROK 7th division at Uijongbu and the 6th Division at Chunchon reported before 5:00 A.M. to ROK Army headquarters in Seoul that the attack was under way. But no senior officers were on duty at Army headquarters at 5:00 A.M. on that Sunday. Nor was there a defense plan that could be put into motion automatically. The high command had been studying four different defense plans and had not yet settled on any of them.

So no help could be expected from the disorganized Army headquarters in Seoul.

It was 6:00 A.M. before the first word of the assault reached the American embassy and the Military Advisory Group at Seoul. It came from five American advisers on duty with the ROK 17th Regiment on the Ongjin Peninsula, the first point of attack.

They reported that in less than two hours the North Koreans had advanced upon them and threatened to overwhelm the division.

Two hours later they sent another frantic message, requesting their evacuation. Two aviators of the advisory group, Major Lloyd Swink and Lieutenant Frank Brown, flew their L-5 liaison planes up to the peninsula and brought out the five American advisers in one trip.

Before the day's end, the regiment had been forced to the end of the Ongjin Peninsula. The next morning most of two battalions and regimental commander Colonel Paik In-yup were evacuated by vessels of the ROK Navy. The third battalion was completely wiped out.

THE SECOND POINT of North Korean attack was the ancient city of Kaesong, once the Korean capital. It lies two miles south of the 38th parallel, on the Seoul-Pyongyang highway, and it was defended by two battalions of the ROK 12th Regiment stationed just north of the city. Colonel Paik Sun-yup, commander of the ROK 1st Division, had decided (with his American advisers) that the only real defense of the area could be made on high ground south of the town and the Imjin River. Most of his troops were concentrated there.

At five o'clock on that Sunday morning, U.S. Army Captain Joseph R. Darrigo was sound asleep in his comfortable house on the northern edge of Kaesong. Darrigo was the assistant adviser to the

ROK 12th Regiment, and he was the only adviser on hand. The others were all down in Seoul on leave. Actually, as the sequence of events indicated, it would have made no difference if every American adviser in Korea had been on the parallel that day. The disorganization of the South Korean forces was so complete that nothing would have helped.

Captain Darrigo was awakened by the sound of artillery fire, soon followed by the rattle of small-arms fire hitting his house. He jumped out of bed, got into his trousers, grabbed his shoes and shirt, and went downstairs. Darrigo and his Korean houseboy got into the captain's jeep and sped to the center of town. There they saw the effects of North Korean planning. From the traffic circle in the center of town, Darrigo could see the railroad station half a mile to the west. There a fifteen-car North Korean train had just pulled in, and North Korean soldiers were unloading and forming up into units. Darrigo estimated that a whole regiment had ridden right into the center of Kaesong without a bit of difficulty. He turned around the traffic circle, took the southern road toward the Imjin River, and crossed over at Musan-ni, where Colonel Paik had placed most of the 1st Division.

By 9:30 A.M. that day, Kaesong had fallen and so had most of the ROK 12th Regiment. The next day two companies of survivors straggled into division headquarters.

THE MAIN NORTH Korean attack was launched down

the Uijongbu corridor, which leads from the north straight down, twenty miles to Seoul, over flat paddy fields. The North Korean troops took two roads south to Uijongbu led by about eighty T-34 tanks, against which the ROK troops had virtually no defense.

At first, some of the South Korean troops took a leaf from Japanese kamikaze tactics: They volunteered to hurl themselves under the tanks with satchel charges of explosives. Some others tried to approach the tanks with charges on sticks. Others tried to lob grenades through the tank openings. But so few tanks were damaged and so many ROK soldiers killed that the number of volunteers quickly dwindled. The tanks rolled south.

Before that first Sunday ended, the people of Seoul could hear the sounds of artillery as the columns converged on the town of Uijongbu.

TO THE EAST, the North Korean Army moved on Ch'unch'on, a railroad center on the Pukhan River and very near the 38th parallel. It is the gateway to the South through the mountainous country of east-central Korea. This city was guarded by the ROK 7th Regiment from mountain positions above the city. Also, the regiment's commander, almost alone among senior ROK Army officers, seemed to have an inkling of danger, for he had not issued any weekend passes to his troops or officers.

Two regiments of North Koreans attacked, but without tanks. Here the ROK artillery and infantry put up a stout defense. The 6th Division commander sent reinforcements from Wonju, forty-five miles to the south, and the North Korean advance was stalled. This was the first serious opposition they had encountered. By the end of the day, they were supposed to have captured the city but they had to change plans and divert troops from a point farther east.

THE LAST NORTH Korean column was awaiting the attack hour on the east coast, across the Taebaek mountain range from Inje. They came in junks and sampans and put ashore near Samch'ok, where they were driven off by artillery, and near Kangnung, where they landed successfully. Their mission was to drive south along the mountainous eastern part of Korea.

Immediately, the American advisers and ROK commanders made plans to withdraw the troops in this area toward Pusan by way of Tanyang Pass. The American advisers prepared to move out to Wonju to connect with the 6th Division headquarters west of the mountains.

The North Koreans also sent a one-thousand-ton armed steamer south, loaded with six hundred troops who were to attack Pusan and cut off that lifeline to Japan. The steamer was moving toward its objective when out of Pusan Harbor came the single modern ship of the South Korean Navy, *PC 701*, under Commander Nam Choi-yong. The patrol boat discovered the steamer, challenged and then attacked, and after a running fight sank the ship. The six hundred North Korean soldiers were lost, and thus was saved the port of Pusan, whose capture would have meant the loss of the single port of entry available for movement of supplies and reinforcements to South Korea. By that narrow a margin, on the first day, was South Korea saved. It was the most important naval action of the whole Korean War.

2.

The American Confusion

AS THE NORTH Korean tanks rumbled southward along the South Korean highways, the North Korean high command was jubilant. The attack was going just as they had expected. Only in one spot, Ch'unch'on, was there any real opposition on this first day. They had control of the military situation on land, and they had control of the air, as became apparent at three o'clock that afternoon. Then a pair of Yak-9 fighters raced across the Kimpo airfield near Seoul and sprayed the area with machine-gun and cannon fire. They destroyed the airfield control tower, blew up a gasoline dump, and damaged an American C-54 transport plane. Shortly afterward four more Yaks flew over Seoul Airfield, damaging seven of the ROK Air Force's tiny fleet of training planes. And later in the day another group of Yaks attacked Kimpo again, this time destroying that C-54.

THE NORTH KOREAN INVASION
25-28 June 1950

There was no response from the South Korean Air Force. It had no fighter planes. For months President Rhee had been asking the Americans to speed the training and turn over to his Air Force those previously promised P-51 Mustang fighters. Now, at last, the Americans listened to him. At least they would as soon as they got organized enough to do anything.

THE NORTH KOREAN invasion was nearly four hours old before anyone on the U.S. side outside Korea learned of it. The first report was received at Far Eastern Air Force headquarters in Japan shortly before 10:00 A.M. The news was flashed then to the Fifth, Thirteenth, and Twentieth air forces, all of which had a stake in the Pacific. But Lieutenant General George E. Stratemeyer, commander of the Far Eastern Air Forces, was in the air between San Francisco and Hawaii, on his way back from meetings in Washington. Major General Earl Partridge, his deputy commander, was spending the weekend in Nagoya and could not be found for two hours. When he was found, what could he do?

Partridge was in charge of the most powerful—and only—American military striking force in the North Pacific. But his only franchise was to carry out the evacuation of American nationals from Korea in case of the outbreak of war. Only if the North Korean Air Force tried to stop the evacuation could he use his fighter planes.

But at least Partridge had a cogent plan for the

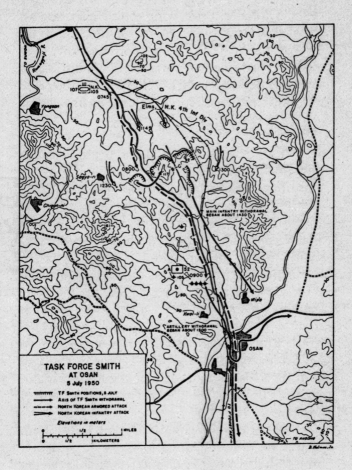

TASK FORCE SMITH
AT OSAN
5 July 1950

	TF Smith positions, 5 July
	Axis of TF Smith withdrawal
	North Korean armored attack
	North Korean infantry attack

Elevations in meters

0   1/2   1 MILE
0   1/2   1 KILOMETERS

B. Holmes, Jr.

evacuation. It was to be carried out by the U.S. 8th Fighter-Bomber Wing. By the end of the day, Colonel John M. Price, wing commander, had assembled 10 B-26 bombers to patrol the sea areas off the Korean coast, 12 C-54 transports and three C-47 transports to bring the Americans out of Korea, and a number of F-80 jet and F-82 fighters to protect the transports and guard the airfields from attack during the operation.

IN WASHINGTON, THIRTEEN hours behind Korean time, the attack began in the middle of a sunny Washington Saturday afternoon. President Truman was taking advantage of the summer lull in government to visit his home in Missouri. The State Department was manned only by duty personnel. So was the Pentagon.

The first reports of trouble came from the press. Wire service reporters began phoning the State Department and the Pentagon for information about reports out of Seoul of a major attack by the North Korean Army. It had taken South Korean government authorities until nine-thirty that morning to decide that what they faced *was* a major attack. The convincing element was the fall of Kaesong.

It took the U.S. ambassador to South Korea, John J. Muccio, almost as long to assess the situation from Military Advisory Group reports and then to radio Washington. Almost simultaneously the assistant military attaché at the U.S. embassy in Seoul sent a message to G-2 at the Pentagon. So it was nine-thirty on Saturday night before the American government could move into action. Before midnight Secretary of State Acheson got President Truman on the telephone in Missouri and passed on the electrifying news. The United Nations was taken seriously in 1950, and the State Department also notified Trygve Lie, Secretary General of the U.N., who immediately called a meeting of the U.N. Security Council for the next day.

All this shocked activity in Washington came as a surprise to the Soviets and their allies. The Americans had made it crystal clear that they would not fight for Korea. Some weeks earlier the Soviets had decided to boycott meetings of the U.N. Security Council, in which they had veto power over action by the international body. So secure were the Soviets in their belief that the United States was unable to rouse itself from self-induced stupor that they disregarded the call for a meeting of the Security Council for the next day. They did not know that President Truman had decided that the North Korean invasion was going to be contested and that action by the U.N. Security Council was to be the first line of American approach.

By the time the U.S. government was beginning to move on the morning of June 26, it was midnight of June 25-26 in Korea, and the North Korean drive had reached a point only seventeen miles north of Seoul. Ambassador Muccio was making preparations for the evacuation of all American women and

children. Several freighters in Inchon Harbor were
ordered to stand by. In Tokyo, General MacArthur
ordered General Partridge to provide fighter cover
over Inchon Harbor. The U.S. Navy was ordered to
send two destroyers to Inchon. But the planes were
not to cross over to the Korean mainland and they
were to fight only if attacked.

As day dawned on June 26 at Inchon, the evacuation began. Overhead, American F-82 fighters circled in flights of four. Below, small boats began
carrying the Americans out to the ships. Most of the
Americans boarded a Norwegian merchant ship.

The evacuation went along without excitement
until one-thirty in the afternoon, when a North
Korean fighter suddenly dived down through the
overcast above the harbor, cannon firing. The fighter went right through a flight of F-82s, which
veered off in evasive action but then gave chase. But
after that one pass the North Korean plane zoomed
up and disappeared into the cloud cover. As darkness fell, the Norwegian freighter moved out and
down the coast toward Japan, still covered by the
American fighter planes.

IN TOKYO AND Washington the dangerous underes-
timation of the enemy continued. At the end of the
first day, reports that the South Koreans were holding at two points gave MacArthur and the Pentagon the wrong impression that the North Korean
drive had bogged down. MacArthur sent an assessment of the situation, stating that American help

was needed to hold but that it could be done with dispatch immediately of one regimental combat team and a buildup of two divisions. President Truman said: send the troops. Thus, to complete the surprise to the Soviets and the North Koreans, the American commitment—they had considered to be so unlikely—was reaffirmed.

During the next two days, quite by accident, the United Nations was able to do for the first and only time what its progenitors had hoped: take strong action to repel outright aggression. The U.N. Security Council passed a resolution that called on member nations to give military aid to South Korea to repel the North Korean attack. This was possible only because of the continued absence of the Soviet delegate. Thus the U.S. decision to defend South Korea was given a moral authority that precluded all the usual international lollygagging. Further, the United States could now call without hesitation on the British and the Australians, who had reasonably substantial forces to offer. The defense of South Korea was converted by chance from an East-West struggle into an international police action, and for the moment at least, the Americans had the force of world opinion on their side.

BUT "INTERNATIONAL POLITICAL action" did not win battles, and the North Koreans were moving right along on this second day of the invasion. On the evening of June 26 the South Korean government began its move out of Seoul, to Taejon. The South

Korean National Assembly disagreed with that move, but that night the South Korean Army high command evacuated the city without telling anyone and left the legislature and the American advisers and embassy high and dry. At nine o'clock on the morning of June 27 Ambassador Muccio and the embassy staff left Seoul also for Suwon, while Colonel William S. Wright, the senior United States Military Advisory Group adviser, went down the road to Sihung-ni, south of Seoul, and persuaded the panicked ROK Army general staff to return to the capital.

That morning General Partridge's planes reached Kimpo and Seoul airfields and began the air evacuation of officials and American refugees from the capital area, while ships at Pusan began taking Americans out of the South.

The evacuation planes were covered from the air by American fighters. During the morning all was quiet, but at noon five North Korean Yak-7s appeared over Seoul and from a high altitude began a long, slanting dive on Kimpo airfield. They were "bounced" by five U.S. F-82 fighters, and in a brief dogfight the Americans shot down three of the North Korean planes in flames. Lieutenant William G. Hudson of the 68th Fighter Squadron was the first American pilot to shoot down an enemy plane over Korea. Major James W. Little and Lieutenant Charles B. Moran also claimed an enemy fighter apiece.

An hour after this incident, the North Koreans

came in again, this time with eight Il-10 fighter-bombers.

The North Korean planes were spotted by a flight of four F-80's of the 35th Fighter Squadron, and they attacked. Lieutenant Robert E. Wayne shot down two enemy planes, and Captain Raymond E. Schillereff and Lieutenant Robert H. Dewald each shot down one. The other four North Korean planes gave up the attack and fled north. The American pilots did not have the authority to pursue them, so they let them go and continued patrol. The North Koreans made no further attempts to interfere with the evacuation that day.

Back in Tokyo, General MacArthur was still under the impression that the South Korean defenses were holding. All he could do to help immediately was employ his Air Force. So he ordered General Partridge to begin air strikes against the North Korean lines of communications and against their troop concentrations as far north as the 38th parallel.

It was easier said than done. The first mission of B-26 bombers set off on the night of June 27, but the planes could not find any targets in the bad weather and returned to Japanese air bases with their bombs. A second B-26 mission was scratched because of the weather.

On the ground, the confusion continued on June 27. Major General Chae Byong-duk, the chief of staff of the ROK Army, ordered a counterattack up the Uijongbu road; it was so badly timed and so

weakly executed that it could not help but fail.
Matters continued to deteriorate. Roadblocks and
demolition teams had been assigned to operate
north of Seoul to slow the enemy advance, but they
simply did not operate except in one or two cases.
By midnight of June 27 the northern defense of
Seoul had virtually disappeared. Shortly after midnight, the Han River bridges just south of Seoul
were blown up by order of the panicked vice minister of defense, thus leaving many ROK troops with
no escape from the city to the south. At the time
some four thousand soldiers and civilians were on
the bridges trying to escape the enemy. Most of these
evacuees were killed or wounded. In effect, the
Republic of Korea's governors and defenders panicked and the catastrophe that followed was nearly
complete. The main element of the ROK Army lost
almost all its transport vehicles, most of its supplies, and most of its heavy weapons. When the
troops arrived at the bank of the Han they had to
swim or get across in small boats. The Army
disintegrated.

On the morning of June 28 the weather improved
a bit and a dozen B-26's took off from Ashiya Airfield in Japan to attack the North Korean railhead
at Musan and destroy North Korean military supplies. On the way back from this objective, near the
38th parallel, the planes strafed enemy troop concentrations and columns on the roads with machine-gun and rocket fire. These planes came in so
low that all of them were damaged by ground fire,

and two crashed on landing, with one crew lost. Another B-26 mission was launched in the afternoon, and all planes returned safely. The F-82s and F-80s gave close support to troops that day, and late in the day four B-29s, which had been ordered up from 19th Bombardment Group headquarters on Guam, arrived to bomb roads and railroad lines north of Seoul.

But the battle for the capital was already lost. Although the troops north of the city held out as long as they could (and valiantly, even according to the enemy), the issue was not in doubt. By the afternoon of June 28 two North Korean divisions had occupied the capital of South Korea.

Before the week was out, everything north of the Han River had been lost by the ROK forces. Colonel Paik of the 1st Division was one of the last to cross the Han, on June 29, near Kimpo. He brought five thousand men, all that was left of his division. When the heads were counted, of ninety-eight thousand ROK troops, only fifty-four thousand remained south of the Han. The South Koreans had lost half their fighting force and 70 percent of their weapons in just a few days.

THIS WAS THE situation that U.S. Brigadier General John H. Church found when he appeared at Suwon on June 28 on the orders of General MacArthur, who wanted a full report. General Church radioed MacArthur that unless American ground forces were committed, there was no way the North

Koreans could be driven back above the 38th parallel. The next day MacArthur arrived to see for himself.

After that day, during which MacArthur went up to the Han to see the blown bridges and the stream of refugees heading south, he announced that American ground forces must be committed immediately.

Actually, they already were. On June 29, the day of MacArthur's visit to Korea, Detachment X of the U.S. 507th Antiaircraft Artillery Battalion arrived at Suwon airfield and set up an air defense. The North Koreans had been attacking the field, and the next time they came over, Detachment X shot down one enemy plane and possibly another.

But that was not what MacArthur meant. As he had advised the Pentagon:

> The only assurance for the holding of the present line, and the ability to regain later the lost ground, is through the introduction of U.S. ground combat forces into the Korean battle area. To continue to utilize the force of our Air and Navy without an effective ground element cannot be decisive.

MacArthur then asked for authorization to commit a U.S. regimental combat team to the battle and to build up a two-division force that would undertake "an early counteroffensive."

Even then, American intelligence had not begun

to grasp the true strength of the North Korean forces. It was going to take a lot more than two divisions to turn the war around.

MacArthur's understanding of the situation was communicated to President Truman, and he lost no time acting. On June 30 the president authorized the dispatch of a regiment immediately and two divisions as soon as possible, and he ordered a naval blockade of North Korea. He then informed Congress of what he had done. By then there could be no further doubt in anyone's mind about what course the Americans would pursue. The president had committed the United States to the Korean War without reservation. Within a matter of hours other nations had followed suit. The British in particular put their forces at General MacArthur's disposal. They had a carrier, two cruisers, and five destroyers in Japan at that moment. The Australians committed a destroyer, a frigate, and a squadron of fighter planes based in Japan.

Already the American task force was in action, shelling North Korean troop concentrations along the coast. The war had been in progress for five days. The North Koreans had been slowed only by logistics. But by July 1, the United Nations forces were beginning to make the North Koreans realize that they had taken on a larger task than they had expected.

3.

Battle for Survival

GENERAL CHURCH AND General MacArthur had concluded that only two South Korean divisions were
good enough to be effective even in slowing the
North Korean advance. After the debacle of the Han
bridges, it was apparent that the ROK Army leadership was in total disarray. At this point, if fighting
was to be done, the Americans would have to direct
it until American troops could be brought up to the
line.

The effective ROK force as of the end of June
consisted of elements of the 1st and 7th divisions—
these units were remnants of the early northern
fighting; the 5th Division, at Yongdungp'o, the
industrial suburb of Seoul on the southern side of
the Han River; and the Capital Division, which still
held Inchon. Of lesser importance, remnants of the
2nd Division were retreating near the confluence of
the Han and Pukhan rivers, the 6th Division was
retreating south of Ch'unch'on toward Wonju, and
on the east coast the 8th Division was retreating

south, toward Pusan. (See the map "The North Korean Invasion.") The 23rd Regiment of the 3rd Division, which had been at Pusan, had moved up along the east coast to Ulchin to block an expected approach down the coastal road.

While the American advisers were doing their best to rally the demoralized South Korean forces, the North Koreans were not standing still. On June 28, the same day that they captured Seoul, the North Korean 6th Division began crossing the Han in the vicinity of Kimpo Airfield. The next day they occupied the field.

Seeing the mess of deserted equipment the South Korean Army had left behind at the Han, the North Koreans sensed a quick victory and began to move.

The North Korean 3rd Division spent a day or so killing South Korean politicians and others designated by the South Korean Communists, then it also moved toward the Han. On the night of June 29 North Korean artillery laid down a barrage. On the morning of June 30 the troops crossed the Han by small boat, by fording, and by swimming. They crossed in sufficient force to rout the disorganized South Korean defenders on the bank east of Yong-dungp'o and then stopped. Their task would be to sweep around to the east as the 4th Division made the direct Yongdungp'o crossing and outflank the defending ROK troops.

That day, U.S. General Church abandoned the role of adviser and became commander: He ordered General Chae to counterattack the North Korean

3rd Division troops. But Chae had no heart for the fight. His troops did not attack. He said they were driven off by the North Korean artillery barrage.

Church insisted that if the ROK forces did not hold at Yongdungp'o there would be hell to pay. The next morning, July 1, the North Korean 4th Division began the frontal crossing of the Han, expecting an easy victory. They did not wait for tanks to be brought across, and that proved to be a costly error. The South Koreans were paralyzed by tanks, which they had not been trained to face, but in the absence of tanks, their tactics were sound. The South Koreans rallied, and in a two-day battle fought briskly. Once again, however, they were beaten by forces better trained and with better weapons. On the third day the North Koreans brought up their tanks, and then it was all over at Yongdungp'o.

On the night of July 3 the town was in North Korean hands, and so was the vital port of Inchon, which had fallen to the North Korean 6th Division.

In fewer than ten days, the North Koreans had taken the South Korean capital, destroyed the fighting potential of the main force of the ROK Army, and captured the port they needed to assure speedy supply of the columns moving south. Their original projection of a two-week campaign to victory still seemed within the range of probability. From here the next objective would be Suwon, less than twenty miles to the south along the main central highway. (See the map "The North Korean Invasion.")

The American command had attempted all along the way to rally the South Korean forces. It seemed, however, that a change of leadership was needed and on June 30 Lieutenant General Chung Il-kwon arrived from Tokyo to replace General Chae as ROK Army chief of staff.

By late afternoon the word had come to General Church that the ROK forces along the Han were disintegrating. He drove 12 miles south of Suwon to Osan-ni, a telephone relay station on the Seoul-Tokyo route, and called supreme headquarters in Tokyo. He spoke with MacArthur's chief of staff, Major General Edward M. Almond, who told him that U.S. troops could be flown in on July 1 to help with the defenses if they could hold Suwon Airfield that long.

Church then returned to Suwon to be greeted by total hysteria. In his absence the American advisory group had panicked at false reports that the North Koreans were coming. The advisory group had abandoned the Suwon headquarters, ordered the anti-aircraft detachment to destroy their guns and abandon the airfield, and told the embassy to move to Taejon. The vehicles were assembled in a column and ready to start the retreat when General Church returned. Furiously he ordered them back to their posts and headed for the headquarters. But some idiot had set fire to it and most of the signal equipment had been destroyed. There seemed to be no hope of restoring the status quo ante, so he led the disorganized force down to Osan-ni and again called Tokyo. He and General Almond agreed that all Americans now would have to move to Taejon (where the South Korean government was already ensconced). The defense of central Korea had to be abandoned, and Pusan had to become the central point of defense.

All that remained in Suwon, then, was the ROK Army headquarters, which stayed there until July 4.

What would have happened if the American advisers had not panicked is debatable. But at least the first American troops would have been flown into Suwon and an attempt would have been made to stem the tide right there. As it was, the American abandonment of Suwon Airfield did nothing to help South Korean Army morale, to say the least.

WITH PERMISSION FROM Washington to engage American ground forces in Korea, General MacArthur moved fast, choosing the 24th Division because it was closest to Korea and thus easiest to move over. The decision might not have been the wisest, for among the four American divisions stationed in Japan at the time, the 24th had the lowest combat efficiency rating: 64 percent (not that the others were so high; the 1st Cavalry, rated 84 percent effective, was the highest). But speed was the goal and haste was the method. General Almond had promised General Church American troops by July

1 at Suwon Airfield. The main body of the 24th Division was sent to Pusan by ship. A small combat team—part of the 1st Battalion of the 21st Infantry Regiment—was sent by air to go into action immediately. It came with two 4.2-inch mortar platoons, one platoon of 77mm recoilless rifles, and six 2.36-inch-bazooka teams. This force was commanded by Lieutenant Colonel Charles B. Smith. A few hours later, the force was followed by Major General William F. Dean, who was immediately named commander of U.S. Army forces in Korea and placed in charge of all troops, including the South Koreans.

DEAN WAS EAGER to get the Americans into action.

On July 4 the North Korean 4th Division began moving down the Suwon road from Yongdungp'o. At noon eleven T-34 tanks led the way into the town of Antang-ni, halfway to Suwon. The road ahead of them from Suwon to Osan-ni was jammed with retreating ROK troops. The ROK 2nd Division's 5th Regiment stopped to fight south of Anyang-ni, but their positions were almost immediately overrun by 14 T-34 tanks. Matters were not helped for the South Koreans by American and Australian fighters in troop support. They were as effective as the North Korean tanks, for instead of striking the enemy, they gunned the South Koreans. Some planes blew up an ROK ammunition train. Others machine-gunned columns of ROK troops on the road, causing heavy casualties and ruining what was left of ROK morale here. (After this incident

General MacArthur ordered all ROK vehicles to be marked with the U.S. white star.)

So the defense of Suwon collapsed in one day. ROK Army headquarters moved south. The North Koreans occupied the town that night.

At Taejon, General Church said he did not intend to retreat farther, a statement made because he now expected troops of the U.S. 24th Division to begin arriving. Obviously he was still thinking in terms of the combat capability of American troops in the Pacific in World War II.

THE AMERICAN TROOPS were on their way—the 21st Infantry Regiment, plus the 34th and 19th regiments. Ahead of all of them came Colonel Smith's little detachment, bent on delaying the North Korean movement down the road to Taejon. It now had the name Task Force Smith.

The troops were brought over from Japan by a half dozen C-54 transports on July 1. They were met at Pusan Airfield by about one hundred Korean trucks, which took them to the railroad station, passing through the city where cheering crowds of Koreans greeted them as the heroes who would preserve them from the North Koreans.

At the moment the troops were feeling very much like heroes. They had every confidence in their ability to knock off the North Koreans with one hand tied behind their backs.

"As soon as those North Koreans see an American uniform over here," said one soldier, "they'll run

like hell." That opinion was more common than
any other among the troops.

THAT NIGHT THE train took the troops up to Taejon.

Colonel Smith reported to General Dean at Taejon and was ordered up the road to engage the
enemy on sight.

"All we need is some men up there who won't
run when they see tanks," General Dean said.

The troops moved up to a point above Osan-ni
where the road runs through a saddle of hills. Smith
selected a position that covered the highway almost
up to Suwon, eight miles north.

There they dug in confidently. Task Force Smith
included a number of combat veterans from World
War II, in all about one man in six. In addition to
the weapons earlier mentioned, they now had four
60mm mortars, and part of the 52nd Field Artillery
Battalion under Lieutenant Colonel Miller O.
Perry. He had six 105mm howitzers and seventy-
three vehicles. They moved into the Osan position
and waited. It was the night of July 4.

Behind them came the next contingent of Ameri-
cans, the 1st Battalion of the 34th Infantry Regi-
ment. This unit came up during the night to
Pyongtaek, the next road town down the line from
Osan-ni. The 2nd Battalion was off to the right, at
Ansong. (See the map "Delaying Action, 34th
Infantry.")

AT 7:30 A.M. on July 5 the North Korean column, led

by thirty-three T-34 tanks, appeared on the road to Osan-ni. At 8:16 A.M. the first American shell was fired. The artillery began a barrage along the road. But the tanks kept coming.

When the tanks had reached a point about seven hundred yards from the American infantry position, the two recoilless rifles began firing. They scored direct hits but the tanks came rumbling on up the road. The artillery fire was ineffective against these weapons.

The T-34s reached a point almost opposite the infantry position. Second Lieutenant Ollie D. Connor took a bazooka then, and working from a ditch alongside the road fired twenty-two rockets at fifteen yard range against the rear of the tanks, where their armor was weakest. This must at least have slowed the lead tanks down, because they stopped just over the pass through the hills. There they came under fire of a 105mm howitzer using high-explosive antitank ammunition. The combination of artillery and bazooka knocked out these first two tanks. The crews moved them off the road. One tank began to burn. One three-man crew came out with hands up. Out of the second tank came a soldier with a burp gun; he fired on an American machine-gun position and killed one of the gunners. Americans killed all three crewmen of that tank.

But the T-34 tanks kept coming. Unfortunately, the American howitzers had only six rounds of high-explosive antitank ammunition. When these were gone they had to use ordinary high-explosive shells. These, they found, ricocheted off the sides of the tanks. The tanks rolled through, firing on the infantry as they came but not stopping. Their assigned objective obviously was the artillery position beyond, and all the tanks moved on toward it, the last of the thirty-three passing through the infantry at nine o'clock that morning. They cut up the telephone lines from infantry positions to artillery. Communication was reduced to radio, and in the wet weather the radios worked spottily if at all. By eleven o'clock communication between infantry and artillery was totally lost.

The American infantry fired everything they had at the tanks, but the tanks moved right on through them, with a loss of only four tanks. They were followed by the North Korean infantry. Task Force Smith did what General Dean had asked: The men stood their ground for four hours. Then they were threatened on both sides by flanking movements.

The tanks seemed to be threatening the artillery, but when the tanks came to the point where the 105mm howitzers had been pulled off the road, they did not turn in but remained on the Osan-ni road. The artillerymen fired constantly, scoring many hits on the tanks, but their shells simply bounced off the sides of the armor and did no damage.

Back by the artillery, Colonel Perry and Sergeant Edwin A. Eversole took two more bazooka teams into action. They scored hits on the turrets, but the bazooka shells bounced off. One 105mm shell somehow managed to hit the track of one tank and disable it. Through an interpreter, Colonel Perry called on the North Koreans inside to surrender. There was no answer. He then ordered the four 105mm howitzers to destroy the tank. They began firing. After the third hit two North Koreans jumped out of the tank and took shelter in a culvert. An American squad moved forward and shot them down.

During this action Colonel Perry was wounded but kept moving, hobbling around the battlefield. When the second group of tanks came up, most of the American artillery enlisted men panicked and took off down the side of the road. Colonel Perry and the other officers carried the ammunition, and the senior noncommissioned officers fired the pieces. Seeing that the guns were firing, the shame-faced men began dribbling back.

Again the tanks ignored the artillery and went on. The 105s could not stop most of them, although another was disabled. But the explosive shells at least wiped the riding infantry off the tanks; that was the best these weapons could do in this situation. Working with what he had, Perry had managed a good deal. He could have done more if he had antitank mines, but there were none in South Korea.

AFTER THE TANKS had passed through the U.S. infantry position up forward Colonel Smith saw a six-mile-long column of trucks and infantry com-

ing down the road toward his position and led by
three tanks. When the column was about a thousand yards away, Colonel Smith ordered his men to
open up with every weapon possible. Mortar shells
were lobbed in among the trucks. Fifty-caliber
machine guns began spitting. Rifles were firing.
Trucks caught fire and began to blaze. The column
stopped. The tanks began to rake the ridge with
their 85mm guns and machine guns. The infantry
jumped from the trucks and began to deploy in
combat formation.

It was now about eleven-thirty in the morning.
The North Koreans did not make a frontal assault,
nor did they seem as interested in outflanking and
attacking the Americans as going around them, but
when Task Force Smith seemed about to be enveloped, the colonel ordered the men to move back. At
two-thirty that afternoon they began a general
withdrawal.

With troops ahead of them, troops on both sides
of them, troops behind them, no communication
with the artillery, and no air support, Colonel
Smith had a tough job ahead. The enemy machine
gunners moved up, and the Americans began to
take heavy casualties. Lieutenant Raymond
Adams, who was captain of the regimental baseball
team, pitched a grenade forty yards into one particularly troublesome machine-gun position and
blew it sky-high. But the retreat was costly and
disorganized. Colonel Smith went on ahead, found
Colonel Perry and his intact guns, and together

they moved back, taking the sights, breech locks, and aiming circles from the guns. The troops ran into enemy tanks at the southern edge of Osan-ni and turned onto a dirt road that should take them to Ansong. The next day Colonel Smith rounded up all the survivors and counted heads. He had two hundred and fifty men left. That meant his casualties had been one hundred and fifty men. Later a few more men straggled through the lines to tell tales of great suffering in reaching the safety of the South. The artillery lost five officers and twenty-seven men. General MacArthur had hoped that this commitment of American fighting troops would stop the North Koreans. When they learned that they were fighting Americans, he had believed, they would reassess their situation. But Task Force Smith had done everything that could have been expected of it, and it had not even slowed down the North Korean advance. (See the map "Task Force Smith at Osan.")

THE LOGICAL MOVE of the North Koreans would be against P'yongt'aek, the next town on the road south to Pusan. (See the map "Delaying Action, 34th Infantry.") When the 34th Infantry Regiment arrived at Taejon by train from Pusan on the night of July 4, General Dean had placed the 1st Battalion of the 34th Infantry at this point, with the 3rd Battalion at Ansong, twelve miles to the east, to cover an alternate route the North Koreans might also use. The regimental command post was at

Songhwan-ni, six miles south of P'yongt'aek. General Dean announced that the regiment must do everything possible to hold the P'yongt'aek-Ansong line.

Altogether, regimental commander Colonel Jay B. Lovless had a force of just under two thousand men, which was more than a third understrength. He had been in command of the 34th for only a month, brought in to replace an officer who had failed to bring the regiment up to even the division's sloppy training standards. Lovless had already complained that he had stepped into a mare's nest: Many of his officers were unfit for command of combat troops, and the state of morale was as dismal as the readiness for action. Lovless had not even had time to begin to rectify the basic wrongs. General MacArthur could not have selected a less apt division in his command, and General Dean could not have chosen a less fit unit for the task at hand.

Dean could not claim the same excuse. He had been a staff officer and had finagled the job of commander of the division eight months earlier. Perhaps his interest was more in costume parties and the trappings of occupation than in the situation of the troops under his command. He could claim that his command in Japan had been so far-flung across the island of Kyushu that he needed a light plane to get around it. For that General Walton Walker, commander of the U.S. Eighth Army, had to take the responsibility. But General Walker had to carry out the missions assigned to him by General MacArthur, whose primary concern was the rehabilitation of the Japanese society and economy. MacArthur was paying very little attention to military affairs these days. Had the offices of occupation commander and troop commander been separated, which was impossible given MacArthur's character, the state of training might have been different. Probably it would not have been, for the "American disease" that suddenly became apparent that Sunday in June was a cultural ailment, a national belief that Americans had proved themselves better and stronger than anyone else in the world and therefore everything was under control. And MacArthur in turn had the problem of insufficient resources to carry out his mission. For that the Pentagon had to take the responsibility. And the Pentagon in turn had too few troops to carry out the worldwide missions assigned it by an ambitious President Truman. For that the politicians of the administration and Congress had to take the responsibility.

On the immediate level, Colonel Lovless' 1st Battalion had a brand-new commander, Lieutenant Colonel Harold B. Ayres, a veteran of the Italian campaign of World War II. His assignment had been one of the first changes managed by Colonel Lovless in his attempts to rebuild the regiment. But Colonel Ayres came to his command with a serious deficiency, one shared by most Americans: a magnification of the contempt that all the American military seemed to have for Asians, even after the

Pacific War. The North Koreans were badly trained, he told his officers, and only half of them had weapons. There would be no trouble at all in stopping them.

Thus informed, the junior officers of the battalion told the noncoms and the men that there was nothing to be concerned about and that in two weeks they would all be back in Sasebo with their "mama-sans," enjoying the delights of occupation of a defeated enemy.

The 1st Battalion moved up to P'yongt'aek in the rain, and when day dawned the troops marched up into the hills north of the town to set up positions to block the road south.

P'yongt'aek lies just south of a small stream that was then crossed by a bridge. The land for two miles north was paddy field, through which the road ran on a ten-foot-high embankment. At the two-mile point, hills stood up above the fields on each side of the road. Colonel Ayres placed A Company on the west side of the road and B Company on the east, with C Company in reserve behind, so it could move either way in need. The men of the two forward companies began to dig in on the hills, although without enthusiasm, for most of them believed they were facing a sort of extended war game.

Captain LeRoy Osburn was commander of A Company. His position ran from the hill to the road. His men dug two-man foxholes along the north face of the hill and down the side into the paddy, to the road. But the position was larger than his force of one hundred forty officers and men could easily command, so the foxholes had to be spread. In the end they were so far apart the men could communicate only by shouting.

A Company was then in position. Each man had either an M-1 rifle or a carbine, and eighty to one hundred rounds of ammunition. Each rifle platoon had one light machine gun with four boxes of ammunition, and one Browning automatic rifle, with two hundred rounds of ammunition. There were no grenades. The weapons platoon had three 60mm mortars and two recoilless rifles. But there was no ammunition for the recoilless rifles. B Company's situatio was similar.

Neither knew anything about the events north of Osan-ni. Nor did Colonel Ayres at the command post know any more.

Brigadier General George Barth, commander of the 25th Division's artillery, was serving as General Dean's senior officer forward at Osan-ni. When Barth saw that neither Task Force Smith nor Colonel Perry's artillery was going to be able to stop the North Koreans he drove down to the P'yong-t'aek area and found Colonel Ayres. Barth reported on the situation at Osan-ni and warned that tanks probably would break through and come down the road, and he told Ayres he ought to send some bazooka teams ahead to intercept them. He also warned Ayres that their position might be enveloped. If that threatened, they were not to try to hold, but to move back slowly, taking delaying positions to gain time.

Lieutenant Charles E. Payne went forward then, with a rifle platoon. At a village a few miles north they saw tank tracks, and after some search they located one enemy tank and opened fire with bazookas. The tank fired back with its machine guns. Private Kenneth Shadrick was killed. Taking his body, Lieutenant Payne returned to the command post to report that his mission had been futile. The U.S. infantry weapons were not effective against the T-34s.

GENERAL BARTH HAD said nothing to Colonel Ayres about the new situation of Task Force Smith, although he obviously knew it had not been able to hold. So when General Dean came up from Taejon that night, Ayres was unable to give him any real information. Dean went back to Taejon with many forebodings but nothing that would cause a change in his plans.

Shortly after Dean left the P'yongt'aek command post, four survivors of Task Force Smith arrived and gave the colonel a highly embroidered account of the loss of the position. Fortunately, just then Colonel Perry arrived with the facts and with General Barth. They decided to hold but to destroy the bridge that led into P'yongt'aek, just in case the tanks got that far. At 3:00 A.M. the troops blew up the bridge.

Now confusion began to set in. General Barth

moved back down toward Taejon, stopping at Colonel Lovless's regimental command post to issue a new set of orders, moving of the 3rd Battalion of the regiment from Ansong to Ch'onan, the next big town down the Pusan road where the roads forked off west to the coast and to the south.

UP ON THEIR hills north of P'yongt'aek, A and B Companies of the 1st Battalion knew nothing of what was happening behind them. They had dug in with the stream and the town behind them, and they sat in the cold rain that night, waiting. They had no facts but many rumors.

It rained all night. No one came up from battalion to give them information. Finally, after midnight, Colonel Ayres sent word to the company commanders that Task Force Smith had been defeated north of Osan. The next information came when the troops heard the sound of the bridge being blown up behind them. That was not conducive to high morale.

At 4:30 A.M. the men were told to break out their C rations and eat while they had a chance. As dawn broke, they looked into their foxholes. They were full of water. So the men sat beside their foxholes, eating. They did not notice when a group of North Korean tanks ran through their area and stopped only at the river where the bridge had been blown up. Soon through the clouds and rain they saw infantrymen. At first the Americans thought these must be men of Task Force Smith, but they learned better. As the light began to grow, they could see a long line of tanks and trucks extending north through the early-morning fog as far as the eye could see.

They opened up with mortars. The tanks responded by turning the 85mm guns against the American positions. The first shell exploded above the center platoon of A Company. The men splashed into their foxholes, landing in water that was neck deep. The North Korean infantry began to move across the rice paddy. Colonel Ayres, who had come up the road, told A Company to withdraw, and he started back to his command post.

The enemy attacked A Company on the left, and the Americans responded. But fewer than half were firing their weapons. There were many North Koreans and few Americans, and the Americans had no effective artillery. Even the 4.2-inch mortar of A Company was out of action because the observer was in shock from a shell explosion nearby, and no one else thought to take over. Soon Captain Osburn ordered a retreat. B Company was already retreating. A Company began a retreat in order, but as the North Koreans increased their fire and opened up with machine guns, the retreat became a panic, and the enlisted men went running down the road and off the road, past their officers, paying no attention to their orders. These panicked riflemen ran two miles south of P'yong-t'aek before they recovered from their fear. They came back into the town and stood, waiting. When Captain Osburn came up, he organized them again and started the march south.

Here at P'yongt'aek some new difficulties began to appear. The platoon sergeant of one platoon decided to find out why his men had not fired their weapons. Of thirty-one members of the platoon, twelve men complained that their weapons would not fire. The sergeant inspected the weapons: All were broken, dirty, or had been incorrectly assembled. So much for the training of A Company, 1st Battalion, 34th Infantry Regiment.

Captain Osburn counted noses. Of his one hundred forty men, he now had about one hundred. Some of the others had been killed (some when they tried to surrender), and some had straggled off in their escape and would join up later. The company had lost most of its equipment and supplies. There was nothing to do but retreat— fast. Osburn ordered a forced march, and he warned the men that anyone who fell out would be abandoned.

With the enemy mounting a steady trail of artillery fire behind them, the men of A Company double-timed south. It was noon before they had outrun the enemy fire and could take a ten-minute rest. Thereafter the captain marched them at a normal pace with a ten-minute break every hour. The men were not used to it; their feet began to give out. Some took off their shoes and wore them around their necks. Some threw away their shoes.

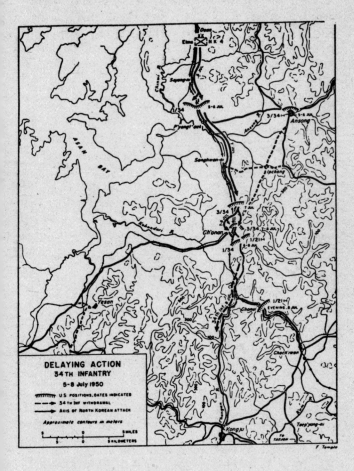

DELAYING ACTION
34TH INFANTRY
5-8 July 1950

||||||| U.S. POSITIONS, DATES INDICATED
— — —▶ 34 TH INF WITHDRAWAL
——▶ AXIS OF NORTH KOREAN ATTACK

Approximate contours in meters

5 MILES
5 KILOMETERS

F. Temple

The company had no communication with any-one, since the radios had been abandoned.

They picked up other stragglers, some of them South Koreans. As far as the men knew, this was the end of their war. They were talking about getting to Pusan and back to Japan.

Late in the afternoon as they were taking a ten-minute break an American plane came over and strafed them. There was only one casualty, a South Korean soldier who had his jaw shot away by a .50-caliber machine-gun bullet. But the strafing just about finished the company's morale. It was evening before they arrived at Chonan (see the map "Delaying Action, 34th Infantry") and there found most of the remainder of the 1st Battalion. It would not have been a pleasant sight for General MacAr-thur: a crowd of tired, disheartened men straggling around the town. The first element of A Company arrived at about dusk. It was two hours before the last of them came in. By that time Captain Osburn had borrowed three trucks from the South Korean Army, and with them he moved his company to defensive positions south of Chonan. There he put them to work digging. But most of them had lost their entrenching tools and almost all their per-sonal equipment. Many were barefoot. Their dis-carded equipment was littered all along the P'yong-t'aek-Chonan road.

A Company, even more than the rest of the 1st Battalion, was as ragtag and bobtail a military unit as existed in the U.S. Army and a good example of how not to put a unit into the field. The battalion was virtually useless as a fighting force.

On the morning of July 7, Captain Osburn tried to pick up the pieces. He sent men to a nearby village to get spades and shovels so they could dig. He got some food from the Koreans. The men sat around in little groups talking about how quickly they could get back to Japan and the soft life of occupation troops.

While the 1st Battalion of the 34th Infantry was having its military nightmare, two troop trains had brought up to Chonan most of the 1st Battalion of the 21st Infantry. General Barth assigned them to defensive positions two miles south of Chonan. Colonel Ayres' troops were ordered to join this defensive position.

This was the situation on July 6. The troops of the 34th Infantry were getting dug in when General Dean came up from Taejon, mad as a wet hen. The P'yongt'aek-Anson defense line had been set up because it was the best natural position north of the Naktong River. Why, he demanded, had it been abandoned without a fight? And who had ordered it abandoned?

There was some uncomfortable silence among the senior officers of the division. Then Colonel Ayres said he would take the responsibility. That was an answer, but was it the real answer? The abandonment of the defense line had been indicated by General Barth earlier as a matter of no great moment. And who, really, was General Barth? He was the artillery commander of the 25th Division who had been sent over to Korea to give Dean a hand as an extra general officer. What he had been doing apparently was moving up and down the line issuing orders that countermanded the spirit if not the letter of Dean's defense plan.

And how could troops with no grenades, no effective artillery, no ammunition for the artillery they had, be expected to hold a position against tanks and highly disciplined troops of the enemy? One thing was becoming clear to the men of the 1st Battalion of the 34th Infantry that was not yet clear to General Dean and the officers higher up: The North Korean soldiers were well-trained, highly disciplined troops with excellent weapons. The American units—forget what they had been in 1945—were soft, undisciplined, and very badly equipped.

General Dean was so unaware of the actual military situation that he considered sending Ayres' troops back up to P'yongt'aek. He thought better of it, but for the wrong reason: He was afraid they might run into a night ambush. He did order a company to go north again after daybreak. No one, obviously, had told him of the rout or the condition of A Company.

On the morning of July 7, Colonel Lovless assigned L Company the task of moving up the P'yongt'aek road to meet the North Koreans. The regiment's intelligence and reconnaissance platoon led the way.

The small force moved up through the virtually deserted town of Chonan. As it moved, Lovless had another message from General Dean, ordering him to send a whole battalion north to engage the enemy. The North Koreans had no tanks south of the blown P'yongt'aek bridge, Dean said.

Lovless ordered up the 3rd Battalion. They came up the road behind the reconnaissance force.

When the I and R platoon was five miles north of Chonan it ran into mortar and enemy small-arms fire. From somewhere, an artillery officer appeared with a single gun. Lovless placed it in a gap of the hills north of Chonan to cover the reconnaissance force.

Hardly had this been done when another message came from General Dean, urging caution because of the enormous number of tanks ahead. Dean also warned that the North Koreans were beginning a flanking movement to come around South of Chonan.

Lovless drove back to Chonan to inform Colonel Ayres of the new situation. He had with him Colonel Robert R. Martin, a good friend of Dean's from World War II, when they had served together in the 44th Division. Martin had been brought over at the general's special command to assist him. Martin had been traveling with Lovless all day long.

When they arrived at Chonan they were greeted by Brigadier General Pearson Menoher, assistant commander of the 24th Division, and General

Church, who had just come up from Dean's headquarters. Menoher handed Lovless an order relieving him and putting Colonel Martin in command of troops he had never seen. Thus out of the battle stepped Colonel Lovless, first senior victim of the chain of events that had brought an unprepared American military establishment into a new war.

4.

Delaying Action

THE FIRST TASK given Colonel Martin was to delay the North Korean advance north of Chonan. If that could not be done it opened a whole new can of worms for the Americans. North Korean armored columns then could turn west on the coastal road and flank the Americans moving up the central road from Taejon.

Martin sent Major John J. Dunn forward to check the situation of the 34th Regiment's 3rd Battalion north of Chonan. (See the map "Delaying Action, 34th Infantry.") Dunn found them moving into a defensive position. While he was there a jeep came in reporting that the I and R platoon and the advance company had been ambushed up front. He investigated, found they had not in fact been ambushed but had retreated from long-distance fire. Martin told him to get them back in position, and he did. Having put out that brush fire, he discovered that the 3rd Battalion had begun an unauthorized retreat from the Chonan position. He started them back to their posts, then went ahead to see how the advance company was doing, taking several other officers with him.

Their jeep was ambushed just ahead of the 3rd Battalion. Major Dunn was wounded and so were others. One officer volunteered to go back for help, and that was the last anyone saw of him. Dunn could see the riflemen of the leading company of the 3rd Battalion, but they made no effort to rescue the wounded, although the enemy force in the area was no more than a patrol. A few minutes later he could hear an American officer crying to the troops, "Fall back! Fall back!" Dunn lay there for two hours before the enemy finally arrived and captured him. He spent the rest of the war as a prisoner.

The 3rd Battalion's abandonment of its Chonan position was ragged and undisciplined—just short of panic. The troops left behind much of their equipment, including some of their mortars. The battalion commander, Lieutenant Colonel David H. Smith, was ordered to go back and defend Chonan. Colonel Martin personally led a patrol north of Chonan to recover the abandoned equipment.

That afternoon of July 7 the 3rd Battalion moved into a position that led from the railroad station to the north along the railroad tracks west of Chonan. One platoon mined a dirt road leading to the northwest so as to prevent enemy movement to the west to flank the main road. The dirt road was mined with antitank mines to prevent a surprise attack from that direction. That evening a battery of the 63rd Field Artillery arrived from Pusan and was put into position south of Chonan to support the battalion. These guns had antitank and white phosphorus shells. Their first fire mission was a success: They destroyed two tanks of a column moving into Chonan.

But by midnight the column had moved into the town, past the thin line of infantry on the north. Colonel Martin took about eighty men into Chonan and was cut off there for an hour or two but fought his way out, clearing the Chonan road to maintain communication with the 3rd Battalion. Colonel Martin was not satisfied that his people would hold, so he went back into Chonan shortly before dawn.

At dawn an American two and a half-ton truck came out of town to get ammunition for the 3rd Battalion. On its return to the town, the driver saw an enemy tank coming down the dirt road from the northwest road. The driver turned around and escaped, going back to report a whole column of tanks advancing behind that leader. The mining of the road had been completely ineffective; either the North Koreans had removed the mines or, more likely, the American soldiers had failed to arm them.

Five North Korean tanks were coming down the dirt road, and they opened fire on the Americans. Troops of the 3rd Battalion destroyed two tanks with bazookas. Private Leotis E. Heater threw five grenades into another tank and set it afire.

The North Korean infantry came into Chonan at about six o'clock that morning, and street fighting began. Colonel Martin took a 2.36-inch bazooka into a hut on the east side of the town's main street. Sergeant Jerry C. Christenson loaded for him. An enemy tank came up and pointed its 85mm gun at them. Colonel Martin fired the bazooka just as the enemy tank fired. The 85mm shell cut Martin in two. His rocket did not destroy the tank. Sergeant Christenson was badly wounded by the explosion and later captured.

The North Koreans were moving in fast. By eight o'clock that morning the 3rd Battalion was completely cut off, and from the rear it seemed improbable that anyone would escape the net. But the artillery laid down a constant fire of white phosphorus shells, and under that cover Colonel Smith and one hundred seventy-five men escaped from the town. They were all that was left of the 3rd Battalion.

Colonel Smith, exhausted, was sent back to Japan. Major Newton W. Lantron took over what was left of the battalion and what was left of its equipment. The battalion had abandoned nearly all its mortars and machine guns, and many of the soldiers had abandoned their weapons.

So the defense of Chonan had failed, and the west road and the south road were now open to the North Korean advance, complicating General Dean's problems considerably. Also, he had lost his

favorite regimental commander, who, after survey-
ing his command, had felt impelled to fight as a
company officer. The 34th Infantry was in total
disarray, although the 1st Battalion, with and
without shoes, still held the blocking position
south of the town.

THE BUMBLING EFFORTS of these two days had at least
enabled Colonel Richard Stephens to bring the 21st
Infantry Regiment into position to support General Dean. Colonel Stephens arrived with the first
trainload of soldiers at Taejon on the morning of
July 7, and General Dean immediately sent him up
to Choch'iwan, about fifteen miles south of Chonan, to establish a defense in support of the 34th
Regiment. The trouble was that five miles south of
Chonan the central road forked; one branch went
straight down to Kongju, and the other veered off to
the east, to Choch'iwon and then joined the main
line again at Kongju. This increase in the number
of roads represents the broadening of the Korean
peninsula in the area. The problem at this point
was that the secondary road structure off the main
road made it possible for the North Koreans to
outflank the Americans on both sides.

GENERAL DEAN NOW relied on the 1st Battalion of the
34th Infantry to defend a position on the direct road
to Kongju, south of the junction near Chonui. But
not for long. Dean was bringing his forces into

position to defend the Kum River line, ten miles
south of Choch'iwon.

Rapidly in terms of logistics, but ever so slowly in
terms of the North Korean advance, additional
American troops and weapons were dribbling into
South Korea. A battery of the 11th Field Artillery's
155mm howitzers came up to Choch'iwon to support the 21st Infantry. A company of the 78th Heavy
Tank Battalion's M-24 light tanks came up. Engineers moved in to do the road mining, prepare the
roadblocks, and mine all the bridges across the
Kum River for demolition.

THE DEFENSE OF South Korea had now developed
into a race. The Americans were banking on holding long enough to bring more forces in from
Japan, more planes, carriers, and ships to bombard
enemy installations. The South Koreans had given
up completely on defense of the western side of the
peninsula and were relegated to the mountainous
east, where the Americans hoped they would stop a
flanking movement toward Pusan.

Washington had sent the U.S. Seventh Fleet to
operate under Admiral Turner C. Joy. The British
had sent their Far Eastern Fleet, and this included
the carrier *Triumph*, the big cruiser *Belfast*, the
cruiser *Jamaica*, three destroyers, and four frigates.
The U.S. carrier *Valley Forge* arrived on the scene.
American and British jets were now flying over
North Korean airfields, destroying the enemy Air

Force on the ground and in the air. Then they began to concentrate on trains, destroying and damaging cars and locomotives. American and Australian planes were also plastering the North Korean soldiers (when they were not hitting their own infantry). The airmen were suffering from insufficient training, just like the ground troops. They had another major deficiency that no one had seemed to consider before: The jet fighters operating from Japanese bases were of such short range that their time over target was just a few minutes. Seldom had an army moving into action been as vulnerable as the North Korean Army was as it headed south down the main South Korean roads. But the U.S. Air Force was unable to take full advantage of these strained logistics. It did not have the weapons.

AS OF THE end of the first week of July, it was apparent to the American military leaders in Tokyo that with the fall of Chonan, General Dean's 24th Division was incapable of stopping the North Korean drive.

In one week General MacArthur had been forced to change totally his appraisal of the North Korean Army. On July 7 he informed the joint chiefs of staff in Washington that what they had been believing for five years was rot.

He admitted that "in some categories" the North Korean forces were superior to the American. He did not say which categories. But by July 7 they had

become apparent: weaponry and leadership up to
the regimental if not the divisional level. A photo-
graph of General Walton Walker and General Dean
in the field in Korea just after the arrival of the
Eighth Army commander is very telling. Walker
appears overstuffed, probably fifty pounds over-
weight. Even the lanky Dean seems to be carrying a
double chin and more than his share of pounds
around the middle. Both men look soft and well fed.
Those five years of the good life had taken their toll
all the way down the line.

MACARTHUR'S NEW ESTIMATE, after a week of fighting, was that it would take four to five full-strength
American divisions supported by one airborne regimental combat team and an armored group with
modern tanks. That meant Washington would
have to send him thirty thousand men immediately.

Assessment of the American and North Korean
weaponry also gave cause for gloom. The American
bazooka, the troops had found, was ineffective
against the T-34 tank. (This bazooka had also been
ineffective from 1942 to 1945 against German
Panther tanks—a fact observed and reported by
scores of field commanders.) The only weapons
effective against the tanks were those that fired antitank ammunition, and antitank mines (more facts
well known since the early 1940s).

With General MacArthur's appraisal, everyone
jumped on the new bandwagon. "I am convinced,"
said General Dean, "that the North Korean Army

and the North Korean soldier and his status of training and the quality of his equipment have been underestimated."

Dean did not add that as deputy chief of the American occupation of South Korea he had been one of the chief underestimators.

Suddenly the joint chiefs of staff in Washington were told that they had produced a "paper tiger" in the Far East and that immediate action had to be taken to remedy that situation.

The news had to be appalling. The entire defense establishment had been whittled down to show form instead of content. The two-thirds-effective division was the rule, not the exception, and that same general ratio existed throughout the armed services. Congress had said "save money," and the defense establishment had saved it at the cost of national preparedness. It was the same old American story.

But what was to be done?

Immediately planes began departing for Japan, carrying specialists and officers capable of leadership. But these were coming in the hundreds while MacArthur's demands were for men in the thousands.

To meet his demands, the Pentagon had to start stripping the Army's general reserve, and this action "greatly reduced the mobilization base for a later buildup. . . ."

In other words, the American military house of cards threatened to collapse everywhere, given this one challenge in one small corner of Asia.

The continental American forces had to be stripped below the safety level to meet MacArthur's immediate needs. They could not send cadres, for it would take six months to work a cadre into a division. They had to send fully equipped fighting divisions and bring these up from the new standard (intolerable in combat) of two battalions to the division to three full battalions and attached troop strength. Immediately battalions were taken from regiments on the U.S. mainland, in Hawaii, and on Okinawa. General J. Lawton Collins, the Army chief of staff, saw that the Army's position would become almost intolerable: It would require 14 months to rebuild the combat units that had to be taken apart immediately. That meant that the only U.S. units that would be up to snuff would be the 82nd Airborne Division and the 2nd Armored Division. And MacArthur was asking for parts of those. Collins resisted giving them, but even so, the Army would not have the capability to carry out emergency missions for at least a year.

There was nobody to blame for this but the politicians, but that was no help to the national defense. What had to be done was to knuckle down in the best American military tradition, one that had always responded splendidly to crisis, and get the troops moving to MacArthur before the defense of Korea became a question mooted by the North Korean drive to Pusan.

The first major unit to be ordered into action was the 2nd Division, located then at Fort Lewis, Washington. That decision was made on July 7, and the division was alerted. But the 2nd Division was still a long way from Korea, and the North Koreans were just a few miles up the road.

WHILE THESE AFFAIRS of state were commanding the attention of official Tokyo and official Washington up to the presidential level, Colonel Stephens of the undermanned 21st Infantry regiment sent Lieutenant Colonel Carl C. Jensen's 3rd Battalion up the road six miles from Chochi'won. Later that day, General Dean sent several messages to Colonel Stephens, announcing that the regiment *must* hold at Choch'iwon until the ROK forces to the east managed to cross the Kum River. The remnants of the 34th Infantry and the 21st Infantry were to delay the enemy approach to the Kum River for four days. There were no reserves, the general added. The only help they could have would be from the Air Force.

On the morning of July 9, Colonel Jensen got as ready as he could for the action to come. The battalion's 4.2-inch and 81mm mortars were registered on the road. The bridges were blown up above the little river, the Choch'on, that skirts the railroad and the road.

All was quiet in the morning, but at around noon Colonel Stephens had a report that enemy tanks were moving south from Chonan.

In the middle of the afternoon the tanks began to come up. But this time the Americans had some things ready for them: artillery with antitank ammunition, and an air-strike capability.

ELEVEN TANKS AND some three hundred infantrymen approached the 21st Infantry position. Captain Charles R. Alkire, commander of the forward position, called for an air strike. It came in. So did the artillery armor-piercing shells. Within the hour five of the eleven tanks were burning—by far the best showing yet made against North Korean armor.

The artillery and the dug-in U.S. infantry were giving the North Koreans a lot to think about. They brought in trucks loaded with troops, and the Americans set the trucks afire. The troops tried to move forward but ran into mortar fields of fire. The Air Force and artillery and mortars knocked out many vehicles that day. Captured North Koreans later put the figure at twenty tanks destroyed north of Chonui. (See the map "Task Force Smith at Osan.")

On that night of July 9, while buildings and vehicles burned around Chonui, North Korean patrols were out, moving around the ridges, discovering the American positions.

That evening, Colonel Stephens came up to the forward command post, which was a foxhole occupied by Alkire and *New York Herald Tribune* war correspondent Homer Bigart on a ridge east of Chonui. Stephens remained there for the night.

When dawn came, so did a great blanket of fog and the North Korean infantry.

If there had been any doubt left in the minds of the American commanders about the proficiency of the North Korean infantry, it was dispelled this day. Using the fog, the enemy launched its attack against the American positions and outflanked them.

At 8:00 A.M., when the fog lifted, Colonel Stephens could see tanks in Chonui. He radioed for an air strike. But other tanks had joined the infantry, moving around to take the American mortars which had done so much damage the day before. They did destroy the mortars and left the American forces up front without that support.

The loss of the mortar support made it possible for the North Koreans to maintain a steady pressure against Captain Alkire's ridge. The North Koreans climbed the ridge, and the American artillery drove them down. The T-34 tanks sprayed the ridge with fire. The North Koreans brought up more troops against the left position held by Lieutenant Ray Bixler's platoon. Bixler called for help. He had suffered many casualties, he said, and the North Koreans threatened to get into his position and overrun him.

Colonel Stephens told him to hold—help was coming. It came in the form of an air strike. Two American P-51 fighters zoomed in, firing rockets and strafing. The rockets hit the tanks but did not knock them out. The strafing killed some enemy troops, but most took cover. When the planes left, the enemy infantry again began their advance up Bixler's hill.

Colonel Stephens' attention was diverted when

"friendly fire" began to come in on Alkire's ridge. By the time he had gotten that stopped, Bixler's position was overrun and no more was heard from it.

This news and the unnerving effect of being fired on by one's own artillery sent many of the men on the right side of Alkire's position into a panic— once more the Americans suffered the effects of inadequate training and a lack of experienced non-coms. Corporal Richard Okada tried to stop the panic on the right but could persuade only a hand-ful of men to stand and fight. With these he formed a tiny perimeter.

Just after noon Colonel Stephens decided the position was hopeless and led the men out of their foxholes, down the ridge, and onto the dikes that separate the rice paddies. Slipping, falling over into the paddies, the men managed to escape. They were a tiny portion of the original force.

At this point came a change that indicated the growing proficiency of the awakening American forces. Colonel Stephens ordered Colonel Jensen to counterattack and retake the Chonui positions.

Jensen counterattacked and did just that, except for Bixler's hill. As small an action as it was, this was the first successful counterattack against the North Koreans so far in the war.

The counterattack also revealed the nature of the enemy. Six American soldiers from the heavy mor-tar company were found with hands tied behind their backs, shot through the back of the head. This discovery did nothing to increase the American desire to take North Korean prisoners.

Colonel Jensen, having retaken the positions around Chonui, held them all day. They were fighting the troops of the North Korean 4th Division, which had been moving steadily since crossing the Han River. Now that division was bypassed by the fresher North Korean 3rd Division, whose advance elements moved into Chonui but went right on through, having seen the tremendous destruction of all useful positions wreaked by the 4th Division.

That day American light tanks were brought up to the fighting for the first time, but they did not distinguish themselves. They were too light, and their guns were too small to do much damage to the far superior T-34 Soviet tanks. The Air Force, however, certainly did distinguish itself that day. That afternoon a flight of American jet fighters dropped down below the overcast at P'yongt'aek and discovered a long convoy of the 3rd Division bound southward. The convoy had stopped while the engineers rebuilt the P'yongt'aek bridge blown up earlier by the Americans. About two hundred tanks, half-tracks, armored cars, and trucks were standing bumper to bumper on the road. The American fighters radioed their base, and the Fifth Air Force rushed out the strongest attack it could mount on short notice. Jet fighters and B-26 bombers found the convoy still standing north of the broken bridge and had the finest field day of the war. They decimated the convoy, claiming to have destroyed one hundred fifty vehicles, including thirty eight tanks, and killing hundreds of soldiers. The results were undoubtedly exaggerated, but also they were undoubtedly very great.

JUST BEFORE MIDNIGHT, Colonel Jensen decided his force was at risk and had held long enough, so he began to pull back to his original position about four miles down the river. To his surprise, the soldiers found their old foxholes occupied by North Korean troops and had to fight for an hour to clear them out.

That night Colonel Stephens moved the 21st Infantry Regiment back to a position two miles north of Choch'iwon, with the agreement of General Dean. Dean also told Stephens that he expected him to hold that position all the next day. All the South Korean forces still had not passed through to safety.

To give Stephens a hand, the Taejon headquarters had brought in two hundred replacements for Colonel Smith's Task Force Smith, and it was sent up into the line on the night of July 10.

Early on the morning of July 11, the North Koreans launched a powerful attack on Colonel Jensen's troops, fallen back from Chonui to their old position. It came as a complete surprise because Jensen, moving back at night and driving a small force of North Koreans out of the foxholes, had believed that these were remnants of the troops they had been fighting at Chonui. Instead, they were a small element of the assault force of the North Korean 3rd Division. They had gone to their command post to report on the exact disposition of the Americans. So on the following morning the North Koreans did not hesitate: At six-thirty they attacked in the fog. There was a minefield in front of the American position, but the Koreans had obviously charted it during the night; four tanks came through unscathed.

The enemy had the battalion command post spotted, and almost immediately they destroyed it with mortar fire. About a battalion of North Koreans very quickly enveloped the position. The American mortar operation failed because forward observers' radios failed.

The result was a total American disaster. As Army historian Roy Appleman put it in his *South to the Naktong, North to the Yalu*, "This attack on the 3rd Battalion, 21st Infantry, was one of the most perfectly coordinated assaults ever launched by North Koreans against American troops."

The attack overwhelmed the battalion before it had a chance to start fighting. During the night, the enemy had placed roadblocks between the battalion and Colonel Stephens' command post. Thus no ammunition could be brought up, and the wounded could not even be evacuated. There were many instances of individual American bravery, but heroes alone do not win battles. Before noon, survivors in small groups were making their way back toward Choch'iwon. Colonel Jensen was killed while trying to cross a stream behind his observation post. Most of the battalion officers were killed or missing in action. When the troops arrived at the rear area, 60 percent of the battalion was missing. Of the survivors, only 10 percent retained their equipment; men came in without rifles, helmets, some again without shoes. Some just gave up and would not fight any more to get back, so completely exhausted they preferred to take their chances on capture.

The problem, of course, went back to the source: The Americans had grown soft.

If General Dean was aware of this deficiency, he had no time to contemplate the philosophical factors. He had just lost half of the effective force that was supposed to delay the North Koreans at Choch'iwon. His next orders were to the 3rd Engineer Combat Battalion to prepare every obstacle possible to slow down the enemy advance in the area. Then he ordered up the 19th Infantry Regiment and the 13th Field Artillery Battalion from Taegu and Po'hangdong. They were to come to Taejon that day. All three of his regiments and all his support forces were committed. The tanks, used on July 10 and 11, had been a disappointment. Four tanks of the 78th Heavy Tank Battalion had been lost without doing anything effective. Again inferior weapons had been laid on without consideration of enemy capabilities. This was not the fault of the tankers. The source lay in Washington.

COLONEL SMITH'S 1ST Battalion of the 21st Infantry was now all together in the line. The colonel was the most experienced man in the field as far as contact with the North Koreans was concerned. He knew their weapons and he knew the deficiencies of his own.

At dawn, an enemy patrol approached the forward position above Choch'iwon. Troops could be seen moving on both flanks. At nine-thirty one whole battalion attacked the left flank, while another entire battalion attacked in the center and on the right. Colonel Smith assessed his situation. There was no way his understrength battalion, made up mostly of untried troops, was going to defeat a force of that size. He communicated this to Colonel Stephens, who agreed and who gave General Dean the bad news that the 21st Regiment was withdrawing from Choch'iwon.

Colonel Smith carried out a masterful retreat, disengaging the battalion one company at a time. They moved down to the Kum River, and most of the regiment withdrew across to the south bank of that river. A small force of about three hundred men took position on the south bank, while the rest of the regiment went on through.

Meanwhile, the remnants of the 34th Infantry had covered the retreat to the east, down the Kongju road with greater success than they had earlier shown in meeting the enemy. Four M-24 tanks had tried to help, but three of them had been knocked out by the enemy. Troops of the 3rd Engineer Combat Battalion had prepared demolition charges for various bridges and strongpoints. The 3rd Battalion had led the retreat, and when it reached Taejon it was reorganized as a composite company—that's all that could be done. Mama-sans back in Japan would have to wait. The men were reequipped and sent back to Kongju. The 1st Battalion recovered a little of its aplomb in covering the retreat from the rear. On June 11 those troops and the 63rd Field Artillery Battalion crossed the Kum River. Colonel Ayres was one of the last to come over, at dusk. A small outpost was left on the north side of the river with instructions to blow up the bridge when the enemy started to cross, and then infiltrate to safety.

Thus ended the first American contact with hostile troops since the end of World War II. In the initial phase, the American performance had been miserable; compounded of surprise, incompetence, and shoddy performance. The weapons with which the American troops had been equipped were distinctly inferior to those of the enemy. The result had been a series of routs. But in a week what was left of the 34th and 21st regiments had steadied down and hardened up. What General MacArthur had termed "a desperate rearguard action" had been accomplished, and thousands of South Korean troops had been saved. The North Korean timetable had been destroyed.

Altogether, the Americans had so far suffered defeat, but it was the sort of defeat that at the end gave General MacArthur hope of overcoming the despair that faced him in the first week of July. As the troops moved steadily back in that first week, it had seemed to him that the North Koreans would run straight through to Pusan and that that would be the end of South Korea.

But now the Americans were safely across the Kum River, having delayed the main North Korean advance for three days. MacArthur was able to say to anxious visitors from Washington that he knew the defense could be stabilized somewhere before Pusan. He could not say exactly when or where, but he could make that promise.

5.

Bolstering the Defense

ON JULY 10 two anxious American generals arrived in Tokyo on behalf of the joint of chiefs of staff to interview General MacArthur on the Korean situation. They were General Collins and General Hoyt Vandenburg, Air Force chief of staff.

The Washington Intelligence apparatus, getting late into the game, had made up for its previous errors of omission by overblowing the North Korean strength. The gloomy possibility that the Americans might be thrown out of Korea altogether was now waved at the joint chiefs of staff. The Joint Intelligence Committee predicted that the North Koreans would overrun Pusan in the next two weeks.

The joint chiefs had been exposed to other nightmare predictions by their loyal subordinates. If the U.S. troops were pushed out of Korea, the political result around the world would be calamity. American alliances would be weakened everywhere. Soviet influence would burgeon. U.S. foreign policy would be discredited, and no one would have much respect for American military capability.

If the United States decided to withdraw from Korea, the effect would be even worse. Other nations would lose faith in American commitments. And for what it was worth (it then seemed quite a bit), American leadership in the United Nations would be lost.

And if the United States was to continue the Korean War, what then? How much military strength could the United States commit to Korea without destroying its ability to meet other emergencies elsewhere? In other words, would the United States have to begin drafting men again on a large scale?

If the United States did opt to remain in the fight, what were the chances of driving the North Koreans beyond the 38th parallel? That and no more was the objective of the moment.

When Generals Collins and Vandenburg arrived in Tokyo, they were prepared for anything.

They met a calm, pipe-chewing MacArthur, who was more than generous with the failings of his subordinates in the operations just past and cautiously optimistic about the future.

The joint chiefs should remember, he said, that his forces had been "tailored for occupation duty and not for combat." Forget whose fault that was.

The immediate problem was to get reinforcements into Korea as quickly as possible. Everything he could spare would be in the line by August. If the joint chiefs would give him the reinforcements he asked for, then he could win the war.

The generals did not much like that answer. They asked a lot of other questions and did not get many answers that pleased them. Their thinking, obviously, was global. Just how important was Korea in the great scheme of things. How important would it be if they lost Korea but gained the strength to prevent any future Koreas?

MacArthur, master military rhetorician, posed them a problem: If your city were divided into four districts, with District No. 1 the most important and District No. 4 the least important, then what do you do if a fire starts in District No. 4? Do you save the fire-fighting equipment for District No. 1? If you do, the fire might spread like the great Tokyo fire of the spring of 1945 until it engulfed the whole city and burned it up.

This analogy suggested that the joint chiefs had everything to win or lose in Korea. If they let Korea go, then they could kiss the world goodbye.

Then General MacArthur offered the two generals his own military-political estimates. If he were given the troops, he said, he would not only drive the North Koreans back north of the 38th parallel, he would also destroy their whole Army and occupy all of North Korea.

"In the aftermath of operations," he said, "the problem is to compose and unite Korea."

Preoccupied with the immediate military problem, the generals apparently did not pay a lot of attention to the implications of what MacArthur was saying. What he promised was to bring to an end the North Korean government established by the Soviets and unify Korea under the aegis of the Republic of Korea—in other words, fulfill Syngman Rhee's dream.

The generals promised MacArthur their support. They went to Korea and talked to General Walker and General Dean and were impressed by the need for immediate action.

And they delivered.

Back in Washington they stripped the general reserve, particularly of experienced specialists. The general reserve was reduced from 150,000 officers and men to 90,000; the rest went to Korea on short notice. Only the 82nd Airborne, the 3rd Cavalry, and a handful of anti-aircraft units were left intact. Obviously it was essential to increase the size of the Army, and this was done by presidential order. Congress, which had been picky about military appropriations for years, turned somersaults to cooperate, particularly after the administration called up elements of the U.S. National Guard for service. Such an action had always been a warning to the American nation.

As of the second week of July 1950, just twenty-two days after the North Koreans had invaded the South without warning, the American reaction had passed the emergency stage and become organized for the long haul. Once more, just as the Japanese had in 1941, an enemy had looked at apparent American disarray and had drawn the conclusion that the big, sloppy republic of the West could not possibly react adequately. Once more, an enemy had been wrong.

ON JULY 9, General Walker's advance party opened the headquarters of the U.S. Eighth Army at Taegu. Symbolically, here was the commitment to remain and fight. Other units began coming into Korea. Major General William B. Kean's 25th Division arrived, beginning on July 10. Lieutenant Colonel John H. Michaelis' 27th Infantry moved into the Uisong area, about thirty miles north of Taegu. Colonel Horton V. White's all-black 24th Infantry came to Pusan, starting on July 12. This was the first full regiment (three battalions) to arrive. Next came Colonel Henry G. Fisher's 35th Infantry.

On the east, the South Koreans were fighting gamely but lamely to prevent the North Koreans from flanking the American force. Actually the North Koreans spent too much time trying to invest too much territory and thus slowed themselves down. Otherwise they could have turned the corner in the east and outflanked the Americans in the second week of July.

It did not happen. General Dean had managed to hold for those important three days north of the Kum River. The South Korean 3rd Division held at Yongdok for the moment. (See map "The Pusan Perimeter, August-September 1950.") General Dean sent the 25th Division there to stem the North Korean advance above the airfield at Yonil.

The United States in that second week began establishing air bases in the South, which improved the defense capability considerably.

The North Koreans by this time were certainly aware that the character of the war had changed. They had been forced to slow down and regroup after the Chonon battle. Air power was making itself felt, the carriers *Valley Forge* and *Triumph* were in the Yellow Sea.

ON JULY 13, General Walker came to Korea to take over command of the ground forces, and on that day the ROK Army headquarters moved down to Taegu to be near the command. The combined U.N. forces in Korea then numbered 58,000 ROK troops and 18,000 American troops.

Walker had his orders from General MacArthur. Walker's first task was to stabilize a defense so that MacArthur could build up a force to launch an offensive as soon as possible.

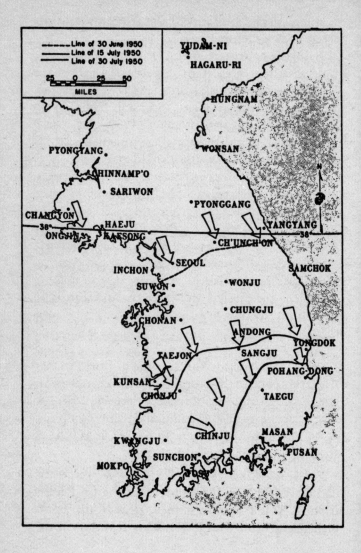

Line of 30 June 1950
Line of 15 July 1950
Line of 30 July 1950

25 0 25 50
MILES

YUDAM-NI

HAGARU-RI

HUNGNAM

PYONGYANG

CHINNAMP'O

SARIWON

WONSAN

PYONGGANG

CHANGYON

HAEJU

38

ONGJIN

KAESONG

CH'UNCH'ON

YANGYANG

38

INCHON

SEOUL

SAMCHOK

SUWON

WONJU

CHUNGJU

CHONAN

ANDONG

YONGDOK

TAEJON

SANGJU

POHANG-DONG

KUNSAN

CHONJU

TAEGU

KWANGJU

CHINJU

MASAN

SUNCHON

PUSAN

MOKPO

General Dean's 24th Division was sitting on the south bank of the Kum River. On the east was the newly arrived 25th Division. The South Koreans were to help where they could. General Chung Il-kwon, the ROK Army chief of staff, was formally placed under General MacArthur's command by President Rhee.

One of Walker's most pressing problems was to rush the training of all Eighth Army troops so they would not make the same mistakes that the first contingent had. Moreover, they had to have modern weapons. Most of the jeeps and trucks were World War II veterans and were worn out. The command radios were worn out also, as had been shown in the early operations of the 24th Division. The troops in the line had no spare parts for their machine guns and virtually no ammunition for the recoilless rifles. Most of the M-1 rifles and carbines should have been discarded as worn out. The same was true of the 60mm mortars. There were very few grenades in all South Korea.

Some of these components could be found in dumps around Japan, and some, such as antitank mines, could be manufactured there. They were. On July 18 the first shipment of Japanese-made antitank mines arrived at Pusan.

For years, American equipment left over at the end of World War II had been rusting on Pacific islands. Now it was reclaimed, cleaned up, refurbished, and headed for Korea. This did not solve the problem of modern weapons, but it helped stop the gaps. And as time went on, the weapons got better. Tanks were modified to use the high-velocity 76mm gun that could be effective against T-34's. The 105mm gun was modified so it could fire at high angle—an important factor in the Korean mountains. The World War II halftrack was modified to use a high-powered 40mm gun instead of the old 37mm.

To get any of this to Korea in time meant an airlift, and one was organized. At the outbreak of the war the Military Air Transport Service in the Far East had consisted of sixty planes. Their number was immediately boosted to two hundred fifty. And, after these first weeks, organized logistics operations were set up in Japan and Korea to start an orderly flow of supplies. The nature of the action had changed completely. The Americans were gearing up to stay.

All these preparations would be as nothing if the troops could not hold the enemy out of Pusan and maintain a perimeter large enough to allow for the buildup. And the Kum River was the first key. The river makes a great arc around Taejon. On the west and north of the river was the coastal plain, which stretches all the way to the Han. On the east are the Sobaek Mountains, and through them passes the main Seoul-Pusan road and railroad. The village of Taep'young-ni stands on the south bank of the Kum, where the road crosses the river. At Kongju, eight miles farther downstream, another road crosses.

The bridges at both places were blown and so was the railroad bridge. All boats along the river were also burned.

The North Korean attack plan was apparent to General Dean's staff. They were facing the North Korean 4th Division on the Kongju road, and the 3rd Division farther east. All the way to the east was the North Korean 2nd Division, deployed against the ROK troops. The North Koreans would launch a frontal attack and then one or two flanking attacks of great strength, as they had earlier.

But knowing what the enemy was going to do and stopping it were two different matters. Troops and weapons were the major problems. The North Korean troops were well trained for their jobs. The same could not be said of the Americans or the ROK Army. And the American weapons were no match for the North Korean artillery or the T-34 tanks. The tank problem was the worst. The United States had adequate weapons, but they were not in Korea or Japan.

GENERAL DEAN ALIGNED his forces roughly as they had been earlier. The 34th Infantry was on the left or eastern side of the great horseshoe of the Kum River around Taejon. (See the map "The Fall of Taejon.") The 21st Infantry was on the right, and the 19th Infantry was in reserve, south of Taejon.

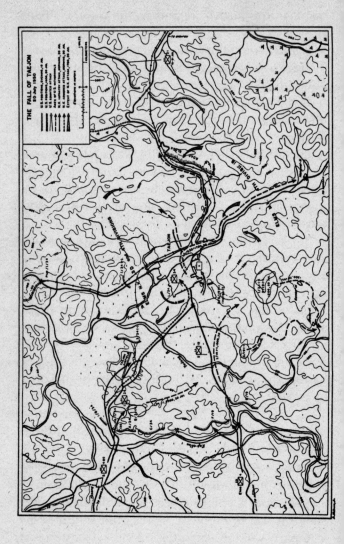

The overall strength of the 24th Division was 11,000 men, but the 21st Regiment, consisted of 1,100 fighting troops, the reinforced 34th was now up to 2,000 troops, most of whom were untried replacements; and the 19th Infantry strength stood at 2,200. The division artillery numbered about 2,000 men. The rest were engineers, special troops, and service troops.

North Korean strength had also been depleted in the recent fighting. The 4th Division, which had taken Chonan, was down to half strength, about 6,000 fighting men. Still the division had about fifty tanks.

The North Korean 3rd Division was much stronger and fresher, having come into the line only at Choch'iwon. However, it had to operate without tanks.

Over to the east, the North Korean 2nd Division had been reduced by heavy fighting but was still superior to the ROK forces it faced.

On the far left front stood the U.S. 34th Infantry's 3rd Battalion, with L Company at the flank. The company commander had tried to secure an operating radio. He did not get it. None were available, and as for field telephones, the shortage of communications wire prevented their use. So First Lieutenant Archie L. Stith might as well have been fighting the Franco-Prussian War as far as communication was concerned. Virtually every unit had this sort of problem. Three miles south of the company was the headquarters and two batteries of the 63rd Field Artillery, but Stith did not seem to be aware of them.

THE NORTH KOREAN attack began to shape up on the morning of July 13. The American troops on the south bank of the Kum could see the North Koreans moving around on the opposite bank. The North Korean artillery began shelling Kongju that afternoon.

The shelling had an immediate effect that even the North Koreans could not have anticipated. K Company of the 3rd Battalion had been reconstituted from whatever replacements came along, and under shelling these men cracked. The entire company, plus the battalion S-2 (intelligence) and S-3 (operations) officers had to be moved to Taejon for medical treatment. In the First World War they had called it "shell shock." In the Second World War they had called it "combat fatigue." Whatever they called the ailment, it represented a physical inability to perform in action. Such men were of no use.

As the North Korean advance built up, two understrength American companies watched them across the Kum. Behind them were mortars of the heavy-weapons company. The nearest friendly troops were the 129th Infantry two miles away.

Early on the morning of July 14 the North Koreans moved. They began with artillery fire on the infantry positions and followed it by sending troops across the river in barges. Some five hundred

North Koreans crossed the river before mid-morning.

Lieutenant Stith watched them come. He also saw an American artillery observation plane in the air. But the artillery did not fire on the barges. That was because the new battalion S-3 had decided to wait for bigger game. A Yak fighter came along and drove away the observation plane.

Soon the enemy organized and began to move toward Stith's L Company. The lieutenant tried to make contact with the machine gun and mortar sections but could not. He became alarmed at the increasing rate of enemy mortar and machine-gun fire against his position and ordered the men to withdraw. They moved back. As they did, one non-commissioned officer encountered a field artillery officer and told him what was happening—that the enemy was moving. He said the artillery officer did not pay any attention.

That sort of confusion seemed to exist everywhere. On July 13, the commanding officer of the 63rd Field Artillery had been evacuated to Taejon for medical reasons. He had been replaced by Major William E. Dressler, and changes had gone down the line. On the morning of July 14, the field artillery knew nothing of what was happening on the river; headquarters was not in touch with the troops on the river defense line.

LIEUTENANT STITH TOOK his company to 3rd Battalion headquarters. The battalion commander relieved him of his command on the spot and threatened him with court-martial.

The damage, however, was done. The North Korean troops were unopposed, as they moved south of the river against the 105mm howitzers of the 63rd Field Artillery Battalion.

The North Koreans moved steadily, and by one-thirty in the afternoon they were on the hill to the north side of the batteries. A soldier at an outpost saw them coming and reported to headquarters battery but was told they were probably friendly troops and not to open fire. The "friendly troops" came up, captured the outpost, and turned the gun against the headquarters battery.

They also used mortars. One of the first shells hit the communications switchboard and knocked out the lines to other batteries. Another shell hit the radio truck and destroyed it. All communication was gone.

Simultaneously a company of North Korean troops attacked A Battery. It was apparent that the North Koreans had reconnoitered the American positions carefully, and that their intelligence was leading them into a very effective attack. At this point it would have made no difference if Stith's company had been in the line. These North Koreans were after the artillery.

They got it because of the default of the artillerymen. The battery commander, Captain Lundel Southerland, was killed almost immediately. Then most of the battery panicked. A few fought like tigers. One such was Corporal Lawrence A. Ray, who used a Browning automatic rifle. He and a few others fought, while most of the artillerymen fled. Ray was knocked out and wounded by a mortar round. When he came to, he crawled into a ditch and there found 15 artillerymen, not one with a weapon. That whole group escaped by fleeing south.

The situation at the headquarters battery grew steadily worse. Major Dressler was killed. Enemy machine guns raked the position, and those still alive fled.

The North Koreans then turned to B Battery. By midafternoon at least three companies of enemy troops were employed in this assault. They came up with machine guns and mortars. The mortars were enormously effective. Captain Anthony F. Stahelski kept his men fighting. At 3:00 P.M. he ordered them to move the howitzers out, but the road was under fire and they could not. They had to abandon the guns.

By four o'clock in the afternoon, the 63rd Field Artillery was effectively wiped out. All that was left was the service battery, which fled south. The 63rd had lost ten 105mm howitzers, all their ammunition, and about eighty vehicles. The five guns of A Battery fell to the enemy intact, so confused and frightened were the artillerymen. The guns of B Battery were incapacitated by the captain's orders before the artillerymen retreated.

Once again, the failure of training showed up. If the American artillery had destroyed the boats reported early in the morning, the attack would never have materialized. If the unknown artillery officer had listened to the noncom from the 34th Infantry's 3rd Battalion as he reported the enemy movement, Major Dressler would not have been surprised and killed in his foxhole by a mortar shell. If the commander of Battery A had listened to his lookout and responded properly, the battery would not have been overrun. And if even one of those things had happened, B Battery would not have had to face a full enemy force that had come through two actions unscathed. It was a question of command and of officers fit to command. The headquarters battery and A Battery had collapsed when their commanders were killed. Few of those American troops were carrying field marshal's batons in their knapsacks.

THAT MORNING COLONEL Wadlington of the 34th Infantry had gone south to Nonsan to look over the area in case he had to withdraw. When he returned to headquarters at Ponggong-ni, south of Kongju, he discovered the fate of the 63rd although he did not then know how bad it was. He ordered Colonel Ayres' 1st Battalion to attack and rescue the guns and men. Ayres set out to do the job but ran into heavy enemy fire and bogged down. His orders had been to withdraw if the mission could not be accomplished by dark, and darkness was coming.

So Ayres turned the men and moved back to Nonsan, which had been designated as the new regimental area.

Back on the Kum River, the 3rd Battalion's I Company kept a lonely vigil. Lieutenant Joseph E. Hicks, the company commander, tried to find L Company, but of course they had fled. I Company was under heavy mortar fire most of the morning. But no infantry attack followed. Hicks held his position until nine-thirty that night, when he had orders to withdraw and rejoin the regiment. So he too went to Nonsan.

WHEN GENERAL DEAN learned of the loss of the 63rd Field Artillery, he ordered an air strike for the next morning. If they couldn't recover the guns, at least he hoped to destroy them so they could not be used by the enemy.

The Air Force was more than willing to comply. Like the ground forces, the air units were beginning to get organized for combat.

On July 10 four Yak 9's attacked troops of the U.S. 19th Regiment near Chongju, and the next day more Yaks attacked a group of American F-80's that were strafing in support of troops. The F-80's were short of fuel and could not respond properly. The same thing happened the next day, and a B-29 was trapped by three Yak-9's and shot down that day. Other attacks on observation planes and B-26's in the next few days caused General Stratemeyer's command to reassess the problem of enemy air power, and out of that reassessment came the decision to wipe it out. This meant that bases had to be established in Korea because of the range problems.

On July 15, General Partridge learned that seven or eight Yak fighters were operating out of Kimpo Airfield. That day he sent a flight of F-80's to attack the field and later a flight of B-29's. These attacks quieted down the Kimpo operations. But then air Intelligence learned that the major enemy airfields were Pyongyang and Yonpo, and orders were given to the carrier *Valley Forge* to take care of them. On July 18 and 19 the carrier ran a "mail run" and in two days fighters and bombers knocked out a claimed 32 enemy aircraft on the ground and damaged another 13. On July 19, F-80 fighters from the 8th Fighter-Bomber Group launched a strike on a field near Pyongyang and destroyed 15 enemy fighters. In the next few days all these fields were plastered by the B-29s and other planes. Between July 17 and July 20, F-80 pilots destroyed six enemy fighters in the air. By July 21, the North Korean Air Force had ceased to become a problem. As soon as enemy planes were discovered, an air raid knocked them out. The Yanks no longer bothered the troops.

BUT IT WAS going to take a lot more than air power to hold the line in South Korea until General MacArthur's major reinforcements could come up. And so far, the American performance still left a great deal to be desired. The North Koreans had breached the Kum River line with ridiculous ease, not even depending on the superior firepower of their tanks but employing about 500 troops with no weapons larger than mortars. The 19th Infantry's left flank was completely exposed. Based on the performance of the 34th Infantry, it seemed doubtful if Taejon could be held.

General Dean was past the point of complaint. He recognized, as had MacArthur, that the troops he had to work with were second-class. At the moment they were all he had and there was no use badgering them.

That night, while the North Koreans moved across the river in force, consolidated on the south bank, and brought their tanks across by barge, General Dean moved around the command working over alternative plans in his head.

What he would do in the next few hours with his inadequate forces could establish the defense of the Pusan Perimeter. Or it could be just another failure.

6.

The Battle for Taejon

ON JULY 17 only the U.S. 34th Infantry remained in contact with the enemy. The North Korean 3rd Division stood above Taejon. The North Korean 4th Division was off to the northwest. Since Taejon was a large market city, the network of roads provided numerous alternatives for the North Korean attack. Their traditional tactics, now well enough known to the Americans, involved envelopment on both sides of a front. Dean's problem was to stop that envelopment with a numerically inferior force that was also inferior in arms. On paper, the 24th Division consisted of three regiments. Actually the regimental commanders could put together about three battalions, or a third of a regiment, to oppose two still strong divisions.

After the loss of Colonel Martin, a new commander had to be brought in for the 34th Regiment. He was Colonel Charles E. Beauchamp. He put his troops out three miles west of Taejon and his command post on the Taejon airfield.

General Dean brought together most of what was left of his field artillery and placed it at the airstrip. On the afternoon of June 17 General Dean ordered his divisional headquarters to move down to Yongdong, but he elected to stay at Taejon and moved his personal headquarters in with Colonel Beauchamp's command post. It was a radical move, but Dean felt that communications were so bad that he must be on the scene for this defensive effort. "It was easier to get a message through toward the rear . . . than toward the front."

General Dean's plan was to hold back the North Koreans as long as possible northwest of Taejon, at the Yusong position, which was built on two long ridges. At the last minute he would move the troops back to another prepared position and try again to hold. This made sense only if the 25th Division and/or the 1st Cavalry could be brought up to help very soon. The 25th Division was just then occupied on the east coast but was expected to be freed momentarily.

Nothing happened on July 17 as the North Koreans consolidated and brought up replacements and weapons for the Battle of Taejon. They also repaired the bridge across the Kum River ten miles north of Taejon. Then they moved tanks and artillery across. If the Americans had been able to keep the bridge down, the attack might have been delayed longer, but at the moment tactical aircraft

could operate from only two fields in South Korea,
so most of the missions had to originate in Japan.
Even so, the Fifth Air Force might have devoted
more effort at that moment to tactical support. A
few B-26 raids on that bridge at Taep'yong-ni
might have made a lot of difference.

On the morning of July 18 General Dean
planned the move out of Taejon, which he expected
to make on the following day. The 21st Infantry
was assigned the task of blowing up the railroad
and road tunnels east of Taejon, which ought to
slow the North Koreans a bit.

General Dean's plans were to come to nothing.
That day General Walker arrived at Taejon and
took over. He had decided that the 24th Division
and the ROK Army to the east should hold as long
as possible as far north as possible. If they had to be
totally expended, well, that was war. This delaying
action would give Walker a chance to bring up the
1st Cavalry to Okch'on, south of Taejon but north
of the Naktong River line.

Walker did not tell General Dean what was on
his mind. He did tell him that the 1st Cavalry had
begun landing at P'ohang-dong on the east coast of
Korea. He wanted the 24th Division to hold at
Taejon until he could bring them up. This would
take two days. At this point, the better part of gener-
alship would probably have indicated that General
Dean ought to move back to his own headquarters,
but he did not. He felt decisions might arrive that

would have to be made on the spot, although in fact his power of decision had just been preempted.

Walker wasn't completely obdurate. At their conference the senior general gave Dean permission to withdraw if it became necessary. But Walker closed by remarking how vital it was to the plan that the reinforcements have those two days to arrive.

General Dean prepared to do the improbable. He went back to Yongdong and ordered the 2nd Battalion of the 19th Infantry to move up to Taejon to reinforce the 34th. The division's intelligence and reconnaissance company was sent up to Taejon too, as was B Battery of the 13th Field Artillery. Dean stopped off to talk to Colonel Stephens and emphasize that the 21st Infantry had to keep the withdrawal road out of Taejon clear for two days. Then, having done all he could with the slender forces available, the general went back to Taejon.

THE NORTH KOREAN attack began early on July 19. The first surprise was an air strike. The U.S. Air Force had not done as well as it believed against the Yaks. The strikes at the source, north of the 38th parallel, were certainly strategically important, but tactically, those strikes cost the defenders of Taejon valuable air support. The proof was that six North Korean Yaks came over the railroad bridge south of Taejon and dropped bombs. They damaged the bridge, but the American engineers had it operating again in a few hours. The attack, however, was a signal that the North Koreans planned to envelop the city and cut off the defenders' retreat.

ONCE ACROSS THE Kum River, the North Korean 3rd Division took position north of Taejon, to maintain pressure there. The major attack was to be carried by the North Korean 4th Division, and as usual it was led by T-34 tanks. Two regiments and most of the artillery and tanks moved south to Nonsan and from there turned east toward Taejon. One regiment moved straight south through Kongju toward Taejon. It was that same flanking movement, but the Americans did not know it and would not because of the dreadful state of American communications. When General Dean had released the intelligence and reconnaissance company from divisional headquarters control it had gone up the line. Therefore, the I and R company was not available for the scouting it should have been doing around Taejon to reveal the nature of the North Korean attack. It probably would have made little difference, since the disparity of forces and weapons between the two sides was so heavily weighted in favor of the North Koreans.

On the morning of July 19 General Dean came up to the 34th Infantry just about the time the North Korean flank assault began to develop. He was with troops of the 3rd Battalion at their position astride the Nonsan road. As the attack began, Colonel McGrail, commander of the 2nd Battalion of the 19th Infantry, came up to help. Two of his companies thwarted the North Korean envelopment plan and took and held some high ground vital to the position. But once this was done, the difficulty of the American situation became even more starkly apparent: There was an open gap of a mile between the 19th's positions and the 1st Battalion of the 34th Regiment on the north.

After the attack had developed on the flank, the North Koreans hit from the north down the Seoul-Pusan highway. Again on a local basis, they used their enveloping technique, which could not help but be effective given their much larger number of troops. Two platoons of the 34th Infantry were cut off, and the soldiers had to fight their way out. Colonel Ayres had to pull his troops back along the road toward Taejon before noon.

The North Koreans had concentrated their heavy artillery on the frontal position, and they delivered a long barrage against the American positions around the airfield. That evening the American positions contracted again, this time into the city of Taejon.

That night the North Koreans moved into the mile-wide gap between the 34th Infantry's 1st Battalion and the 19th Infantry. From the west came the flanking movement, and by midnight the North Koreans had reached the road south of Taejon. Two incidents indicated this: At one point Colonel Ayres sent a patrol out to investigate tank noises on his flank. The patrol never came back. At another point a patrol from the I and R Company went south to investigate along the main road. They were stopped by enemy troops six miles south of Taejon. They reported back. On the basis of these reports, Colonel Ayres suggested to Colonel Beauchamp that they ought to withdraw from the city. Beauchamp, however, was mindful of General Dean's intense desire to hold another day, and he rejected the idea. Somehow in a failure of communication—perhaps it was because General Dean was moving around the line so much—he did not learn of the existence of the roadblock.

The situation seemed to quiet down during the early hours of morning, but at 3:00 A.M. the North Koreans began to move. Their first strike was against the forward position of the 34th Infantry's 1st Battalion on the main Pusan road north of Taejon. Infantry and armor came down the road and struck the battalion's right flank. As usual, the North Koreans went after the weapons before they hit the men. They got into the 81mm and 4.2-inch mortar positions and then struck the headquarters company. This meant they had excellent intelligence, and it meant the Americans were being betrayed, again and again, by Koreans.

All through this defensive campaign the Korean civilians had moved freely among the Americans. It was easy enough for a "refugee" to observe where the command post was located, see the mortars and artillery go into place and then, out of sight, throw down his refugee bundle and proceed to the first North Korean outpost and report. How often this occurred is impossible to say, but an examination of the North Korean attack patterns shows a knowledge of the changing American positions that indicates either that the enemy was receiving assistance from behind the lines or that its intelligence officers were clairvoyant.

One mission of the North Korean tanks that morning was to take infantry into Taejon and set them up as snipers to harry the Americans. Five tanks were assigned this task.

The North Koreans again showed the importance that treachery played in the campaign. When the tanks entered Taejon that morning, unerringly they went to the position occupied by the service company of the 34th Infantry, which meant the kitchens and motor pool. They shot up this compound, destroyed the vehicles and an ammunition truck, and moved out.

General Dean and his aide had spent the night in Taejon. They awoke at five-thirty to the sound of small-arms fire. The general got up and found a pair of bazooka teams (armed with the almost useless 2.36-inch rocket) and went out tank-hunting.

WITHIN AN HOUR after the beginning of the North Korean assault, it became apparent to Colonel Ayres that he was going to have to evacuate his command post. Enemy troops had come down through the bazooka teams (which apparently had failed to hold for any time at all) and through the rifle companies (of which the same had to be said).

By dawn the battalion headquarters and heavy-weapons company were on the move, going south.

Yes, the North Koreans were moving fast.

But that morning, something positive happened for a change. Colonel Beauchamp, commander of the 34th Infantry, heard from Colonel Ayres that the enemy was on the road near Taejon Airfield. Beauchamp got into his jeep and started up to the 1st Battalion command post to see for himself. On the way he ran into a T-34 tank and very nearly got himself killed. One bullet grazed him, and others set his jeep afire. He crawled back along the road and found part of the answer to the T-34s. Finally the Americans had received a weapon that was effective against the T-34s armor—the 3.5-inch bazooka. A few of these had come to Korea in the past day or two, and Beauchamp lucked onto one of them, operated by a team of C Company of the 3rd Engineer Combat Battalion. He sent the team forward. The men found the tank at a road intersection and promptly set it afire with rockets. The team then took up position at the intersection and waited for more tanks.

The Americans at last had a really modern weapon, but they had very few of them. The ammunition for these bazookas had been put into production fifteen days before. This dismal fact seems hard to believe, given the history of American warfare. Back in 1943, when the U.S. 82nd Airborne Division dropped into Sicily, Brigadier General James Gavin had noted officially the vast superiority of

German bazookas over American. In the Normandy invasion the standard American bazooka had proved of so little worth against German Panzer tanks that the American bazooka men considered it an enormous prize to find an enemy bazooka and the ammunition for it. Six years later, the Americans were just getting ready to fight the German tanks of World War II.

That one weapon did not make a big dent in the North Korean advance. The 1st Battalion was in deep trouble, cut off from the rear by the North Korean flanking movement. Beauchamp ordered the 3rd Battalion to attack in that gap between the 19th and the 34th, but when they came up, they found no gap existed—it was occupied by North Koreans, who had half a dozen tanks. The Americans were very nearly trapped until saved by a single soldier, Sergeant First Class Robert E. Dare, who took up a defensive position and sent the advance platoon back while he covered them. Dare was killed, but not before he had saved his company and perhaps the battalion from annihilation.

By midmorning the North Korean frontal assault unit, the 5th Infantry Regiment of the North Korean 4th Division, had captured the airfield. Here the regiment stopped, waiting for the enveloping force to do its work west and south of the city. The American forces at Taejon moved south.

The American command was completely confused and misinformed about the situation that existed by noon. Colonel Beauchamp did not know that his 3rd Battalion attack had failed or that the North Koreans had interposed themselves between the 1st Battalion and the 19th Regiment troops in the mile-wide gap northwest of Taejon. So when General Dean inquired, Beauchamp indicated that all was well. Actually the American position could hardly have been much worse.

What happened was that the 1st Battalion found itself surrounded and Colonel Ayres led a move that brought the men into the mountains and out of the fight. The alternative was captivity or death for every man.

THE LOSS OF the 1st Battalion of the 34th Infantry meant the American front had no cohesion at all. General Dean did not know what was happening and was out of communication with Colonel Beauchamp except by messenger. Colonel McGrail, commander of the 2nd Battalion of the 19th Infantry, was also out of communication with Beauchamp. The bazooka team at the crossroads near the airfield had knocked out another T-34 tank and was then joined by an infantry platoon and another of the good 3.5-inch bazookas. This was probably the strongest American position anywhere around Taejon. The trouble was it was in the wrong place, almost entirely surrounded by the enemy and out of communication with everybody.

General Dean came up to the position that morning having failed to knock off any tanks with the old-style bazookas. But tanks were falling. By nine o'clock four of the five tanks that had entered Taejon had been destroyed.

IN THE CONFUSION that accompanied the failure of communications, Colonel McGrail's 19th Infantry, 2nd Battalion was cut off and it, too, moved into the mountains and out of the fight. By midafternoon not a single unit of the battalion was in the position that showed on General Dean's map.

In the fighting in Taejon that morning one building went up in flames, and the fire soon spread through the city. The only effective defenses were small enclaves of troops knocking out a tank here and there with one of their 3.5-inch bazookas.

General Dean spent most of the day tank-hunting. His purpose was not personal glory but the necessity of inspiring his men, who had become almost as leery of the enemy tanks as were the South Koreans. Now that the Americans had a weapon that could knock out the tanks, Dean wanted it used to the utmost. He knew that one of the strongest factors in the North Korean advance was their ability to penetrate at will with the T-34s.

As the day wore on, the troops became more enthusiastic about the new bazooka. The word was passed, and morale in Taejon went up. Inside Taejon they destroyed an estimated ten tanks. The Air Force also was helping. In the morning, as the tanks rumbled down the road toward Taejon, the fighter planes were on them with rockets and napalm. They destroyed five or six tanks. The positive result of all this newfound activity was that for the first time the North Korean tanks failed completely in their mission, which had been to terrorize the Americans in Taejon and force them to run in panic into the arms of the North Korean flanking force coming east over the roads south of the city. Instead, all the North Korean tanks in Taejon were destroyed. General Dean had proved a point.

However, the battle inside Taejon was not the decisive action. The fate of the city was being decided outside to the north and west, where both American defensive battalions had been scattered. General Dean and Colonel Beauchamp lunched together on C rations at noon, confident that the battle was going well. It *was* going well for the North Koreans. The American defenses had completely evaporated into the mountains south of the city.

At lunch the two commanders decided they had given General Walker his two days and it was time to withdraw. Since communications were so bad, runners were sent to inform the battalions involved. But the runners to the 2nd Battalion of the 19th Infantry and the 1st Battalion of the 34th Infantry were swallowed by the war, and General Dean still did not learn that those units had disappeared to the south.

The 3rd Battalion of the 34th Infantry did receive the withdrawal order. That unit and various miscellaneous units soon prepared to move down the road. A platoon of tanks came up from the 1st Cavalry Division to escort the column.

All this while the senior officers were receiving reports from various sources outside the city about "enemy" units moving toward Taejon from the east, west, and south. They did not believe the reports, preferring to understand that these were friendly troops. Once again failures in communications proved virtually fatal, because all these columns were enemy.

As the Americans began to move south toward Taegu, the North Koreans were on hand to ambush them. On the north and west the North Koreans were moving in to take the city.

From this point on, the American defense of Taejon dissolved in total confusion. (See the map "The Fall of Taejon.") Colonel Beauchamp went out in his jeep to try to restore some order and ended up down at Okchon reporting to General Menoher, the assistant division commander, on what was happening to the north. Menoher could make no sense of the conflicting and erroneous reports.

All this time, General Dean was moving around the edges of Taejon, believing that the battle was going splendidly, until he discovered that Beauchamp was missing. At that point Dean began to have the feeling that something definitely was wrong, and, attempting to hurry the evacuation of Taejon, he told Colonel Wadlington, the regimental executive officer, to get the show on the road.

That meant, among other things, getting the artillery out. This proved to be a problem, because the North Koreans had moved up until they were almost close enough to take the batteries. A counterattack was organized, the North Koreans were forced back, and as many guns were saved as the Americans had tractors to attach them to. The others were wrecked.

By late afternoon it became apparent that the North Koreans were thick along the road south and that the convoys would have to run several gauntlets of fire. General Dean sent a message back to his headquarters calling for armor to come up and clear the area. By this time the North Koreans were pouring shells into the city and causing casualties among the troops still there.

It was six o'clock that evening before Colonel Wadlington led the main convoy out of town. Even before they got outside the limits, they came under fire from North Korean machine guns alongside the main road. Wadlington got lost in the city, came to a dead-end schoolyard, burned his jeep, and headed into the mountains. Fifty more vehicles of the convoy later took the same wrong turn, ended up in the schoolyard, abandoned their vehicles, and also went up into the mountains. The groups became separated during the night. Some made it back to the U.S. lines. Some were captured. Some were killed. Many were betrayed by the Koreans.

General Dean's jeep started traveling with the convoy but took a wrong turn and ended up on the

Kumsan road. (See the map "The Fall of Taejon.") The main convoy went down the Okch'on highway. The North Koreans were on both sides of the road and kept knocking off vehicles. The troops got out and fought, then got back in and rode a little farther. Each time a group of vehicles stopped there was more loss, and more men burned their vehicles and moved into the hills to make their way in little groups toward the American lines as best they could.

BY NIGHTFALL THE convoy was in shambles. Enemy mortars searched out every vehicle. This dreadful time is best described through the experiences of Sergeant George D. Libby of C Company of the 3rd Engineer Combat Battalion.

Sergeant Libby was riding out of Taejon in a truck when it came to one of the roadblocks. The truck was disabled, and everyone in it was killed or wounded but Libby. He jumped off into the ditch alongside the road and began giving first aid to the wounded. He stopped an artillery tractor that was going through the roadblock, put the wounded from his truck aboard, and got in next to the driver on the enemy's side. He knew that only this driver could operate the tractor, and he wanted to protect him.

The tractor moved on south, running the gauntlet of fire. Libby was wounded several times. They came to another roadblock. Libby was wounded again, but they got through. He lost consciousness and died from loss of blood. However, the driver got the tractor through. Libby was later posthumously awarded the Congressional Medal of Honor.

That night an effort was made to break the road-block from the Okch'on side. Colonel Beauchamp rounded up a number of infantry and five tanks. They moved forward, but the enemy had been given too much time in a roadblocking position. Their engineers had set mines in the road. One of the U.S. tanks hit a mine. Then a string of antipersonnel mines was detonated. Every foot of the way north was contested. Beauchamp's improvised unit fought as long as its ammunition held out and then had to give up and retreat south. The roadblocks stood.

During the night many of the Americans escaped by walking east through the mountains and skirting the roadblock. The highways were strewn with abandoned vehicles and guns and equipment, and the road to Okch'on was, to all effects, impassable.

AFTER GENERAL DEAN'S jeep took the wrong turn and headed down the Kumsan road, there was no turning back because they were under fire. Another jeep was accompanying him. They went along until they came to an overturned U.S. truck with several wounded men lying nearby. Dean loaded the men into the jeeps and sent them on. He then climbed into an artillery half-track that came by. It moved south but soon ran into another roadblock, and the men got out alongside the road when the firing became intense. Several were wounded.

Dean and the others lay in a ditch for a while, then crawled through a bean patch to the bank of the Taejon River. They remained there until dark and then began climbing the mountain north of the village of Nangwol. Dean decided to go down the mountain to get water for the wounded, and he set off by himself. He fell down a steep slope and passed out. When he came to, he had a broken shoulder and cuts and bruises. He was disoriented, but he began to walk.

The rest of his party waited on the mountain for two hours, then went on and finally made their way back to the American lines. General Dean wandered in the mountains for thirty-six days, but he was moving right along with the North Korean Army. Finally he met a pair of South Koreans who promised to take him to safety. Instead they betrayed him and led him into a North Korean ambush, where he was captured. His weight had dropped from one hundred and ninety pounds to one hundred and thirty. (His betrayers later were caught and convicted. One of them was executed and the other sentenced to life imprisonment.)

The Battle of Taejon ended in the complete rout of the American forces. They lost their general and eleven hundred and fifty of four thousand men engaged. As was the way in the Korean War, the casualty totals were confusing. Only about fifty men were known dead. Over two hundred were wounded, but about nine hundred were missing in action. Most of these were killed, many of them after they had been captured.

7.

The Road of Defeat

GIVEN THE FORCES available to him and the situation in which the U.S. Army found itself in Korea, traditional military strategy would have dictated an immediate retreat to Pusan and evacuation of the Americans until General MacArthur could prepare for a reentry into Korea by amphibious landing.

But MacArthur had been along that road before. The loss of the Philippines in the early days of World War II had been a major psychological defeat for the United States and a great propaganda victory for the Japanese. The stakes in 1950 were even higher, and the evacuation of the Americans might have created crises in half a dozen parts of the world.

Further, General MacArthur had confidence that he would be able to get enough troops and equipment into Korea to stop the North Korean advance short of Pusan. It was a gamble, but one in which

MacArthur was joined by the authorities in Washington and backed by most of America. The price, as everyone familiar with the military situation knew, was going to be more losses before the tide was turned.

Already the Americans had accomplished one major strategic victory. General Dean's 24th Division, despite its deficiencies in leadership and training, had held long enough for two more divisions to be brought into South Korea. True, these divisions were scarcely better trained or officered than the 24th, but at least the Americans had slowed the North Korean advance and destroyed the enemy master battle plan.

At this point the Americans had about 39,000 men in South Korea. In itself this was a remarkable accomplishment, considering that a month earlier the entire American force in South Korea had consisted of a handful of military advisers. And better-trained and better-equipped U.S. troops were on the way to Korea: two battalions of the 29th Infantry, the 5th Regimental Combat Team (striking force), two regiments of the 2nd Infantry Division, and the 1st Provisional Marine Brigade. Besides this, the Navy was recommissioning fifty World War II warships for service in Korea. Each day these forces came closer. Five other nations had promised to send troops to Korea on the U.N. side. Time was the vital factor. If the Americans could hold for a few weeks more, the war could be turned around.

ON THE EAST coast, the South Koreans were retreating steadily, but fighting hard on their way south. They were helped by naval bombardment carried out by American and British ships, which delayed the advance of the North Koreans down the coastal road. In one daring raid on July 12, Commander William B. Porter, the executive officer of the cruiser *Juneau,* took a party ashore far north of the 38th parallel to blow up a strategically important railroad tunnel near Songjin on the Chongjin-Wonsan railroad.

But the major effort of the naval forces had to be directed at support of the South Korean retreat, and this meant working over the North Korean 5th Division as it advanced down the coast.

It also involved the first amphibious operation of the war, the landing of the 1st Cavalry Division at Pohang. The use of this minor port was necessary because the facilities at Pusan were enormously overworked trying to bring in replacement troops and supplies for the 24th and 25th divisions. The landing was well within the territory controlled by the ROK forces, so there was no opposition. And as General Dean's force was taking its beating on the Seoul-Pusan road, the 1st Cavalry was moving north and west.

Otherwise affairs were going badly on the east coast. On July 17, the North Koreans drove the ROK forces out of Yongdok. General Walker was distressed by this failure and attempted to change the situation. The Navy began bombarding the town. A battery of the 159th Field Artillery was brought up to help the South Koreans, and for the next two weeks they fought the Battle of Yongdok, in which the town changed hands several times.

This fighting was marked by "unusually accurate" mortar fire from the North Koreans. Again there must have been a reason for this; the suspicion is inescapable that spies in the South Korean camp were responsible. To bring spies into the South Korean lines was not nearly so hard as it might seem to a Westerner. The South Korean Army depended on all sorts of camp followers. Most of the meals were cooked by women. Most of the supplies were carried by civilians on A-frame packboards. It was not strange to see numbers of civilians moving in and out of the camps without question. Such a situation lent itself to espionage and certainly contributed to the North Korean strength.

But in the end, the Allies held the North Korean 5th Division at Yongdok and cost the North Koreans casualties adding up to 40 percent of the division.

West of the North Korean 5th Division, the North Korean 12th Division was moving south toward Andong on the Naktong River. The terrain was so rough that the South Korean troops were able to put up a fair defense. Still, everywhere but on the far eastern coast the South Koreans and Americans were being pushed back.

Next to the North Korean 12th Division, on the west side, was the North Korean 8th Division, then the North Korean 1st Division, the North Korean 13th and 15th divisions, the 2nd Division, then the 3rd and 4th, and finally on the western side of the peninsula, the North Korean 6th Division.

At this point in the war, Kim Il-sung, the generalissimo-president of the North Korean People's Republic, was very unhappy with the progress of the war. He sensed that on the east his troops were being slowed down, and perhaps he even had the feeling then that this invasion was not going to work out quite as he had expected. The big surprise had been the decision of the United States to fight for South Korea. The question that remained was how hard and how competently the softened Americans would fight. The North Koreans mounted an enormous propaganda campaign, vowing to drive "the American aggressors" and the "Syngman Rhee puppet troops" out of South Korea altogether. They were bringing four more divisions down from North Korea to speed the task.

An interview at that point with General MacArthur or General Walker would not have helped Kim Il-sung's digestive processes. Although the battles were going badly, the determination of these commanders to succeed was even stronger than it had been earlier; and the total support they were receiving from Washington meant everything.

WITH THE DISAPPEARANCE of General Dean, General Walker appointed General Church to command the U.S. 24th Infantry Division. But the 24th was in no condition to bear the brunt of any fighting at this point. Others would have to carry the load.

OVER ON THE east coast, the North Korean objective was P'ohang-dong, with its big half-moon bay, and Yonil Airfield south of the port, where American fighters were now operating. The ability of the Korean-U.N. Allies to hold Yongdok prevented the loss of that town.

To the west in the last part of July a desperate battle was fought for the city of Andong, which lies on the upper part of the Naktong River. The Naktong starts about one hundred miles north of the southern tip of the peninsula in the Taebek Mountains and meanders its way south down the center of the peninsula until it is joined by the Nam River from the northwest. This river provided several natural defense lines, including one for Taegu, and most important, one for Pusan.

The North Korean battle plan called for the 12th Division to seize Andong and then start down the road to Uisong. For ten days at the end of July the ROK 8th Division fought a series of bloody battles against the North Koreans in this mountain country. The failure of the 12th Division to capture Andong straightaway and the failure of the North Korean 5th Division to capture Yongdok caused a major shake-up in the North Korean field command, with Major General Kim Hwang-hyop removed as II Corps commander and replaced by Lieutenant General Kim Mu-chong. Generalis-

simo Kim Il-sung issued orders: P'ohang-dong was
to be captured by July 26 without fail. But on July
26, the North Korean 12th Division still had not
reached Andong. The North Korean impetus had
definitely been slowed down.

Finally, on August 1, by exhausting itself, the
North Korean 12th Division did manage to capture
Andong. But in that effort it lost its division commander (killed), lost half its tanks, and burned out
its division artillery. The month ended with the
North Korean 12th Division immobilized at Andong.

AT THIS JUNCTURE, the ROK Army finally had
enough respite to pull itself together and reorgan-
ize, a move that the Americans had been urging
since the fall of Seoul. The "new" ROK Army
consisted of two army corps, each consisting of two
divisions and auxiliary troops, and one independent division on the east coast. The ROK II Corps
position abutted that of the Americans at Hamch'ang. The ROK I Corps headquarters was at
Sangju. On paper the Army had rebuilt its strength
to 85,000 troops, taking in thousands of recruits. In
fact, wherever there was serious threat, General
Walker interposed an American unit.

That was the case at Sangju. It was obvious that
the North Koreans intended to continue their
advance down the middle of the peninsula, even if
the North Korean 12th Division was stopped for the
time being. General Walker ordered the U.S. 25th

Division to stop the North Korean movement in the upper Naktong Valley. The Americans penetrated north as far as Yech'on, about twenty miles west of Andong, and then turned this area over to the South Koreans for defense. The South Korean line in the last days of July ran from a point just south of Andong, west to Hamch'ang, then south just east of the road that led to Sangju, Hwanggan, and then to Kumch'on. Backing up the ROK forces were the U.S. 25th Division on the north and the U.S. 1st Cavalry Division on the southwest. Below them, west of Taegu, was the recovering U.S. 24th Division.

THE FIRST ACTION of importance in this area came on July 22, when troops of the North Korean 1st Division began an assault near Hamch'ang. The assistant commander of the 25th Division had decided it would be a good idea to strengthen the ROK troop units there by putting a company of Americans in the middle of the South Korean line. Colonel Henry Fisher, commander of the 35th Infantry Regiment, protested. He said his troops were untried, and if something happened, he could not guarantee their performance. He was overruled.

So F Company of the 2nd Battalion of the 35th Infantry was put into the South Korean line. On the morning of the 22nd, when the North Koreans attacked, "something happened," as Colonel Fisher had feared. The South Koreans fled without giving any warning to the American company. The

Americans learned they were alone when the enemy began firing at them from hills at their rear. They wanted to retreat, but the way was blocked by a rushing stream. Two officers tied telephone lines around their waists and tried to swim the stream but failed. Finally, a platoon of U.S. tanks on the other side of the stream held the North Koreans down long enough for the survivors to escape, but some were drowned and many were killed or captured.

On the morning of July 23 enemy tanks came up toward Hamch'ang. The American 90th Field Artillery Battalion began firing on the tanks. The Americans had the right sort of ammunition, and in short order four of the five tanks involved were destroyed. The other tank moved back but was knocked out by an air strike. What a difference that was from the earliest action, when Task Force Smith watched helplessly as Colonel Perry's artillery shells glanced off the sides of the advancing North Korean tanks.

The trouble was that there was not enough of this sort of strength to go around. Much of the South Korean Army was fighting almost exclusively with hand weapons. They had few mortars, and most of them were inoperable. They did not have enough machine guns. They had lost their artillery for the most part. Consequently, in the face of the push from the North Korean 1st Division, the South Koreans fell back steadily, and the 35th Regiment had also to fall back. It retreated to set up a position, discovered that the line had dissolved, and retreated again. Where the South Koreans had modern weapons, they did very well. Indeed they made better use of the outmoded 2.36-inch bazooka than the Americans did. The ROK 6th Division reportedly destroyed seven enemy tanks with those bazookas.

The North Korean 1st Division came on. The cost was enormous; the divisional commander was wounded and replaced. Five thousand casualties was the price of the move along the central plateau. But they moved.

THE AMERICAN 24TH Infantry Regiment's 2nd Battalion was badly shot up in an encounter with the enemy west of Sangju. The 24th was the only force guarding the western approach to Sangju, and it was not very effective. The men were not ready for combat, and at the slightest sign of trouble, they panicked. On one occasion one battalion ran away from a fight, leaving behind almost all its machine guns, mortars, 3.5-inch bazookas, and more than 100 rifles. When an infantryman abandons his weapon he is either untrained or in real panic. The men of the 24th Infantry qualified on both counts, and they panicked not once but several times. On July 29 the whole 1st Battalion fled, leaving Colonel Horton V. White, the regimental commander, to hold the line with one combat engineer company and a field artillery battery. Hold it they did, firing 3,000 rounds of ammunition that night while Colonel White found and reorganized his

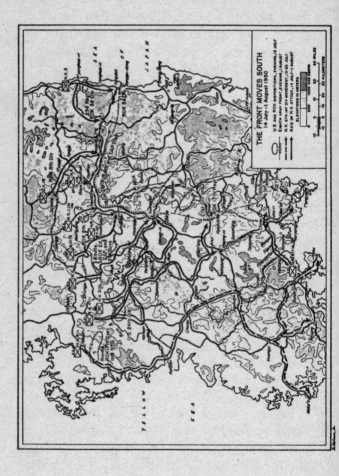

THE FRONT MOVES SOUTH
14 July–1 August 1950

U.S. AND ROK DISPOSITIONS, EVENING, 14 JULY
Eighth Army FRONT, EVENING, 1 AUGUST
N.K. 6TH DIV. OF MOVEMENT, 13–25 JULY
AXIS OF N.K. ATTACK, JULY–1 AUGUST

ELEVATIONS IN METERS

200   1000 AND OVER

men. The performance was so disgraceful that the regiment command established a roadblock east of the regiment's troops and stopped every vehicle coming from the battle area, taking off what they called "stragglers" (in an earlier war they would have been called deserters) and sending them back to the line.

By July 30 the regiment was so disorganized that General Kean, the division commander, brought in part of the 35th Infantry to support the 24th. In one action a lieutenant and fifteen men fled their positions. They were ordered back into the line but the lieutenant refused to go, saying he was scared. The senior sergeant took the soldiers back to their position and assumed command of the platoon.

Finally, on the last day of July, the 24th Regiment was withdrawn from the line, and the 35th took over the defense position west of Sangju.

FARTHER EAST THE newly arrived 1st Cavalry Division was in trouble. At the opening of hostilities General Walker had transferred seven hundred fifty noncommissioned officers from this division to the 24th and 25th divisions. Possibly these transfers were all that made it possible for the divisions to fight at all. The 1st Cavalry Division got replacements, but they were not trained, and part of them were out of the divisional punishment stockade. Victor McLaglen movies to the contrary, in real military life men with disciplinary problems do not usually make very good soldiers. This unusual transfer indicated just how hard General MacArthur was scraping the bottom of the barrel in Japan. The 1st Cavalry was one battalion short and had only two firing batteries of artillery and one M-24 light-tank company.

When the division arrived, General Walker told Major General Hobart R. Gay that he must protect Yongdong, an important road center about twenty miles west of the end of the South Korean line at Kumch'on. There were no friendly troops left to send between the 1st Cavalry and Taegu, so Gay would have to keep his own lines of communication open.

On July 22, the 8th Cavalry Regiment relieved the 21st Infantry Regiment of the 24th Division at Yongdong.

At Yongdong, however, General Gay learned that he was not a free agent. An officer of the operations section of the Eighth Army indicated that he must place one battalion of his troops northwest of Yongdong and another battalion southeast. These battalions would have no contact. Thus they could easily be surrounded and cut off. The general said he would not do this unless General Walker's headquarters confirmed the demand. Walker's headquarters did confirm it. So the troops of the 8th Calvary Regiment were placed in that fashion. The 5th Cavalry Regiment was placed east of Yongdong to protect the town.

ON JULY 22, the North Korean 3rd Division moved

out of Taejon along the main highway that leads to Yongdong and then to Taegu beyond. That division was relatively fresh, having had only a frontal assault to carry out against Taejon.

The 1st Battalion of the 8th Cavalry Regiment was in place to face them on that road. On July 23 the first tanks came up against the American positions, and three of the tanks were knocked out by the 3.5-inch bazookas.

Once again the North Koreans moved to envelop. One element launched a frontal assault on the 1st Battalion, while a second moved around to the southwest of the 2nd Battalion and placed a roadblock a mile and a half in the rear. This was just what General Gay had been worried about in the establishment of positions.

On July 24 the 8th Cavalry brought up tanks, but the M-24s were not good enough for the job. Four attempts to break the roadblock behind the 2nd Battalion failed. General Charles Palmer, the divisional artillery commander, had been given responsibility for these positions west of Yongdong. He sent in reinforcements built around the 1st Battalion of the 5th Cavalry. But once more the enemy had moved its major force into the flanking position, and the reinforcements found themselves heavily engaged while the North Koreans went after the artillery. It is too bad that General Walker's headquarters did not have better intelligence and better contact with the 24th Division during its early fighting. The enemy had used this maneuver successfully three times already, and with adequate communications Walker would have been warned and forearmed.

Here, however, for the first time the Americans began to understand why the enemy seemed to have second sight about the American positions. Among the hundreds of refugees who crowded the road, for some reason one pair—a man and his pregnant wife—caught the Americans' attention. The pair were stopped and searched. The big bulge in the woman's midriff turned out not to be a baby but a radio transmitter. From that day on General Walker began to pay more attention to the flow of refugees and to limit their traffic in the combat zone.

By the morning of July 25 the North Koreans were all around the American positions west of Yongdong. General Palmer called for a general retreat. The 8th Cavalry's 1st Battalion managed an orderly withdrawal. It was in the least endangered position. But the bulk of the enemy were southwest, engaging the 2nd Battalion. By putting up a heavy artillery barrage on the roadblock area, the 99th and 61st Field Artillery battalions managed to extricate most of the battalion. However, two companies and one platoon and the tanks were cut off. Four tanks managed to force the roadblocks, but seven did not. Those tankers abandoned their vehicles and walked over the mountains to escape. So did the infantry, abandoning all its equipment save individual arms.

On the road close to Yongdong, F Company of

the 5th Cavalry ran into an enemy ambush, and only 26 men came back from it. On the night of July 25 the North Koreans took Yongdong. They had suffered heavy casualties, but they had the territory.

MEANWHILE, THE U.S. 27th Infantry had been given the task of protecting the Ch'ongju-Kunch'on road, which, below Hwanggan, became the main road to Taegu. (See the map "The Front Moves South.") Their task was to stop the North Korean 2nd Division, and that was not going to be easy. The North Korean 2nd Division was under enormous pressure from the high command because it had failed to arrive in time for the Battle of Taejon, having been engaged in hard mountain fighting against the South Korean Army. Now the North Korean 2nd Division was trying to prove itself.

If that force could move down to the Kumchon road, it would be behind the U.S. 1st Cavalry. The commander of the 27th Regiment was Lieutenant Colonel John Michaelis, known generally as Mike. The regiment's Korea odyssey to this point was an indication of the furious activity at Eighth Army headquarters, where General Walker seemed much like the little Dutch boy trying to stuff up innumerable holes in the dike with his fingers. Michaelis's regiment had first been sent to Uisong, then to Sangju, then to Hwanggan as General Walker perceived new dangers in the steady drive of eight North Korean divisions toward Pusan.

Michaelis gave to his 1st Battalion the job of

making contact with the enemy. Lieutenant Colonel Gilbert H. Check took that battalion north on the road. They encountered ROK troops coming through but could get no information as to the size or armament of the North Koreans. The ROK troops were totally demoralized and moving back as fast as they could.

A strong patrol from the 1st Battalion encountered the enemy on the night of July 23, in the form of a column marching down the road. The patrol ambushed the column and put up an enormous amount of small-arms fire. The enemy stopped. The patrol returned to the battalion command post and reported. So at least Colonel Michaelis had some warning.

The morning of July 24 dawned with the typical morning fog of South Korea. Two American rifle companies were posted along the road on ridges on either side. Moving through the fog, the North Koreans came up along the road close to the American positions before they were spotted. The Americans began to fire. The enemy responded with rifle fire and mortars. Then several tanks appeared. The tanks came through, but the rifle companies stopped the North Korean infantry and held their positions. The fighting there went on all day, and the ridges changed hands several times.

The tanks burst through toward the battalion command post. They opened fire, destroyed several vehicles, and killed the battalion medical officer at his aid station. Captain Logan E. Weston, the commander of Company A, got a bazooka and knocked out one tank. Tank fire deafened him, but he refused to quit the action.

More tanks came up, and the battalion position was definitely threatened. Colonel Check called for an airstrike, and as if delivered by a genie, just then several F-80s appeared, saw the tanks, and went after them. They destroyed three.

The fighting went on all day. The North Korean 2nd Division had gone into this battle with eight tanks. That night they had two left. After dark, the 27th Infantry's 1st Battalion disengaged and withdrew through the 2nd Battalion. Colonel Michaelis may not have been involved in the earlier fighting, but he expected an enemy attempt to encircle his battalion during the night and thus avoided the danger.

How right he was. Early the next morning the North Koreans sent two battalions in a double enveloping move against the positions earlier held by the 1st Battalion. That put the North Koreans directly in front of the 27th's 2nd Battalion, and the Americans opened fire with everything they had. They caught the enemy flat-footed and caused serious casualties. The two North Korean battalions finally disengaged and limped back north. But mindful of the pressure from their own higher authority, the North Koreans came back again that day. The second time they threatened to envelop the regimental command post, so Colonel Michaelis ordered another withdrawal to high ground. The withdrawal was orderly and successful, covered by American tanks.

That withdrawal put the 27th infantry very close to Hwanggan, which the enemy had been ordered to take at all costs. On July 26 the fighting began all over again. The 35th Infantry sent a battalion to the right flank of the 27th, which helped prevent a new envelopment. But the trouble was the same as always: too many enemy troops, too few Americans, and not enough firepower. On July 27 the enemy tried the left flank. There was a large gap between the western unit of the 27th and the nearest unit of the 7th Cavalry Regiment of the 1st Cavalry Division. The fighting was extremely heavy, and the 27th Regiment's B and C companies suffered many casualties in holding the position all day before the pressure forced them to withdraw.

At this point the regiment was badly hit, and Colonel Michaelis asked for permission to withdraw and regroup. It was granted. The 27th withdrew through the 1st Cavalry Division and went into reserve near Taegu on the Naktong River. The regiment had made the best record of the American forces in the war so far: It had held the enemy for five days, smashed one encircling move to pieces, knocked out a significant proportion of enemy armor, and retained its own equipment and organization. It had suffered three hundred twenty-five casualties while inflicting about three thousand casualties on the North Koreans. Its operation had been a classic example of the successful delaying action.

8.

"There Will Be No More Retreating . . ."

THE STIFF FIGHT put up by Colonel Michaelis's U.S. 27th Infantry outside Hwanggan was a milepost in the Korean War. Until this point no U.S. regiment had managed a completely orderly engagement. A few more victories like this for the North Korean 2nd Division and there would be no division left.

ON JULY 26, General Walker warned his divisional commanders that they might soon have to fall back farther to a defensive position. That was not an order of moment but a provision of information.

Having done so, General Walker then telephoned MacArthur's headquarters in Tokyo, asking for permission to move Eighth Army headquarters down to Pusan. The divisions would hold along the Naktong River. He did not know at the time that General MacArthur had just concluded some ringing statements about the success of the delaying action and the American determination to stand fast.

The result of that telephone call was another visit by General MacArthur to Korea. He came in by plane to Taegu on the morning of July 27, and for ninety minutes MacArthur and Walker conferred.

There could be no such move, MacArthur said. The Eighth Army had to hold. There could be no withdrawal.

THE PROBLEM OF fighting a delaying action remained, and the uneven quality of the divisional and regimental officers involved contributed to the difficulty. For example, during the fight of the 27th Infantry on the Hwanggan road, the U.S. 7th Cavalry regimental headquarters panicked at reports that they were about to be overrun and in the early hours of July 26 ordered a general withdrawal. When the word reached the regiment's 2nd Battalion, the men scattered in fear and, by nightfall more than one hundred of them were still missing. The regiment's organization was shot to pieces.

On July 26, elements of the North Korean 3rd Division started another wide flanking movement, this one aimed at Kumch'on. But the 1st Cavalry Division discovered them and repelled the flank attack. At this time General Gay felt that his position was growing ever more dangerous, so he elected to withdraw to the vicinity of Kumch'on. On July 29, after the 27th Regiment had retreated through his lines, he began packing up. In a few hours the 8th Cavalry was astride the Sangju road north of the town. The 5th Cavalry was southwest of the town, and the 7th Cavalry was pulling itself together six miles northwest of Kumch'on.

The American defense was definitely stiffening. One indication was the performance of the 16th Reconnaissance Company that day.

Lieutenant Lester Lauer of that company drove southwest through the town of Chirye, which lay below the 5th Cavalry Regiment's position. He was informed a little later that after he drove through, an enemy unit moved into Chirye. He radioed the company commander, Captain Charles Harvey, who took another platoon down to help. At the outskirts of Chirye, Harvey's group encountered North Koreans and killed several of them. The two platoons then joined up south of town.

Coming back, in the northern part of Chirye they surprised the enemy in their usual process of building a roadblock behind the Americans. They had an M-39 armored vehicle with them, and this heavy vehicle knocked down the roadblock and went on through. But only one jeep made it before strong machine-gun fire destroyed the next vehicle and stalled the retreat.

The patrol pulled back to the south edge of the town and set up 81mm mortars. The men began firing on the enemy machine-gun positions. After Captain Harvey was killed in this action, the rest withdrew, abandoning their vehicles. But their encounter was a warning that a large enemy force was coming, and they got that word back to General Gay at his headquarters in a schoolhouse in Kumch'on.

On July 29, General Walker made a tour of his divisional headquarters to pass the word that he had received from MacArthur.

General Walker was thoroughly displeased with the performance of the troops of the 25th and 1st Cavalry divisions. He told General Gay that much after Gay had retreated to Kumch'on. Gay admitted that he had not known what to do, and when a divisional commander says that to his chief, that army has plenty of problems.

It was apparent to General Walker that Gay was only saying what his other commanders were feeling. None since General Dean had shown a real appreciation of the desperate nature of the current situation, or the need to hold on at all costs. A Japanese or a German general would have understood the problem, but American commanders had since 1942 operated in an aura of victory, not defeat.

The North Koreans were advancing rapidly all along the Korean peninsula. Only on the extreme east, where the Battle of Yongdok still raged, was there any positive look to the United Nations situation. What was needed desperately were fresh, well-trained troops, and they were on their way. But the morale of most of the Americans in Korea was very low. Since the days of World War II the GIs had had an immediate sense of the true nature of their wars. So far, Korea was the "bugout" war. Their commanders were constantly using phrases such as "temporary withdrawal" and "readjustment of the lines"—phrases reminiscent of the Japanese and Germans in the second half of World War II. These phrases did not conceal the fact that the enemy was winning and that the American and ROK forces were not putting up a very good defense.

"Bugging out" was the phrase the soldiers used to describe the actions. They had bugged out at Cho'nan, Ch'ongju, Taejon, Yongdong, and Chirye. The men of the 25th Division said their regimental theme song was the "Bug-Out Blues."

Daily, the officers at General Walker's headquarters watched the blue and red lines on the situation map and saw the perimeter shrink. Aboard the transports that were bringing supplies and the new troops from America, the officers kept situation maps of the conflict across the Pacific. They were dismayed to see how that perimeter shrank day after day. On July 29, the maps showed that the American and ROK forces had been squeezed back into an area eighty miles wide and fifty miles long in the southeast corner of the Korean peninsula. At this point in the relief convoy, five would get you ten that the Americans would have been driven into the sea before the convoy ever got to Pusan. In spite of those positive statements made by General MacArthur for American home consumption at the end of July, the tactical situation in Korea seemed desperate.

Almost unnoticed came a new threat, the movement of the North Korean 6th Division down the west coast of Korea. Driving the ROK 7th Division before it, the North Korean 6th Division had gone from Kunsan to Chonju to Namwon and then to Kwangju. There one element had split off to take Mokp'o, a port on the southwest tip of the peninsula. (See the map "The Front Moves South.") Another column had taken Posong, and on July 28 the main force had reached Sunch'on, a little over one hundred miles from Pusan on the south coast. At this point they were prepared to move for the final blow against the Americans and the almost completely demoralized South Koreans.

Major General Pang So-hang, commander of the North Korean 6th Division, issued an order of the day to his troops as they prepared:

"Comrades," he said, "the enemy is demoralized. The task given us is the liberation of Masan and Chinju . . . the liberation . . . means the final battle to cut off the windpipe of the enemy."

Was that military hyperbole?

General Walker did not think so.

That day the general made it clear to General Gay and General Kean of the 25th Division and to General Church of the 24th Division what they had to do. It was a statement worthy of a Rommel.

> . . . There will be no more retreating, withdrawal, or readjustment of the lines or any other term you choose. There is no line behind us to which we can retreat. Every unit

must counterattack to keep the enemy in a state of confusion and off balance. There will be no Dunkirk, there will be no Bataan, a retreat to Pusan would be one of the greatest butcheries in history. We must fight until the end. Capture by these people is worse than death itself. We will fight as a team. If some of us must die, we will die fighting together. Any man who gives ground may be personally responsible for the death of thousands of his comrades. . . . I want everybody to understand that we are going to hold this line. We are going to win.

General Walker gave this particular statement to General Kean to put out to the troops, hoping to bolster them. But the same sentiments were expressed up and down the line.

ON JULY 30 General Gay sent a strong force to Chi-rye, and the Americans forced their way into the town. Still, the North Koreans held the hills above the town. On July 31 the North Koreans began shelling the town; this forced General Gay to pull back to the northeast. The North Koreans then mounted a major offensive toward Kumch'on (see the map "The Front Moves South) and pushed the Americans back. But notice the difference in these actions and the earlier ones: The North Koreans gained ground, but at high expense these days. The drive on Kumch'on brought a series of U.S. air strikes that destroyed several tanks, and the artillery and the 3.5-inch bazookas destroyed more. The 1st Cavalry Division in its first ten days of action in Korea had suffered nearly one thousand casualties, but the North Koreans had taken about two thousand. The slowdown asked for by General MacArthur was occurring. U.S. naval forces were organizing powerful strikes against such North Korean strategic targets as the big oil refinery at Wonsan. These attacks had to hurt the enemy's war potential. More important at the moment: Planes from the carrier *Valley Forge* caught about fifty enemy aircraft on the ground and destroyed many of them.

Still, the question at the end of July was: Could the North Korean advance be brought to a halt before the enemy reached Pusan?

General MacArthur had given the reply to General Walker, and like a good field commander, General Walker had given it to the troops. No matter what the cost might be, they had to hold.

IT WAS A sign of the softness, disorganization, and undisciplined nature of the American forces then in Korea that the Walker remarks aroused more than a little resentment and furore. Later the war would arouse resentments because it was a "no win" situation. But this was not the case in the summer of 1950. It was true that the high command had not had time to propagandize the troops, as had been done in World War II, arousing personal fury against the Japanese and Germans. And this lack of personal feeling against the enemy was an important contributor to the low state of morale that the first three divisions to arrive on Korean soil brought with them.

However, as General Walker had put it, there was no place else to go, past the Naktong line, except to Pusan and the sea. As Walker told a *New York Times* reporter, for five weeks the Americans had been trading space for time. Now space was running out.

The situation had all the elements of a war movie. The Marine and Army reinforcements were only two days away. This new force included the 5th Marine Regiment and Marine Aircraft Group 33. Brigadier General Edward A. Craig, the commander of the 1st Provisional Marine Brigade, was already in Taegu, conferring with General Walker and his staff and getting the lay of the land. The troops at sea were at a disadvantage because there was no military intelligence available on the North Korean forces. All they knew was what they read in the newspapers. But they got out the manuals on Soviet tactics and learned how the North Koreans could be expected to operate.

The Marines were coming better prepared to fight than any other outfit. And behind them, Washington was reactivating divisions. So for the long haul, the prospects for the Americans in Korea were taking a turn for the better.

For the short term, with the land running out, there was enough to worry about to keep General

Craig up nights wondering if by the time his men got to Pusan there would be anything left to defend, for two days after General Walker's strong statement that there would be no more retreat, the 25th Division made another withdrawal. Elements of the 1st Cavalry abandoned equipment and guns and hurried back beyond Kumch'on. In General Walker's flat language, "the war had reached a critical stage."

ONE OF GENERAL Walker's problems was to keep track of the movement of the North Korean forces in the Southwest, because the South Koreans were fleeing in such panic that no coherent information could be secured from them. Walker's eyes were the reconnaissance planes sent out to find the enemy along the roads and in the towns. Only thus was he able to be informed, and then after the fact. By July 23 Walker had become aware that the North Korean 6th Division was preparing to roll behind the left flank of the Eighth Army, but he could not do much about it with the troops on hand. He did tell General Church that the battered 24th Division would have to come out of reserve to try to stop the North Koreans, but the front was sixty-five air miles long, and no one believed it possible.

At least General Walker had provided for the defense of the Chinju area. The U.S. 19th and 27th Infantry regiments were moved to a point east of Chinju to oppose further North Korean advances from the west. The 21st Infantry and division headquarters were moved to Sanje-ri and Hyopch'on. How long they could continue was debatable. The first task General Walker conceived for the Marines who would be coming in was to stop the enemy and the disaster that threatened the left side of the American line.

Also coming were various Army units in a far less satisfactory state of readiness.

Two battalions of the 29th Infantry Regiment at Okinawa were also on their way. Their duty just previous to the Korean War had been much the same as that of the three divisions in Japan: the pleasurable life of occupation. When the decision to send them was made, their commanders had been promised that they would have six weeks' infantry combat training in Japan before being committed to combat. What happened now was an indication of the crisis outlined by General Walker: The battalions were brought up to strength in Okinawa by replacements who were raw recruits. Nor would the battalions have six weeks of training but ten days, said Eighth Army headquarters. That was all they could promise.

When the two battalion commanders of the 29th arrived at Taegu on July 22, they learned the troops would have no training at all and only three days in which to draw weapons and zero them in.

When the men of the 29th arrived at Pusan on the morning of July 24 they were marched immediately into vehicles and moved to Chinju. So the highly trained and well-armed North Korean 6th Division found itself up against raw recruits who had new rifles they had never fired, mortars that had not been calibrated properly, and new .50-caliber machine guns with the Cosmoline still sticking to the edges.

Five would get you ten that Pusan could not last until August 2, when the Marines were expected.

WHEN THE FIRST stage of the battle for the Kum River line was fought on July 15, the fresh U.S. 19th Infantry Regiment was deployed on the flank of the 34th Regiment.

When the 19th came up it had a large area to worry about: The main position was astride the Seoul-Pusan road where it crossed the Kum River, but the defense zone extended from the railroad bridge eight miles north of Taejon, along the river to a point three miles west of Kongju. Actually the ROK troops were responsible for the railroad bridge. At that point the 19th's flank rested against that of the ROK units. (See the map "The Fall of Taejon.")

ENGINEERS HAD DESTROYED the railroad bridge across the Kum and the highway bridge. The command post of Lieutenant Colonel Otho T. Winstead's 1st Battalion was in the village of Kadong, a mile south of the Kum River on the main road. Colonel Guy S. Meloy's regimental command post was a mile south on the road in the village of Palsan. The companies of the 1st Battalion were posted along the big loop of the river too far apart for comfort. The 2nd Battalion was in reserve behind the 1st Battalion. For once the Americans had plenty of artillery: two batteries of the 52nd Field Artillery, two batteries of the 11th Field Artillery's 155mm howitzers, two batteries of the 13th Field Artillery. The 26th Anti-Aircraft Artillery and A Company of the 78th Heavy Tank Battalion were at Taejon, but their tanks were light M-24s. The tankers knew what they had and what they faced, and they were extremely nervous and depressed.

IN SPITE OF several calls for air strikes, the American and Australian planes failed to prevent the buildup of North Korean tanks on the north side of the Kum River. The T-34s with their 85mm guns dug in and began to fire to support the infantry crossing. The artillery had begun at 1:00 P.M. on July 14, but the enemy failed to make any crossing that day. There was a good reason for that failure: The enemy's 3rd Division did not like those air attacks. The division had been on the march, with a brief rest, since June 25, and the troops wanted to know why they had not already won the war as promised. Their officers told them that once they had taken Taejon the Americans would surrender and the war would be over.

That was before the collapse of the 34th Infantry's defense on the left.

By nightfall on July 15, some advance patrols of the North Korean Army had infiltrated into Nonsan, where the U.S. 34th Regiment was trying to make its stand. Once again the North Koreans made good use of the darkness to establish the American positions for their next attack. It was an extremely professional army.

That evening, Colonel Meloy alerted all units of the 19th Regiment to watch for enemy attempts to make a night crossing.

Just before dusk on July 15, several tanks came down to the edge of the river on the north side. They were first seen by Lieutenant Charles C. Early of the 19th's B Company. He counted nine tanks about two miles away and reported to his company commander just about the time the tanks opened fire on his position. The company commander got onto battalion, and battalion ordered an air strike. It came in and left one tank burning on the road. The other eight took refuge in woods nearby. The planes circled overhead until darkness drove them off. Then the infantry began to move toward the river near the highway bridge. American recoilless rifles and machine guns caused heavy casualties, but some of the North Koreans made it to the south side of the Kum River.

Upstream at a point called Hill 200 another enemy unit began to cross. The men of C Company tried to stop that but weren't helped a lot by the Heavy Weapons Company behind them, which put several rounds into the company mortar position, destroying two of the 60mm mortars and breaking the base plate of the last one. One of the enlisted men improvised a base plate, held the tube in his hand, and fired three hundred rounds thus. The enemy attack stopped. Unable to cross under the cover of the tanks' guns alone, the North Koreans brought up their artillery.

At three o'clock on the morning of July 16 (another Sunday), the attack began in earnest, preceded by a very heavy artillery barrage from the North Korean guns. The American artillery and infantry returned the fire. The problem once again was that the American line was too thin. The North Koreans managed to make an effective crossing between C and E companies on the right-hand side of the line. C Company managed to hold Hill 200, but the North Koreans had outflanked them and now marched around the east end of the 19th Regiment's 1st Battalion.

At the same time the North Koreans sent an even larger force to the west end of the American line, downstream, and outflanked that line as well. Two few troops, too few guns: It was the old story of the past two weeks.

Colonel Meloy watched from his command post as the enemy moved inexorably across the Kum. They seemed to be crossing everywhere, and it was not long before they had penetrated deep into the center of the American line. They threatened the 1st Battalion command post until Colonel Meloy organized a counterattack. The troops he had for this move were cooks and bakers, drivers, mechanics, company clerks, and anyone else who happened to be around headquarters. These soldiers comported themselves very well and managed to drive the North Koreans from the high ground they had captured in the center. Some of the North Koreans swam back across the river to the north side.

The colonel was quite proud of his men, and he reported to General Dean that they had pushed the enemy out and that the position was safe. He intended to hold until dark and then pull back to a position closer to Taejon.

In fact the enemy who had outflanked the defenders on the right made a broad turn and put up a roadblock three miles behind the battalion command post on the main highway. Once again the North Koreans were after the artillery. Colonel Meloy called for his reserve companies to come up and break the roadblock. He also called for an air strike.

The North Korean confidence that they would take Taejon in a hurry and their setting up of a roadblock were postulated on facts of which the Americans were not aware. For several days the North Koreans had been infiltrating guerrilla troops into Taejon. The guerrillas were to serve as a disruptive and flanking force. And this is precisely what they were doing at this time, aided by a number of North Korean regular troops who had come around the American right end.

Colonel Perry, the commander of the 52nd Field Artillery, saw a large number of men in white coming toward his positions. He ordered A Battery to fire on them. Part of the troops headed for B Battery, coming up from the south. The men of B Battery turned their guns around and began firing. The North Koreans, however, proved that their intelligence—much of it secured from the guerrillas—was superb. They set up mortars, and their first shots killed the battery commander of B Battery and his first sergeant and wounded five of the six section chiefs. It was almost as if they knew where they would be. Colonel Perry saved the day. He organized another of his volunteer-fire-department forces, made up of mechanics and wiremen and drivers, and launched a counterattack on the force besieging B Battery. The fire from B Battery, under Lieutenant William H. Steele, who had assumed command, plus Perry's attack drove the North Koreans south into the hills and saved B Battery.

These troops joined others and reinforced the roadblock that Colonel Meloy had been warned about, not far from the village of Tuman. The enemy chose a beautiful spot for the block. At this point the Yongsu River, which was much swollen by rain just then, came up against the cliff on the west side of the road. River and sharp bank left no room for vehicles to pass on either side of the road. South of this point a succession of high hills flanked the highway on the west. The North Koreans moved in here.

COLONEL MELOY CAME down south to see what was happening, and he was wounded shortly after he arrived. He turned command of the regiment over to Colonel Winstead of the 1st Battalion. Soon the battalion was in touch with General Dean, who announced that he was organizing a relief force but that it would be three-thirty before he could get there. He instructed Winstead to move the men out. After that conversation was finished, the radio truck was hit by a shell, and communication with division was cut off.

Winstead ordered the troops at the roadblock to continue to try to break through to make contact with Dean's force. Then he went back up toward his 1st Battalion to pull them out.

This proved difficult. The North Koreans had surrounded Hill 200 and were pouring mortar fire into it. The Americans had a hard time getting out of their foxholes and moving. The sunlight was hot that afternoon, as it always was on a Korean summer day when the rain was not pouring in. A and B companies managed to stick together and move slowly south. C Company got entrapped by North Koreans who had six machine guns. The company was badly chopped up. It split into small units, and the men tried to make their way south. Soon the road was filled with American troops moving more or less aimlessly. Attempts to organize counterattacks against the North Koreans in the hills along the road did not succeed. Major Logan could not get the men to move up into the hills to attack the enemy automatic weapons pinning them down. Their failure to do so resulted in total American disorganization and defeat at this roadblock.

The men were in poor condition from months of occupation duty, and the heat of a Korean summer afternoon was too much for them.

Several American tanks showed up, but they did not seem to have any command direction or any plan of operation. To add to the confusion, several P-51 fighters flew over and strafed American positions.

Down south at the roadblock, Major Logan decided to take a patrol out to skirt the enemy and find out how far the North Korean position extended. He made it in two hours back around to the Pusan road, where the 13th Field Artillery had been emplaced. He came up just as the artillery was getting ready to move south. A few minutes later Logan encountered General Dean, who had a force that included two light tanks and four antiaircraft artillery trucks mounting multiple .50-caliber and 40mm guns.

Dean sent Logan south to establish a new position, and Lieutenant Colonel Thomas M. McGrail, commander of the 2nd Battalion, went forward toward the enemy roadblock. About a mile to the north, when the column rounded a bend in the road it ran into an ambush. The force was ripped apart by enemy fire from machine guns and antitank guns. The men in the four antiaircraft trucks suffered 90 percent casualties, and all four vehicles were destroyed. The U.S. tanks fired all their ammunition and turned and went back down the road.

Meanwhile, American troops were piling up on the north side of the roadblock. General Dean ordered another attempt to break the roadblock, but the enemy had dug in along a Y-shaped hill about a mile and a half long and could not be dislodged with the forces at hand. The attempt had to be abandoned.

When Major Logan had gone off from the northern edge of the roadblock seeking help, he had left Captain Edgar R. Fenstermacher in charge. The captain now decided to send vehicles to run the blockade, to get Colonel Meloy and other wounded through to safety. He put Colonel Meloy in a tank and sent the tank through in the lead. Twenty other vehicles came through after it, speeding down the road. They made it.

A few miles south of the roadblock the column stopped when the tank's engine failed. They all got out, destroyed the tank with a grenade, and went on south to deliver Colonel Meloy to Yusong.

By this time back at the roadblock the American force had built up to about five hundred men and one hundred vehicles. Captain Fenstermacher decided the only way to get out was to go overland. They burned the vehicles. While doing this Fenstermacher was shot in the neck.

One group of about one hundred men took forty wounded soldiers and started east of the road. The going was rough, and many of the wounded could not continue. Chaplain Herman G. Felhoelter and

Captain Linton Buttrey, the medical officer, stayed with them. When they heard North Koreans coming, Felhoelter told Buttrey to escape, which he did, although he was wounded in the effort. From afar, through binoculars, First Sergeant James W. R. Haskins of the headquarters company watched the group of North Koreans come up and shoot down the chaplain as he prayed and then shoot all the wounded Americans.

All that night of June 16 the stragglers made their way across the hills, trying to avoid North Korean positions. Only two rifle companies of the 19th Infantry were left intact. One of them was ordered to dig in at Yusong. Their position became the farthermost north of the 24th Division.

IN THIS SECOND phase of the battle for the Kum River line, the 19th Infantry lost most of its vehicles and heavy equipment. Its personnel casualties were also heavy. C Company of the 1st Battalion lost one hundred twenty-two of one hundred seventy-one men. The 19th then moved down to Yongdong, twenty-five miles south of Taejon, to rebuild. G Company was replaced at Yusong the next day by a company from the 34th Infantry.

The 52nd Field Artillery lost eight of its 105mm howitzers and most of its equipment. The 11th and 13th Artillery managed to withdraw early and got away without losses.

THUS THE KUM River line was lost. Taejon was now open to attack, and beyond that Taegu, the temporary capital of the Republic of Korea.

Even so, the U.S. high command in Tokyo was feeling better about the prospects. They did not expect General Dean to hold Taejon. Taegu might even fall. But General MacArthur's chief of staff said that American plans were developing and that the enemy was suffering heavily for the ground gained. Meanwhile, even in Korea the Americans were becoming better organized to stop the drive. There would be more sacrifices—for all practical purposes the 24th Division was written off. But out of this would come the turnaround of the war.

9.

Back to the Naktong

THE OFFICERS AND men of the newly arrived American 29th Infantry Regiment were assigned to the command of the 19th Infantry on the east flank of the American line. Colonel Dennis Moore, commander of the 19th Infantry, could not possibly have known of the actual condition of readiness of the new troops. Otherwise he would never have assigned them on the moment of their arrival to take the offensive and capture an important point on the Chinju-Pusan road.

On the evening of July 25 the men of the 3rd Battalion of the 29th Infantry were just getting into place at Chinju, hardly back on their land legs after the sea voyage from Okinawa, when Lieutenant Colonel Harold W. Mott received orders from Colonel Moore to seize Hadong, a road-junction point about thirty-five miles southwest of Chinju.

Hadong was just a place name on the map to Colonel Moore and the other Americans. But Major General Chae Byong-duk, the South Korean officer who had presided over the collapse of the ROK Army at Seoul, said it was vital to the defense of Pusan. The available intelligence indicated that the North Koreans had sent about five hundred troops that way. Thus, according to the book, a battalion that was at least eight hundred strong, even if understrength, should be able to handle the job.

General Chae was nearly jumping with anxiety and eagerness. He volunteered to accompany the troops and to act as Colonel Mott's interpreter and geographical guide. The offer was accepted by Colonel Moore, and General Chae joined up. No one thought to provide the 3rd Battalion with radio communication facilities to keep in touch with Colonel Moore's command post.

Shortly before one o'clock on the morning of July 26, the 3rd Battalion of the 29th Infantry started out in truck convoy for Hadong. There was no new intelligence about the situation there. Colonel Mott expected to find a few North Korean troops in the town.

General Chae reported that the main road to Hadong was washed out and that heavy rains had made it impossible to ford the river. Therefore they should travel by a circuitous detour using back roads with which Chae was familiar. They headed for Konyang over back roads and then turned north to meet the Chinju-Hadong road at Wonjon.

Colonel Moore had expected the troops to be ready for action at dawn. But dawn found the long column in disarray. The roads Chae had chosen were scarcely more than cart tracks through the rice paddies, scarcely passable for heavy Army trucks. Many vehicles fell off the road into the paddy fields and had to be pulled out. The going was very slow.

Daylight came and they had not yet reached Wonjon. On the road, however, they encountered a truckload of South Koreans. They stopped to get information, General Chae translating.

These men, said the general, were the only survivors of a force of four hundred South Korean militia that had been chewed up by the North Koreans on July 25.

This sobering news indicated that Colonel Mott was going to find a lot more than a handful of North Koreans at Hadong. When finally the column reached Wonjon he called a halt. He set up a perimeter and announced they were stopping for breakfast. He also sent his executive officer, Major Tony J. Raibl, back in a jeep to Chinju to inform Colonel Moore of this latest intelligence development. When Raibl arrived at Chinju he argued for establishment of a defensive position at a suitable roadblock site east of Hadong. Colonel Moore insisted that the 3rd Battalion must take Hadong. Raibl brought that unwelcome word to Colonel

Mott, and the troops moved on that afternoon to a point about three miles east of Hadong at the village of Honegch'on. There the column was overtaken by an Air Force captain with a radio jeep. He and his men had been sent from Chinju to control air strikes to aid the battalion. But the radio was not working. That night the battalion bivouacked at Honegch'on while the Air Force technicians repaired their radio.

The next morning, July 27, the column moved again, with a rifle company in the lead, then the heavy weapons company, followed by the other three rifle companies. The road climbed east up the flank of a mountain in a series of dogleg turns. Near the top of the pass that led down into Hadong town, a patrol of North Korean troops appeared on the road ahead. Captain George Sharra, commander of L Company, alerted the heavy weapons company, which opened fire with their two 75mm recoilless rifles. But these untested weapons had never before been fired, and the shots passed harmlessly by the enemy troops. The North Koreans ran back over the pass.

Captain Sharra rushed his company to the top of the pass, where they fanned out and took positions on both sides of the road.

Below them they could see a road similar to the one they had come up leading by sharp turns a mile and a half into Hadong. To the right above the pass the terrain was dominated by a high peak. Captain

Sharra could see people moving around up above them. To the left, the mountain fell sharply down to paddy fields along a river.

All was quiet on the road. The North Koreans had completely disappeared.

Captain Sharra's company secured the pass at nine-thirty that morning. A few moments later Colonel Mott came up accompanied by the Air Force men and most of the battalion staff. Since the radio was working, they had called for an air strike on Hadong town, and it was scheduled to begin at nine forty-five. Everybody at the battalion command post wanted to see it. Soon the road around the pass was filled with people and jeeps.

Captain Sharra pointed out the people on the mountain to the right. Colonel Mott said he had ordered K Company up there.

Everybody waited for the air strike.

Captain Sharra was a little concerned about the heavy concentration of people at the pass. But it was his job to defend the position, not tell the battalion commander what to do. Soon he saw a company of troops winding their way up the road from Hadong. His machine gunners looked up, but Captain Sharra said the column was too far off to wait until they came closer.

Major Raibl, who had been at the rear of the U.S. column, had been ordered to the command post by Colonel Mott. Major Raibl came up and joined the party standing on the road in the middle of the pass.

He saw soldiers moving around near the base of the mountain to the right. General Chae said he could not tell whether these people were North Koreans or not. Some of them were wearing the mustard-brown cotton uniforms of the North Korean Army. But some seemed to be wearing the green of the Americans and South Koreans. Perhaps they were friendly. He advised waiting. Colonel Mott concurred. They stood in the middle of the road, waiting.

When the approaching column was one hundred yards away, General Chae shouted at them in Korean. The column broke and the soldiers dropped into the ditches on the sides of the road.

Captain Sharra gave the word and his men began firing on the troops below as they deployed. As soon as the American machine guns opened up, return fire started—from the mountain on the right came small-arms, machine-gun, and mortar fire. The North Koreans on the higher ground had zeroed in on the middle of the road at the pass.

Bullets from the first burst of North Korean machine-gun fire caught General Chae in the head, and he died. The same burst caught Major Raibl, who rolled down the road to get out of the line of fire. Colonel Mott and several others were also wounded by this first burst. The battalion staff had been virtually knocked out of action.

The mortars had been aimed expertly, and shells began falling all around the pass. Just as the fighter planes began to appear above Hadong, circling and asking for information, the radio jeep was destroyed. The planes circled for a few minutes and then disappeared. The Air Force captain who had originally arrived with the radio jeep picked up a rifle and joined the platoon on the north side of the road, facing up the hill against the enemy troops.

Colonel Mott was only slightly wounded, and he went back to the rear of the column to help unload ammunition. While doing so, he dropped a box on his foot and broke the foot.

At the top of the pass, Captain Sharra's company was pinned down by the enemy on higher ground. Enemy infantry charged down on K Company, which was trying to climb the mountain. Sharra's company provided covering fire for K Company and also held against the North Koreans above them.

The North Koreans were moving to rake the road behind the pass. A soldier dug a foxhole for Colonel Mott.

The fight continued all morning and soon involved every element of the battalion. Colonel Mott, in his foxhole nursing his broken foot again, could not move very well, and Major Raibl was wounded again and sent back in a convoy with other wounded. Mott told Captain Sharra to take command of the battalion. His task was to extricate them from what had obviously been a trap.

By midafternoon Captain Sharra had assembled

all who could move, and they started back down the road to Chinju. The last to come out were Lieutenant J. Morissey of the platoon on the left side of the pass and his eleven surviving riflemen. The Air Force captain was not among them. So busy had they been in the past twenty-four hours that no one ever learned his name.

During the retreat some men threw away their weapons and fled through the paddies and into the hills beyond. Some of them made it back to the U.S. lines several days later. One group of about one hundred marched to the coast and was rescued by a South Korean fishing vessel that took them into Pusan.

Many men did not make it at all, although east of Hadong G Company put up a roadblock. It held until the morning of July 28, when it was withdrawn by Colonel Moore of the 19th Infantry.

Later, the Americans discovered that about one hundred prisoners had been taken here by the North Koreans, and when the territory had been recaptured by the Americans, about a third of the battalion's strength was found, the bodies mostly in the rice paddies and along the river. In other words, those men who had stood and fought survived, for the most part. Those who had fled were killed, for the most part.

On the road back to Chinju the main party met B Battery of the 13th Field Artillery, which had been making its way slowly toward Hadong to support the battalion. Since there was no position to support, B Battery also turned around. On the way back, one 105mm howitzer and two trucks fell off into the paddies and were abandoned.

When the 29th Infantry's 3rd Battalion arrived at Chinju there was little left. Both recoilless rifles, all the mortars and machine guns, all the communications equipment, and most of the battalion's rifles were missing. Of the battalion staff only the commanding officer and the supply officer remained. Four company commanders had been lost. On July 28 the healthy survivors were reorganized into two companies and attached to the 19th Infantry Regiment.

AFTER THE DISASTER at Hadong there was nothing to stop the North Korean 6th Division's drive until it reached a point about four miles just west of the Nam River, where the Americans were dug in along a line of hills.

The North Korean 4th Division had remained in Taejon for several days after the capture, resting and taking replacements to restore its troop strength. The division moved down to Kunsan, where its tank remained behind for maintenance. So confident were the North Koreans now of quick victory that they relaxed. It seemed hardly likely that tanks would be needed until they reached the Naktong River line, and there they could be brought up in a hurry. The infantry moved down to

Chian and then toward Koch'ang. Their assault was to be made in coordination with that of the North Korean 6th Division, coming around from the west. It was at this point that the high command made the serious error of judgment that gave the Americans the extra time they needed in their most desperate hours. The North Korean high command ordered the seizure of all the southwestern Korean ports before the final drive on Pusan. The purpose was to assure an orderly supply route by sea to Pusan. The result was that the North Korean 6th Division did not immediately exploit the victory at Hadong. Nor did the North Korean 4th Division move briskly against Koch'ang.

THE SITUATION OF the 34th Infantry Regiment of the U.S. 24th Division typified what was happening in Korea in the month of July. On July 28, in position at Koch'ang, the regiment consisted of about eleven hundred men. The two fighting battalions, the 1st and the 3rd, comprised about three hundred fifty men each, or less than a third of normal battalion strength. This was all General Walker could give them.

The general saw, however, that the 34th could not hold Koch'ang alone and also defend the road junction at Anui, a few miles to southwest. Fortunately he did have one fresh element of troops at his command: the 1st Battalion of the 29th Infantry, which had come in with the 3rd Battalion from Okinawa. The 1st Battalion was ordered to Anui to relieve a battalion of the 19th Infantry, which was then withdrawn to the Chinju area.

This 1st Battalion was commanded by Lieutenant Colonel Wesley C. Wilson. If anything it was even more badly prepared for battle than had been the 3rd Battalion of the 29th Infantry. It had no communications equipment of any importance, virtually no ammunition for its mortars, and no recoilless rifles or other artillery.

Colonel Wilson's men relieved the soldiers of the 19th Infantry at Umyong-ni, south of Anui, on July 27. Other troops went up the road to Anui.

Meanwhile, an advance element of the North Korean 4th Division cut the road between Anui and Koch'ang, to the northeast. Checking out his situation, Colonel Wilson sent a two-jeep patrol up to Koch'ang to make contact with the 34th Infantry there. The patrol was ambushed on the road. The first jeep was riddled by machine-gun fire, and all in it were killed. The second jeep was traveling one hundred yards behind the first to avoid dust, and the driver jammed on the brakes, all four men in that jeep piled out, and when a number of North Korean soldiers came up to investigate the wreckage of the first jeep, Private Sidney D. Talley stood up and sprayed them with fire from his M-1 rifle. He killed two and raised the morale of his companions, who

now got up and started firing, also. The North
Koreans ran off. The Americans got back in their
jeep and hurried to the Anui command post to tell
their story.

Meanwhile, off to the southwest, another patrol
of the 29th Infantry ran into North Koreans on the
Hamyang road. Later that day the moving 19th
Infantry troops ran into a fire fight on the road back
to Chinju and had to abandon their vehicles. They
got lost and ended up the next day north at
Koch'ang along with a number of ROK troops.

As of July 28, then, the North Korean 4th Division had units in the countryside all around these
road junctions but had not yet made a frontal
assault. The first one came at Anui, where B Company and D Company of the 29th Infantry were
overwhelmed by a superior force. Part of B Company got across the upper Nam River to a high hill
east of the town, but North Korean machine-gun
fire cut off the rest and they were forced to fight their
way out as best they could. They were fighting in
the streets until midnight. The survivors again took
to the hills. Eventually about half the men of these
two companies came into the U.S. lines.

On July 28, the North Koreans of the 4th Division began another envelopment, moving around
on trails behind Colonel Wilson's position at
Umyong-ni. On July 29 he was aware of it and
began a series of withdrawals and successfully made
it down to Sanch'ong, the next major point on the

Chinju road. Here Colonel Wilson had orders to dig in and hold.

But while elements of the North Korean 4th Division moved toward the south, the major force turned left to attack Koch'ang. That brought them up against Colonel Beauchamp's 34th Infantry, which was disposed in a semicircle around the town.

After the hard fighting of early July, the 34th Infantry's communications were in shambles, and they had remained that way. The regiment had only a handful of radios and no regimental switchboard. Like all the other U.S. units, it was short of mortars, mortar ammunition, bazookas, and machine guns. Too many had been left behind on too many roads. Some of the men no longer had complete field uniforms or entrenching tools. Some did not have steel helmets.

They did have some other attributes of war that they had acquired the hard way. They had learned about roadblocks, and this day they put up one of their own. On the afternoon of July 28 North Korean troops began moving toward Koch'ang from Anui and ran into that roadblock. The men of the 34th directed artillery fire on the position and pinned down the North Koreans until dark. At that point Colonel Beauchamp abandoned the roadblock and brought the troops closer to Koch'ang.

Colonel Beauchamp planned to withdraw slowly to a point south of Koch'ang and continue the delaying tactics. He so informed General Church, commander of the 24th Division. The admonitions of General Walker were still ringing in General Church's ears. He told Colonel Beauchamp he must hold Koch'ang. So in the middle of the plan it was disrupted, and the 3rd Battalion was held at Koch'ang. Because of the quick change in plan and because of poor communications neither battalion knew what the other was doing or what it was to do next.

That night the North Koreans, who knew exactly what they were doing, sent two columns toward Koch'ang splitting the American force there and enveloping part of it. Once again a change in orders by a higher commander had set up an enemy envelopment.

General Walker's concern and General Church's orders were based on the realization that the Naktong River line was the last natural defense position before Pusan. If the North Koreans managed to cross the Naktong River, then the chances of stopping them would be sharply diminished, even with the expected reinforcements. General Walker knew what he was asking of the soldiers, and so did General Church. They had no alternative.

THE CONFUSION IN orders to the battalions of the 24th Regiment cost the regiment one platoon. The 3rd Battalion, which had no orders, fell back that night through Koch'ang, leaving I Company as advance guard, isolated on the north. This company was surrounded by the North Koreans. The next morning the 1st Battalion forced its way along the road and rescued all but one platoon of the company. However, one platoon was lost.

By this time the morale of the 24th Division was at a low ebb. On that morning of July 29 a patrol of North Koreans approached the positions occupied by A Battery of the 13th Field Artillery. The men awoke to the sound of small-arms fire coming from a point about a quarter of a mile away. The artillerymen and the infantrymen panicked and deserted the guns. They announced that the enemy had overrun the artillery. The battalion executive officer finally brought up some volunteers. When they reached the artillery they found the guns deserted. A BAR man and three riflemen guarded the artillerymen, who began firing the guns. The Americans then hitched the artillery pieces to their tractors and made an orderly withdrawal without losses.

The artillery followed the 34th Infantry, which withdrew that day to positions just outside Sanje-ri on the Taegu road. This withdrawal also was orderly, and the engineers blew up all the bridges and set demolition charges along the road. It was another indication that the Americans were improving, although the morning's panic showed that they still had a long way to go.

The blowing up of the bridges prevented the North Koreans from bringing their artillery as they advanced under the urgings of their high command, which was now becoming obdurate about the slowdown in the rush for Taegu.

General Walker fully expected another encircling move around Taegu, carried out by troops coming south to Cho'gye and then crossing the Naktong. Meanwhile, other troops would head down the Uisong road and make a flanking movement on the American right while three other divisions carried out a frontal assault. At the same time, General Walker had virtually no troops to stop the North Korean 6th Division's drive from the southwest.

In this emergency, the general called on the Navy for maximum support of infantry operations. For the past two weeks the Navy had been carrying out strategic bombardment of North Korean ports, factories, and troop concentrations. On July 25 Task Force 77 started attacking bridges, traffic, and troop concentrations. The trouble was that the Navy's intelligence was two or three days old, and the North Korean 6th Division had moved far to the east of the points attacked.

The Navy's attempts to assist were hampered by red tape wrapped around the Air Force and Army commands in Tokyo, but some help did get through. A flight of attack planes and two flights of fighter planes hit Yongdong and the Yongdong-Taejon road and destroyed a large number of vehicles and routed many troops. Two days later more

Navy planes knocked out enemy concentrations at Mokp'o on the southwestern coast. This activity may have prevented an attempt by the North Koreans to launch a seaborne invasion south toward Pusan.

But the real danger area was the Southwest, and here the Navy operated on July 29. They covered the retreat of the 29th Infantry troops, knocking out enemy convoys on the roads. They were helped by the planes of the Fifth Air Force, but the attacks succeeded only in slowing down the North Korean 6th Division.

On July 29th the North Koreans began their assault on Chinju. Knowing it was coming, General Walker had done some more frantic shuffling of troops. He sent the ROK 17th Regiment to back up the 34th Infantry west of Hyopch'on.

That day the 1st Battalion of the 19th Infantry was in place at Kuho-ri, blocking a secondary road from Hadong. Battalion? Colønel Rhea had only two hundred riflemen. The other troops around Chinju were the remains of the 3rd Battalion of the 29th Regiment, which had been decimated at Hadong, and the 2nd Battalion of the 19th Infantry.

The North Korean attack came late that morning of July 29. The attack was slowed for a while by a number of air strikes that did considerable damage to vehicles on the road. But by nightfall the North Koreans were up to their old trick, cutting roads around Chinju. The next morning they exhibited a new trick: foliage camouflage. About a battalion of troops moved up against the American defenders west of Chinju, wearing camouflage. When aircraft passed they sat on the ground and could not be seen. Then they advanced again. The American artillery fired on them but soon ran out of ammunition.

That afternoon the American defenders retreated to the east bank of the Nam River. There were, at that point, about fifteen hundred Americans in the 19th Infantry between the North Korean 6th Division and Chinju.

About seven hundred replacements were coming in. These were all green troops, but there was no time to do anything but throw them into the line. A number were shot down before they ever reached their assigned positions. Those who did arrive were of very little assistance. Several company officers pleaded with battalion headquarters not to send any replacements at all during the action.

By nightfall on July 30 the North Koreans had infiltrated the American front positions and were moving tanks along the road to Chinju inside the U.S. lines. There was very little that the short-handed infantry companies on the west side of Chinju could do; there were too many North Koreans coming in too many directions. The Americans killed a number but did not even slow the North Korean advance.

The final assault against Chinju began before dawn on July 31 with an enemy artillery barrage. The infantry followed. By 5:00 A.M. the Americans were retreating again, this time to the edge of the town of Chinju.

Part of the U.S. 19th Infantry was located north of Chinju. The men saw North Koreans come toward the town, but they were told that a ROK battalion was going to attack, so they were not to fire. They did not fire. Three hours went by. The ROK troops never showed up. The North Koreans surrounded the 1st Battalion of the 19th Infantry.

The battalion held a rocky promontory, however, and refused to be dislodged. Eventually the North Koreans abandoned the struggle and moved off to the northwest.

But elsewhere the North Koreans moved steadily toward Chinju, using tanks and self-propelled guns. By eight o'clock that morning the Americans were moving all service troops and supplies out of Chinju by train. A few hours later all the Americans had left the town, moving east. They crossed the Nam River three miles east of Chinju. By nightfall the North Koreans had moved four thousand troops into Chinju. They were now less than fifty miles from Pusan. Their next objective would be Masan, and then there seemed to be virtually nothing to stop them on their march to the sea.

But General Walker still had one reserve regiment to send into the battle: Colonel Michaelis's 27th Infantry, which at Hwanggan had done the most professional job of delaying the North Koreans of any American unit yet employed.

On the afternoon of July 31, the regiment moved

south to take up a defensive position between Chinju and Masan. That evening Colonel Michaelis was assigned to set up a roadblock at the pass three miles west of Chungam-ni, on the north road from Chinju to Masan. The 19th Infantry was south of that position, west of a fork in the road that created the center road to Masan. The southern road to Masan was guarded by the 27th Infantry.

In the next few hours, however, the situation became much more complicated, largely because of the wavering of the 19th Infantry. The 27th and 19th regiments changed positions.

On the night of August 1 some important reinforcements arrived at the Masan area: 54 M-4 medium tanks of the 8072nd Medium Tank Battalion. These were not equal to the T-34 by any means, but they were the best armored weapons the U.S. troops had yet been given in this struggle.

The 1st Battalion of the 29th Infantry, now attached to the 19th Infantry, was assigned to reconnoiter the enemy positions westward on the north Chinju road on the morning of August 2. The column would be led by five M-4 tanks and four M-8 armored cars. Next would come the motorized battalion in trucks and jeeps.

Early on the morning of August 2 the column set out and moved up to the position of the 19th Infantry's 1st Battalion at a defensive point called The Notch, a pass southwest of Chungam-ni. Infantrymen were riding on the outsides of the tanks and the armored cars. They moved through, reached the pass, and started down. A dozen vehicles had begun the descent when they were suddenly hit by enemy fire. Unknowing, they had moved into an attack just launched by the North Koreans. Soon the first tank was immobilized by a mortar round that went down the hatch and killed all the crew. The column stopped. Enemy machine-gun fire swept the tanks, knocking off the infantrymen. The soldiers who were not hit jumped off the tanks and into the ditches. There they landed on top of North Korean troops, and hand-to-hand fighting began. The North Koreans captured some Americans, bound their hands, and forced them ahead of them as they tried to advance up the hill to the pass.

But behind the tanks came the 1st Battalion of the 29th Infantry. Colonel Wilson's men began to fight back. Recoilless rifles knocked out the enemy machine guns. Mortarmen worked their weapons hot, firing back at enemy bursts.

The fighting spread to the high ground on both sides of The Notch. One company of the 19th Infantry was nearly wiped out because of its commander's negligence. The company had been assigned to climb the peak on the west side of The Notch, but the men had grown tired and the commander had stopped the ascent short of the crest. The men had gone to sleep. They were caught the next morning by the North Koreans, *still asleep!* The company commander was bayoneted to death in his blanket.

So were several of the troops. The rest of the Americans were driven off the high ground.

The fighting continued all day. West of The Notch, Americans of the 29th Infantry drove the North Koreans back. On the east side there was more confusion, much of it caused by a force of ROK troops who appeared in the wrong position. By late afternoon, the North Koreans had withdrawn. At this place the North Korean 6th Division's drive had been halted, if only temporarily.

While the 29th Infantry was making this reconnaissance of the upper road to Chinju, Colonel Check's 1st Battalion of the 27th Infantry was doing the same along the lower road. His group was led by four medium Sherman tanks. His objective was the crossroads at Much'on-ni.

The troops pulled out at 4:00 A.M. After traveling for several miles out of Chindong-ni, the column encountered a platoon of North Koreans, still in their blankets in bivouack. The Americans played havoc with them. Behind the North Korean infantry a column of trucks was stopped for the night. A few trucks escaped, but ten were captured along with their loads of uniforms, food, and ammunition.

The appearance of a U.S. armored column when none was supposed to exist created the same sort of panic among the North Koreans along the Chinju road that the first sight of T-34s had done among the Americans early in the campaign. Scores of enemy vehicles moving east suddenly turned around and headed back to Chinju. American fighter planes coming in to support the U.S. troops found these columns and wrecked a large number of vehicles.

The American column moved on until it ran into heavy resistance. Colonel Check dismounted the men and sent the trucks back so they would not be captured. He also sent runners to find and inform Colonel Michaelis, but none of them arrived. The North Koreans had moved in behind the column and cut the road again.

Two of the U.S. tanks were knocked out by enemy antitank guns, whose shells killed the crews, but the antitank guns in turn were destroyed by American artillery. The tank commander said that the damaged tanks would run, but he did not have enough men to run them. Colonel Check called for volunteers to operate the two tanks, and many former bulldozer operators volunteered. The surviving tank men gave them a quick course of instruction. The force moved on, westward against the enemy.

At about 5:00 P.M. a liaison plane appeared overhead and dropped a note from Colonel Michaelis. The note told Colonel Check to return and warned him that the road had been cut behind him all the way back to the lines. He was to lead with the tanks. As soon as the column came into range it would have support from the U.S. artillery.

The column turned and started back to the U.S. position. The two damaged tanks would not run properly and had to be towed by the undamaged tanks to get them started. Then they went along. The infantrymen moved along the sides of the road, fighting off the North Koreans as they went.

Just before dark Colonel Check decided to make a run for it. He mounted all his infantry aboard the tanks (thirty-five men on each tank) and more men aboard the mortar and artillery vehicles, and they started back in a hurry. All the way along they met enemy troops. When they encountered a concentration, the tanks stopped and the infantry jumped off and knocked out the enemy machine guns. Then they got back on the tanks and rode some more.

Overhead planes of the Fifth Air Force zoomed down to strafe enemy concentrations ahead of them. When darkness fell, they had reached the range of the 89th Field Artillery, and the artillerymen fired 155mm howitzer shells along both sides of the road as the Check column came through. At midnight, the Check column reached Chindong-ni. It had suffered about thirty casualties in carrying out the most distinguished offensive action of the U.S. forces in Korea to date.

THAT DAY—AUGUST 2—the North Koreans infiltrated the roads all around Chindong-ni. The 6th Division's 14th Regiment had expected to take the town easily that day, while the 15th Regiment went on that same day to capture Masan.

That night, the troops of the North Korean 14th Regiment moved around the town and especially to a hill overlooking the 27th Regiment's command post in a schoolhouse on the edge of town. On the morning of August 3 they attacked. The American troops started to panic but were quickly brought under control by Colonel Michaelis. The North Koreans, who had the usual intelligence advantage of spies in the enemy camp, had expected to attack a regimental headquarters but had not expected to find rifle companies at the spot, and certainly not armor.

Company A, which had distinguished itself earlier up north, did so again, and its commander, Captain Logan E. Weston, did so particularly, taking two machine-gun positions himself.

What turned the tide was the armored column that had come back the night before. The tanks and armored cars surprised the enemy and drove them off. The enemy sent in a second battalion, but it was caught on the road by the American artillery, which had a field day decimating the North Korean trucks. By midafternoon the enemy had withdrawn and the Americans counted four hundred North Korean dead on the field. The U.S. troops had suffered a total of sixty casualties, and they had frustrated the enemy plan. When the 14th Regiment failed to take Chindong-ni, the North Korean 15th Regiment, which had infiltrated the high ground around Masan, held back its attack. And while this desperate fight was occurring around Colonel Michaelis' command post, General Walker was rushing the 25th Division out of the center of the U.N. line to Masan. By the end of the day the division was moved, and the virtual vacuum in the Southwest was closed up. The 25th Division's absence was not noted by the enemy, luckily. It had been backing up four ROK divisions in which no one had much confidence, against five North Korean divisions. General Walker's move here was the most daring and the riskiest he had taken, for if the North Koreans had attacked south of Hamch'ang as the 25th Division was moving south, it seems most unlikely that the South Koreans could have held them for more than about 10 minutes. But the North Korean 2nd and 3rd divisions were unaware of the move, so no attack was launched.

The North Korean 6th Division discovered then that fresh troops had moved into Masan and the going was not as clear as they had expected. They paused to reconnoiter and replan. The fast-moving drive on Pusan was halted, and the momentum was lost. The North Korean 6th Division's casualties had been so enormous that various officers were being upbraided for losing so many men. The division was down to about half strength. It took the corps commander a few hours to realize what had happened, and by then it was too late: The Americans had organized a whole new defensive line along the Naktong River.

10.

Pusan Perimeter

AS OF AUGUST 3, 1950, the Korean War changed character. No longer were the South Koreans in headlong flight, and the Americans were attempting vainly to stem an advancing tide without armor, without weapons effective against armor, and without organization. Help was now only hours away, and General Walker had retracted his lines to defensive positions that could be defended, given the materials. This was where he meant to "stand or die."

The defense line to the north was manned by ROK troops in the mountains from Yongdok on the eastern shore to Naktong-ni, where the line joined the Naktong River. From that point the line ran almost due south, on the eastern bank of the Naktong down to the juncture of the Naktong and Nam rivers, where the augmented Naktong turned east and then meandered to the sea at Pusan. At the juncture of the rivers, the line deserted the river and followed the roads, with strong American positions at The Notch, Chungam-ni, and around Masan. The whole area measured about one hundred miles north and south and fifty miles east and west.

The last days of July and the first days of August were enough to make a general bite his nails. The Eighth Army had begun to receive useful supplies, but the troops were in bad shape. General Walker did not have a lot of confidence in the fighting capabilities of the 25th Division. The 24th Division was shot, and General Walker said it would have to go back to Japan for a complete reorganization before it would be ready to fight again. But the division could not be released from Korea until replacing troops came in. And they were coming at a snail's pace.

On August 1 the 5th Regimental Combat Team from the United States arrived at Pusan and immediately was hustled west to the line to strengthen the 25th Division. The skeletonized 2nd Division was scheduled to become the Eighth Army reserve. At least, then, General Walker did have a little something in reserve.

The Marines were still on the high seas. There were nearly forty-seven hundred of them, and most of them were combat veterans from World War II. As the ships neared Korea, General Craig was waiting anxiously for them at Pusan. On the morning of August 2 he learned that the ships would be in that evening. The Marine brigade's air arm had already landed at Kobe, Japan. Two squadrons of fighter planes and one squadron of night fighters were preparing to go into action in the next few days. The fighters would operate from carriers. The night fighters would operate from Korean land bases.

As always, there was a serious difficulty in bringing Marine units into an Army theater of operations. The command problems had not begun to diminish: General Craig had sent a message to the troop commander of the Marines at sea, describing the general situation and telling the commander that his men would probably have to move out as soon as they hit land. The message had never been delivered, and the troops aboard the transports had absolutely no idea of what would be asked of them when they landed. They had not been issued ammunition or rations. No advance guard had been set up. Nothing was ready for action.

General Craig was waiting for them on the dock as a South Korean band tried valiantly and failed to execute the Marine Corps hymn in salute to the reinforcements. The general was shocked to learn that nothing was ready for action and called an immediate meeting of the responsible officers of the brigade.

That evening the newcomers had the whole dismal situation laid out for them. They were told of the condition of the ROK forces, of the depletion and weakness of the U.S. Army forces. They were informed that the Marines would move out at six o'clock the next morning by truck and train. They still did not know where they were going. General Walker had not yet decided where they were needed most of all.

Craig did know one thing: The Marines would be asked to conduct the first American offensive of the war. He and his officers had expected this; it was the proper role for the Marines. And although the general could not tell the officers where they were going, he could assure them that they would have their own Marine air arm in close support, a matter they had come to view during the years of the unification troubles as of major importance.

Late that night, the battalion commanders and company commanders met with the junior officers and the noncoms and told them what the general had said. They had to get ready, but nobody knew quite what for.

That night the Marines assembled on the docks of Pusan and were issued C rations and bandoliers of bullets, grenades, and machine-gun ammunition. It was nearly dawn before they moved back aboard the ships to be fed the last hot meal they might have in a long while.

It was nearly midnight before General Craig learned that General Walker wanted them to move to the village of Changwon on the northern road out of Masan, in the area of the Army's 25th Infantry Division. This move was the result of frantic planning on the part of the Eighth Army staff, which hardly knew which way to turn. In the last few hours it had begun to appear that the North Koreans were preparing to drive against Taegu, now that their lightning thrust against Pusan in the Southeast had been stopped. General Walker believed that by sending an offensive force out in the Southeast he could relieve the building pressure against Taegu by North Korea's crack 3rd and 4th divisions, augmented by the 2nd Division.

The Americans underestimated what they were facing. For months Premier Kim Il-sung in North Korea had been claiming that before the end of summer he would unify Korea under the North Korean People's Republic. The promise had seemed so near fulfillment until a few days earlier; Premier Kim was not willing to sacrifice it now. The field commanders were ordered to take Pusan at any cost before the middle of August, and they responded by preparing to throw all the strength of their eight divisions in South Korea into the battle. The North Korean I Corps on August 3 was ordered to take Taegu and Pusan by August 6.

To face this foe, General Walker now had a numerical superiority over the enemy, although no one in the U.N. command seemed to realize it. The Republic of Korea Army had been reorganized into five divisions. Walker also had four skeletonized U.S. Army divisions and the Marine brigade. Walker probably would not have been terribly comforted if he had been aware he outnumbered the enemy, for he knew the miserable condition of three of those four U.S. divisions and the continued weakness of the ROK forces. The Marines represented the only really superior force that had been brought in. The other elements of strength the U.N. command possessed were the Navy and the Air Force. The latter was just now in difficulty: The push of the North Koreans to the Naktong line threatened to make the Air Force remove its operating bases back to Japan and its joint operations center from the Eighth Army headquarters area at Taegu back to Pusan. This change would make it much more difficult for the Air Force to give troop support on short notice.

The North Koreans were prepared to move against four key points along the U.N. defense line. First was at Yongdok, down to Pohang. So far they had been frustrated, but the new orders were absolute: No cost was too high. The second point was at Waegwan, about fifteen miles northwest of Taegu. Two good roads led into Taegu, and these could be used by tanks to lead the drive. The third point was at Yongsan, where the relatively fresh North Korean 3rd Division was poised. Fourth, and the most dangerous as far as General Walker was concerned, was on the Masan-Chinju front. And it was to this area that the Marines were brought to make their countermove.

Meanwhile, the Navy and the Air Force were trying to keep the North Koreans off balance. On August 3 the pilots of VMF 214 flew their planes aboard the escort carrier *Sicily*, and that day, as the

Marines moved out of Pusan, the Marine fighter planes flew their first missions against North Korean troops around Chinju. They repeated the strikes the next day.

On August 5 the big British cruiser *Belfast* and the cruiser *Kenya* bombarded North Korean installations in the Inchon area, hoping to reduce their supply route south. The *Sicily* was there too and so were Marine fighter pilots.

On the east coast, the cruisers *Toledo* and *Helena* conducted a series of bombardments of troops in the Yongdok area that kept the North Koreans from advancing. Air Force planes also attacked the North Korean positions with rockets that were very effective against troops and supply dumps.

The ROK Navy's *YMS 502* was probably the ROK's most successful fighting unit. That ship destroyed a number of boats loaded with North Korean troops who were planning a seaborne flanking movement from Yongdok southward.

BUT ON AUGUST 3 the major danger was perceived to lie in the Chinju-Masan area, and so the Marines were hustled out of Pusan in that direction. They traveled light. All personal baggage was left at Pusan. Each Marine carried only his pack, his weapon, ammunition, and rations.

The 1st Battalion was the advance guard. Shortly after 6:00 A.M. on August 3 the battalion set out in Army and Marine trucks for a forty-mile trip to Changwon. There the Marines jumped out of the trucks, and at the orders of Lieutenant Colonel George R. Newton, dug in along the Changwon-Masan road to cover the arrival of the rest of the brigade.

The other troops came by road, and the trucks, M-26 tanks, and other heavy equipment by rail. By 4:00 P.M. all but one tank platoon had arrived in the Changwon area. The 2nd Battalion took position on a hill south of the town. General Craig's command post was on the edge of Changwon. The artillery and the tanks were scattered between the outlying battalions and the general's position.

Although the brigade's officers were nearly all combat veterans and more than 60 percent of the enlisted men were too, that first night at Changwon showed how much can be forgotten by fighting troops in five years. As darkness descended, shadows lengthened and seemed to move, and rifles began to pop. Around midnight the area sounded like small-town America on the Fourth of July. Two machine guns joined the rifle chorus. Most of this firing came from the headquarters area, but even the combat troops of the 5th Marines were affected, and before the noncoms could quiet the men down, several were shot accidentally. General Craig was furious and dressed down his officers for such unprofessional conduct. The next night all was quiet on the perimeter.

A day or so after the Marines arrived at Changwon they noticed a number of people atop a nearby mountain that commanded the whole Marine area.

A little observation indicated that these were not hunters or foragers, and a platoon of riflemen were dispatched to deal with them. By the time the platoon arrived at the top of the mountain the intruders were gone. And not all of the men of the platoon arrived. The intense humid heat of the Korean countryside and the rugged terrain of the mountains took their toll in heat prostration, as they already had of the U.S. Army troops. The North Koreans had one great advantage in this war: their adaptation to the local conditions. They had grown up with the heat and the humidity, the stink of the human excrement (heavily laced with the Korean condiment kimchee) of the rice paddies, the flies, and the diseases. To be sure, the ROK forces had the same advantage, but their effectiveness as troops was not the same. As for the Americans, they suffered from the heat and from disease as they had in no previous war since the Spanish-American. This summer of 1950 was unusual, too, worse luck for the foreigners: The monsoon rains failed, and the temperature rose as high as 120 degrees Fahrenheit in the hot sunlight.

THE MARINES HAD one great advantage over the previous Army unit rushed into Korea: They had a little time. On August 4 the troops patrolled and worked on their field discipline. Communication was set up between the brigade headquarters and the air units, on land at Chinhae and at sea aboard the *Sicily* and the escort carrier *Badoeng Strait*. As noted, the planes of VMF 214 struck the enemy on August 3, 4, and 5. The Corsairs of VMF 323 went into action on August 6, bombing, strafing, and firing rockets at North Korean troop concentrations along the Naktong River line.

And as the air units went into action and the ground troops prepared for it, General Craig went down to Masan to meet with General Walker and General Kean, the commander of the U.S. Army's 25th Division. The Marines, Walker said, would be attached to Task Force Kean.

This task force consisted of two regiments of the 25th Infantry Division (each recently brought up to three-battalion strength), the 5th Regimental Combat Team, and the 1st Provisional Marine Brigade. These units were strengthened by two medium-tank battalions, an Army unit equipped with M-4 tanks, and a Marine unit that used M-26 Pershing tanks.

Task Force Kean, General Craig learned, was to attack westward along those three roads to Chinju, seize Chinju Pass, and then secure the Nam River line, which the North Koreans had breached in their first rush toward Masan. The 35th Infantry would attack from The Notch on the northern road. The 5th Regimental Combat Team would take the middle road from the village of Chindongh-ni, and the 5th Marines would attack along the southern road that separates from the middle road about 3.5 miles west of Tosan. That southern fork was the long way to Chinju, skirting the coast and passing through Kosong and Sachon. The 24th Infantry would come along behind and cover the ground between the roads, clearing the enemy out of the mountains between the 35th Infantry and the 5th Regimental Combat Team. A regimental force of ROK troops called Task Force Min was to help them. They were to strike on August 7.

The major North Korean elements in this area were the 6th Division and the 83rd Motorcycle Regiment, an unusual unit that had been born as part of the North Korean Peoples Army 105th Armored Division. Its equipment consisted of Soviet-made jeeps (modeled after the lend-lease version of World War II) and motorcycles with sidecars, an adaptation of a German vehicle. Both types of vehicles were mounted with fixed machine guns. The crews carried submachine guns. They formed a sort of mounted infantry shock force, useful as long as the battle moved along arterial roads but far less so if the battle bogged down in the rice paddies.

These two units had fought their way into Chinju on July 30, and forward elements had penetrated nearly to Chindong-ni, while the main force had been in a relative position of rest since.

On the morning of August 6, the 3rd Battalion of the 5th Marines moved into Chindong-ni to relieve the U.S. Army's 27th Infantry, which had been holding the village. The North Koreans threatened on the north and on the west but had not managed to break through. But the North Koreans had been exercising a steady buildup in the past few days, bringing armor and heavy equipment into the area north of Chindong-ni.

The 27th Infantry then moved back to go into the Eighth Army's reserve. Their key position was a piece of high ground a mile and a half out of the village and east of the Haman road. Lieutenant Colonel Robert D. Taplett set up his command post on this hill. Higher up the hill he posted Captain Joseph C. Fegan's H Company. Fegan wanted to move even farther north, to a piece of higher ground, but that would have put him a quarter of a mile out in front of the rest of the battalion, and Taplett said no.

G Company guarded the Haman road from a small knoll at the bottom of Hill 255 and Hill 99 next to it. And part of H Company looked out southward to the sea to guard against encirclement.

That was the defense. There was no third rifle company in the battalion, in adherence to the peacetime practice of cutting the armed forces to cadre strength. Taplett did have the weapons company, some headquarters troops, the reconnaissance company, and a platoon of the mortar company on hand. His immediate tactical commander for the time being was Colonel Michaelis of the Army's 27th Infantry.

Shortly after the beginning of August 7, Colonel Michaelis ordered Colonel Taplett to commit a reinforced platoon to Yaban-san, which the Marines called Hill 342 and the Army called Fox Hill.

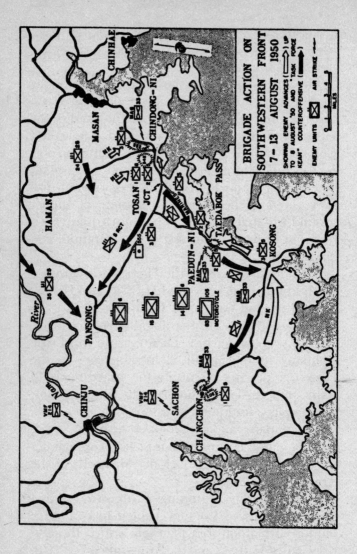

BRIGADE ACTION ON
SOUTHWESTERN FRONT
7 – 13 AUGUST 1950

SHOWING ENEMY ADVANCES (⟶) UP
TO 8 AUGUST '50 AND "TASK FORCE
KEAN" COUNTEROFFENSIVE (⟹)

ENEMY UNITS ☒   AIR STRIKE ⟶

CHINHAE

MASAN

CHINDONG-NI

HAMAN

TOSAN JCT.

TAEDABOK PASS

PAEDUN-NI

PANSONG

KOSONG

CHINJU

SACHON

CHANGCHON

River

MILES

It lies just across the Haman road from Hill 225. This prominence had been occupied by an Army company, which had lost most of its strength in a series of mini-actions. Taplett objected to having his small force strung out farther but was informed that General Kean himself had given the instructions. Hill 342 was to be held "at all costs." (See the map "Brigade Action on Southwestern Front.")

Second Lieutenant John H. Cahill was given the job of holding Hill 342, with the 1st Platoon of G Company, reinforced by a machine-gun squad and a radio operator. The platoon was supposed to be met by a soldier who would guide them to the hill, but the soldier got lost and the platoon came under fire from Marines. Two of Cahill's men were wounded. They stopped and waited for dawn. Then they began the ascent of Hill 342. The 1st Platoon then had its baptism into the Korean War. As the men climbed, the heat became oppressive and they began to drop even though it was not yet 8:00 A.M. Cahill went on ahead, into the Army company's perimeter, and came under fire from the North Koreans around the hill.

There he was briefed on the Army's problems. This unit, F Company of the 5th Regimental Combat Team, had been besieged for four days. The company commander had moved his men out into a broad fan shape during the day but moved them back into a tight perimeter on the hilltop at night. That is how Cahill found them. His own troops began moving painfully to the top. They came under machine-gun fire, stopped, returned the fire with automatic weapons, and then came up farther. On the way up they lost one man killed and six men wounded, including the platoon sergeant. Besides the official losses, a number of men were still on the hillside, suffering from heat exhaustion. Only 37 of the 52 Marines reached the top.

It was not long before Lieutenant Cahill saw why General Kean had ordered his unit to the hilltop. The Army troops were virtually exhausted. That morning during a North Korean movement, a whole section of the perimeter collapsed, and soldiers came running back in panic from their foxholes. The Army platoon commander rounded them up and got them back into position. It soon became apparent that the North Koreans were around the hill in great force, and when the 5th Regimental Combat Team was informed, the Army company was ordered to remain up there with the Marines. Cahill began moving his men into position around the Army troops. Two Marines were killed by snipers during this operation. Then all settled down to a state of siege while down below Army and Marine commanders made plans to relieve the men on the hill.

From the hilltop, Lieutenant Cahill called for artillery fire to silence the enemy mortars. It did not work. He called for an airdrop of water and ammunition. The airdrop fell into enemy hands. Another airdrop came in with five-gallon jerry cans, but they burst on impact, and the thirsty men on the hill got virtually no relief. A third airdrop at four o'clock in the afternoon finally brought them water and ammunition.

As they stayed up there, firing and being fired upon, the 2nd Battalion of the 5th Marines was moving down to Chindong-ni from the Changwon area. The battalion stalled on the road, came under fire, and took some casualties. But it moved on into Chindong-ni and reinforced the positions. General Craig soon arrived by helicopter for consultation. His 1st Battalion troops were to move out on the morning of August 7 after the Army troops of the 5th Regimental Combat Team had taken the Tosan junction. Then the Army troops were to take the right-hand fork, and the Marines would move down the longer Chinju southern road. Farther north, the 2nd Battalion of the Army's 35th Infantry had moved out of The Notch along the northern road on schedule but had run into a North Korean unit supported by several self-propelled guns. All that morning the fight continued.

DURING THE NIGHT of August 6-7, as Lieutenant Cahill's men had stumbled around on the bottom of Hill 342, the North Koreans had moved strong forces around the hills that overlooked Chindong-ni; these forces had caused all the trouble for the Marines moving down from Changwon.

As the time came for the 5th Regimental Combat Team to move out along the road toward Chinju that morning, a heavy fog rolled in as usual, preventing the scheduled air strike. A twenty-minute barrage was put along the road by the artillery. At seven-twenty that morning the Army troops moved down the road to launch the offensive to the south, and the Marines awaited their turn.

The Army troops reached the junction without difficulty, but then instead of maintaining a force to guard the fork and sending the remainder along the right-hand or upper road, the commander turned left, down the southern road.

Not knowing that the junction and the hills around it were unguarded, the 1st Battalion of the 5th Marines started down the road.

On the morning of August 7, Lieutenant Cahill's Marines and their Army allies were in a pickle. The North Koreans had brought up many troops during the night and were bent on the capture of Hill 342 that morning. Just before dawn they attacked. The Americans held and threw the North Koreans back down the hill.

Lieutenant Colonel Harold S. Roise's 2nd Battalion of the 5th Marines had started out on the night of August 6 to relieve the Army and Marine riflemen on Hill 342. Captain John Finn, Jr.'s, D Company was given the job. When that had been done during the night, no one had expected any resistance going up the north side of the hill. Lieutenant William E. Sweeney's E Company was to go around to the west side of the hill and ascend. But as they discovered, during the night the North Koreans had augmented their troop strength considerably. Roise's men ran smack into a large force of North Koreans who had assembled on the front of the hill. The fighting was conducted all day long in one hundred and twelve-degree heat, and the Marines suffered more from climate than from enemy fire. Late in the afternoon both relieving companies bogged down on the sides of Hill 342 and settled in for the night.

THE NORTH KOREANS had done a good job of infiltrating the whole area north and west of Chindong-ni in preparation for their new drive to take Pusan. They had, in fact, launched a new offensive at the same time that the Americans had begun theirs, and the two forces had run smack into one another.

The key position at Hill 342 still was not totally secure; it had to be for the U.S. offensive to continue.

Only the 35th Infantry was where it was supposed to be at the end of the first day. By evening the Americans had driven the North Koreans back along the northern road to Chinju and were near the Much'on-ni road fork, their first objective. They had destroyed several tanks, antitank guns, and one self-propelled gun. They had captured so much radio equipment and so many documents near Pansong that Colonel Fisher believed they must have overrun the North Korean 6th Division command post. But in all this fighting they only took three prisoners. Memories of all those dead Americans with their hands tied was taking its toll on the North Koreans.

The rest of the American attack units were nowhere near their objectives.

The 1st Battalion of the 5th Regimental Combat Team was stalled on the wrong road to Chinju, through its own errors. The 1st Battalion of the 5th Marines was backed up behind it at the crossroads.

Troops of the Army's 27th Infantry who were supposed to be going into reserve were suddenly engaged in fighting. The 24th Infantry, which was assigned to scour the mountain ridges between the roads, was soon bogged down in a number of individual fire fights.

Furthermore, in a typical flanking maneuver the North Koreans had slipped around in the mountains during the night of August 6 and occupied high ground east of the town of Chindong-ni. They then dominated the road to Masan and created a roadblock there, with enough soldiers to hold it. All day long, elements of the 24th Infantry and the 3rd Battalion of the 5th Marines tried to take that high ground and failed.

The American counteroffensive was stalled at the end of its first day. But then so was the drive of the North Korean 6th Division on Chindong-ni and Pusan.

11.

Counterattack

ON THE MORNING of August 8, the 35th Infantry on the northern road to Chinju was ready to move ahead. But by the time the battalion neared the Much'on-ni road junction, Colonel Fisher had word from General Kean that he was to stop. The drive had bogged down elsewhere, and he must not get out in front and be isolated. He dug in on the high ground just east of the road fork and waited. (See the map "Brigade Action on Southwestern Front.")

A new problem had been discovered off to the north and east of the task force. North Korean troops had moved into the mountains in great strength, and when the 24th Infantry began what had been supposed to be a simple job of routing out a few patrols in the area around Sobuk-san, the Americans had run into several hornet's nests and come out badly stung. Sobuk-san, which was not supposed to offer any problem, remained in enemy hands, and the American units that were supposed to fan out from there into the mountains were stalled without even a good idea of what they faced.

The bogdown continued on August 8. The roadblock east of Chindong-ni stubbornly resisted all efforts to dislodge it. The Americans brought up artillery, but the North Koreans continued to hold. Every North Korean company was under enormous pressure from above to meet Kim Il-sung's deadline of mid-August for control of all Korea.

ON THE NIGHT of August 7 the North Koreans surrounded the perimeter at the summit of Hill 342, but Captain Finn's men of D Company relieved the beleaguered Cahill and his Army comrades. Then Finn had the problem: to hold his hill against determined enemy attempts to take it and thus control the main road that led from Chindong-ni toward Chinju. Two of Finn's platoon leaders were killed, and the surviving lieutenant was badly wounded in the action of that day. Finn was wounded while trying to recover the body of one of his lieutenants. He gave up control of the company of Lieutenant R. T. Hanifin, Jr., who was in charge of the mortar platoon. Hanifin took the mortars up the hill and beat off another North Korean attack. At the end of it, the company had lost six men killed and twenty-five wounded. In the heat of the day Hanifin collapsed from heat exhaustion, and command was taken over by Master Sergeant

Harold Reeves, the gunnery sergeant of the company. D Company continued to hold the position all day without a breach. By the end of the day the whole of the 2nd Battalion of the 5th Marines was occupied in the battle for Hill 342. Captain Andrew M. Zimmer, a regimental staff officer, came up late in the day and took over D Company. By the end of the day, the edge of the Communist attack here had been blunted. The North Koreans had committed at least two companies plus mortar units and had failed to take the position. That night of August 8 the enemy withdrew to the north.

MEANWHILE, THE NORTH Koreans had moved in all around Hill 99 and Hill 255 near Chindong-ni, and on the morning of August 8 they were able to block the relief of the Marines by the 24th Infantry by controlling the Haman road north of Chindong-ni. The Marines fought hard to dislodge them from that position and finally did so during the afternoon.

But the North Koreans still held the top of Hill 255 and thus could control the main line of supply between Chinju and Masan.

The North Koreans attempted to reinforce their position on Hill 255. Their troop column was spotted by Marines of G Company, and they stopped that reinforcement with machine-gun and small-arms fire. On the night of August 8 the Marines kept up a constant mortar barrage at the base of Hill 255, preventing the enemy from reinforcing its position or bringing up troops for a flank attack. The next day artillery and air strikes reduced the enemy further, and by midmorning the Marines were moving up the hill to the summit. By noon they could see troops of the 24th Infantry Regiment along the ridgeline of the road and knew then that the way was clear for the counterattack westward that had been held up for three days.

The problem at this point was to catch up to the 35th Infantry, which was waiting ahead on the right. The difficulty was the narrowness of the road as far as the Tosan junction, where the Marines would swing off to the left while the 5th Regimental Combat Team continued along the main road down the center toward Chinji. General Craig ordered the advance to begin on August 8. Little progress was made because the 5th Regimental Combat Team ran into heavy resistance along the road, and the unit's vehicles backed up behind the forward echelon. Behind them came the 5th Marines, who had to use the same road as far as Tosan.

By nightfall the problem still existed. The Army troops controlled the road, but the North Koreans were in the rice paddies on both sides. A fight was developing at Hill 308 south of the road, and the men of the 1st Battalion of the 5th Regimental Combat Team were becoming dispirited. That night, General Kean ordered the Marines to relieve the 5th Regimental Combat Team men and take Tosan without further ado. At ten o'clock that night the 1st Battalion of the 5th Marines reached a rendezvous point arranged by the Army. There they were supposed to meet guides who would take them up Hill 308 to find and relieve the Army troops. But the guides did not show up, and the Army soldiers were already abandoning the hill, so the Marines went on to prevent the enemy from filling a vacuum. About half a mile east of Tosan they came to a dike road that led south to Hill 308. The 5th Regimental Combat Team troops were returning along this narrow road.

The Marines waited until the Army came down; then they could use the dike to reach the hill, three quarters of a mile away. Slipping and sliding and often falling into the stinking muck of the paddy fields, the Marine infantry made its way toward the disputed hill. At dawn on August 9 they had completed the trip without encountering a single North Korean. Then it became a question of climbing two thousand feet in sunlight that came up over the mountain and immediately became broiling hot. By noon they had taken the hill against minimal opposition, mostly sniper. The road was then clear for the 5th Regimental Combat Team to move on through Tosan, and the Marines came up behind them and made the left turn along the southern road.

The first objective of the Marines was the village of Paedun-ni. Lieutenant Colonel George Newton, commander of the 1st Battalion of the 5th Marines, was told to get going. Immediately he encountered two problems peculiar to the Korean War.

The first was the problem of heat exhaustion. Half the men of his two rifle companies were suffering from it and were in no condition to lead an advance. Newton went down Hill 308 and formed up an attack unit from the headquarters and weapons companies.

The second was the problem of maps. The Americans had occupied South Korea from 1945 to 1949, but the Army had never thought to map the terrain. When the war broke out the Americans had to depend on old Japanese maps, which had a number of inherent difficulties. The Koreans, in a surge of nationalism, had ignored all the Japanese geographical names that had been forced upon them in 1910. So most of the place names on the Japanese maps were useless. During forty-five years of occupation of Korea the Japanese had believed their empire inviolate, and they had never bothered to keep the maps up to date or to mark them with terrain contours. Where Colonel Newton went wrong was in the reading of a road junction at Oso-ri, a spot about a third of a mile south of Tosan. Both roads led to Paedun-ni, but one was improved and the other was a cart track. Since only the cart track showed on Newton's map, he took that route. He had started the unit down that road when Colonel Murray came up and told him he was on the wrong route. So the Marines backtracked and lost an hour and then began to move forward. They were slowed by a single North Korean machine gun, which was knocked out by a bazooka

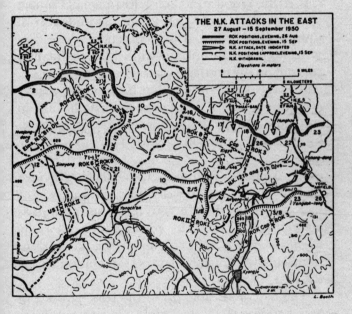

THE N.K. ATTACKS IN THE EAST
27 August – 15 September 1950

team. Late that afternoon of August 9, the column reached the top of a four-hundred-foot pass south of Hill 308. Here Newton halted the column and took up defensive positions for the night.

THAT MORNING OF August 9, after the Marines had cleared the Toson area, the 5th Regimental Combat Team column moved on along the middle road toward Much'on-ni, a road junction where they were supposed to link up with the 35th Infantry column on the northern road. The going was easy, and by the end of the day they had not met serious opposition. The 35th Infantry was also having an easy time of it just then and waited at Much'on-ni for the 5th Regimental Combat Team to come up.

ON THE EVENING of August 9, General Craig decided that the North Koreans were either running away or had abandoned the southern road from Chinju as an artery of advance. He ordered a night attack by the 5th Marines' 2nd Battalion, to start at the position held by Colonel Newton's 1st Battalion astride the pass.

The battalion came up to the pass by truck at about nine o'clock that night. They headed out immediately to attack Paedun-ni. General Craig was right: There was no resistance along the road.

But there were difficulties. The column was led by three M-26 tanks. The first fell through a weakened concrete bridge into a stream and wedged tight between the bridge supports. The second threw a

The traffic circle at Kaesong. From here the American military advisers could see the North Koreans at the railroad station, disembarking from their train on the morning of June 25, cool as cucumbers.

Americans of the 21st Infantry arriving in South Korea, sure that they will stop the North Koreans and be back in Japan in two weeks. The Americans were in for a rude shock.

(above) General Walker, left, and General Dean. This photo, taken at the outset of the Korean War, shows the effects of five years of high living. A few weeks later General Dean, a North Korean prisoner of war, was skin and bones, and General Walker had trimmed down to size.

(right) Major General Paik Sun-yup. He was commander of the ROK 1st Division, which caught the force of the North Korean attack on the west.

American soldiers advance through a rice paddy. One of the problems with the paddies was the oriental practice of fertilizing them with human excrement. It was another hurdle for the Americans, and anyone who ever experienced it would never forget the stink of secondhand kimchee.

Looking back toward Pohang-dong, South Korea. This area was North Korean-controlled when this photo was taken on August 20, 1950.

(left) A 76mm howitzer captured from North Koreans by 5th Cavalry Regiment, 1st Cavalry Division, in Waegwan.

(below) Captured North Korean equipment (front to rear): .25-caliber Soviet submachine gun; .25-caliber Soviet carbine; .31-caliber Japanese rifle; .31-caliber Soviet automatic rifle; .61-caliber Soviet antitank rifle; other weapons not identified. August 1950.

A Leatherneck sniper and spotter ot the 1st Marine Division work together picking off the enemy in Korea.

American tanks in action in the Bowling Alley above Taegu, August 21.

(above) Waégwan bridges over the Naktong River. Hill 303 is at the lower right. Both railroad and road bridges are down, but it would not take much to restore them.

(below) The Naktong River, with the town of Andong and the Andong Bridge.

An American machine gun ready at the Yusong position overlooking the Kap-ch'on River and the highway.

American engineers prepare to blow up a bridge in the face of the advancing North Koreans. Note the ever-present Korean refugees on the road. They were a source of constant concern because of their potential for espionage.

American howitzers in action. This battery of 155's was firing on the town of Chonan on July 10, 1950, after it was captured by the North Koreans.

Brigadier General John H. Church (left) on his arrival at Suwon Airfield, with E. F. Drumwright, counselor of the U.S. embassy; President Syngman Rhee of the Republic of Korea; and Ambassador Muccio.

MacArthur visits the front. Early in the campaign, General MacArthur flew over to Korea from Tokyo with Major General Edward M. Almond (right) to see for himself what had to be done. Here MacArthur is talking to the U.S. ambassador to South Korea, John J. Muccio, outside ROK Army headquarters at Suwon.

track at a light bypass at the same crossing and stalled the column for two hours while temporary bridging was constructed. It was eight o'clock in the morning before the column reached Paedun-ni. Again, General Craig's hunch appeared to have been proved correct: There were no enemy troops in Paedun-ni. The general came up by helicopter that morning and ordered more speed in the advance on Kosong, so heavy trucks were brought up to carry the infantrymen the eight miles to Kosong. The tanks were far behind. The motorized column set out: four jeeps carrying part of the reconnaissance company; six jeeps carrying part of D Company; five trucks carrying more men of D Company and the 60mm mortars; and one machine-gun section.

A little over two miles outside Paedun-ni the road turns and begins the ascent up Taedabok Pass, just before the village of Pugok. The pass is overshadowed by a tall hill. The first four Marine jeeps were in the pass and opposite the hill when the North Koreans sprung an ambush. Machine guns began firing from the high ground above the pass and from the hill. The column jerked to a halt, and Marines began pouring out into the ditches beside the road. An antitank gun scored a direct hit on one jeep.

The whole column had come to a sudden halt. The commander of D Company ordered a platoon to take the high ground on the right side of the road. They did so without opposition and set up automatic weapons to return the North Korean fire.

Captain Andrew Zimmer, the leader of D Company, sent his second platoon up on the right to clear the enemy firing from there. He had spotted the location of the antitank gun that had destroyed the jeep, and soon 60mm mortar fire put an end to it. But in doing so the mortarmen used up all their ammunition, so Zimmer waited at the pass for reinforcements. They came in the form of two tanks, which arrived at four-thirty in the afternoon. Their 90mm guns soon drove the North Koreans into hiding.

Meanwhile, more Marines were coming up: the rest of the 2nd Battalion on foot and the 3rd Battalion by truck. They all stopped at the pass while Colonel Murray conferred with his battalion commanders. He found Lieutenant Colonel Taplett, and they went up on the hill on the left. Below they could see Kosong, which appeared to be very quiet. Murray ordered the 3rd Battalion to move on through and attack Kosong.

WHILE MURRAY AND Taplett were conferring on the left-hand hill above the pass, Lieutenant Colonel Roise of the 2nd Battalion was looking over the positions on the right. He did not see anything very serious ahead. Major Morgan McNeely took a jeep, a radio operator, and a fire team up the road to patrol. He ran into a spate of small-arms fire on the other side of the pass around a bend where no one could see what was happening. Lieutenant Jack Westerman took the lead in the advance with his platoon of G Company. Now, for the first time in this war, the Americans gave the North Koreans a taste of their own tactics. Lieutenant Edward Duncan's platoon made an enveloping sweep to the right, outflanking the enemy on the high ground above the road. Westerman moved up to see Major McNeely's battered jeep ahead but no sign of McNeely's patrol. Westerman made a dash to the jeep. He found the patrol huddled underneath it and Major McNeely mortally wounded. He brought back McNeely, but further rescue attempts were stopped by North Korean fire on the jeep.

Part of the difficulty was a pair of machine guns at the far end of the road, just before it bent again around a hill. Two platoons spent the rest of the daylight hours routing out those machine guns. Then Colonel Taplett called a halt for the night. No attempt was made in the darkness to get back to the men beneath the jeep, because Taplett had to assume the North Koreans had set up an ambush there.

When morning came, two companies of the 3rd Battalion prepared to continue the attack, but as dawn broke a platoon of North Koreans dashed out of the fog to attack Lieutenant Robert Bohn's G Company. In half an hour the attackers were driven off and the advance could begin. The American line moved up to the jeep, and two survivors were rescued. The other three men of the patrol had been killed outright by that first burst of enemy fire that caught the jeep as it rounded the bend.

The Marines were showing how it should be done:

The two battalions were now moving in a column, with G Company's 3rd Platoon in the lead. Corporal Raymond Giaquinto was the point man, with flank guards slightly behind him on each side. About a mile along the road, Corporal Giaquinto saw ground ahead that could be troublesome, with places for an enemy to hide. The flankers moved out on each side, and then Giaquinto raced up the road. Sure enough, they came upon a machine-gun emplacement, but so quick was their reaction that they killed all five North Koreans in the position before they could fire a shot.

They repeated this action three more times along the road to Kosong, hardly holding up the advance of the column behind them.

Meanwhile, the Marine artillery was sending 105mm shells into the town, and these flushed out an enemy column of one hundred vehicles, which began a hasty retreat. Just at that moment a division of Corsairs from the carrier *Badoeng Strait* happened to fly over Kosong after a search mission on the road ahead of the town. They swooped down along the column to strafe. The column stopped; vehicles crashed into one another or overturned on the side of the road. The North Korean troops scattered into the ditches. F4U fighter planes came in with 20mm guns and rockets to attack the jeeps and motorcycles of the motorcycle regiment. As they were running out of ammunition, along came more planes of VMF-323 and Army P-51 fighters, which continued the strafing.

The North Koreans fought back with machine guns and small arms. They damaged one Corsair, and Lieutenant Doyle Cole ditched in the bay south of the town. He was rescued by General Craig's helicopter.

Captain Vivian Moses's plane was also badly damaged, and he had to put it down in a rice paddy in enemy territory. He had done the same thing the day before and had been rescued by a helicopter. But in the latter landing Moses was thrown out of the cockpit and knocked unconscious. When the rescue helicopter arrived, the crew found him drowned. He was the first casualty of Marine Air Group 33. But his actions and those of the other pilots of MAG 33 that day showed how effective air-ground cooperation could be.

AT TEN O'CLOCK that morning of August 11 the Marine column reached the bridge north of the town, and H Company passed on through to take the town. With two tanks the riflemen moved in easily against light resistance and drove out the enemy. The men of H Company then occupied all the high ground and set up the command post in a schoolyard. General Craig came up by jeep to check on the situation. There was some sniping and a few minor actions at Kosong but nothing that threatened the position.

G Company moved west across the town to a hill

below the Sachon road—Hill 88. The North Koreans were dug in there, but that situation was remedied by an air strike from Marine Air Group 33. At one-thirty in the afternoon the infantrymen of G Company reached the crest of the hill and found no enemy, just abandoned equipment, evidence of hasty retreat.

That afternoon General Craig ordered the brigade to move on toward Sachon without searching out every possible enemy holdout position around Kosong. Up ahead of the Marines on the Sachon road were two enemy antitank guns. A medic jeep made a wrong turn and rushed out along the Sachon road, where it was blasted by the antitank guns. That little tragedy may have saved a tank, because two M-26 tanks came up to the bend in the road, where they remained and knocked out the two antitank guns without further ado.

The column moved up then and not long afterward came upon the scene of destruction wrought by the Air Force. But many of the vehicles that had been abandoned on the road were in perfectly good condition.

The brigade moved on through the wreckage, covered above by planes of MAG 33, who reported seeing enemy troops retreating rapidly toward Sachon. At 6:00 P.M. the column was held up by an enemy machine gun ahead, which wounded three Marines. It took the tanks a little time to deal with the machine gun, and at that point Colonel Taplett decided to call a halt for the night. The 3rd Battalion dug in on the Sachon road, with the 2nd Battalion not far behind.

AS THE MARINE brigade took the southern road to Chinju, the 5th Regimental Combat Team moved ahead along the center route. On August 10 the going was easy. The 1st Battalion was on the right side of the road, and the 2nd Battalion was on the left side.

Virtually no troops were encountered on the road to Pongam-ni until the 1st Battalion ran into opposition on the hills near the town. The enemy was routed; the 1st Battalion entered Pongam-ni, and Lieutenant Colonel John P. Jones established his command post there. (See the map "Brigade Action on Southwestern Front.")

Pongam-ni and the village of Taejong-ni were almost abutting at a crossroad on the east side of a mountain pass. A quarter of a mile out of Pongam-ni lies a steep barren ridge about half a mile from the east-west road. The ridge parallels the road on the right-hand side. Directly north of Pongam-ni lies a valley about a quarter-mile wide, occupied by a narrow dirt road leading down from the north, and a stream that runs into another at the edge of Pongam-ni. There a modern concrete bridge crossed the stream. West of the two villages another pair of ridges meet in the apex of a V about a half mile away. The east-west road runs along the southernmost of these ridges and crosses at a pass into a three-hundred-yard-wide valley on the western side.

When the 5th Regimental Combat Team battened down for the night on August 10, the Americans controlled the southern ridge and the eastern part of the northern one. The enemy held the rest of this ridge, and the hill northeast of Pongam-ni, on the right-hand side of the road.

That afternoon the artillery came up and occupied positions in the valley around the two villages. That night the North Koreans attacked the artillery positions and the headquarters command post of the 5th Regimental Combat Team, and the command post of the 2nd Battalion. The attacks were repulsed, and on the morning of August 11, air strikes pushed the North Koreans back onto their mountaintops and kept them quiet.

In the night fighting, Lieutenant Colonel John P. Jones, commander of the 1st Battalion, was wounded and the next day was replaced by Lieutenant Colonel T. B. Roelofs. That afternoon Roelofs was assigned to clear the north ridge of the enemy, secure the pass, and protect the advance troops as they moved through to the west. After that the 1st Battalion would follow along the road.

Colonel Roelofs did clear the north ridge. Before dusk B Company had possession of the high ground north of the pass. A Company and several tanks remained on the little road up the valley to the north to protect that area. So the battalion settled down for the night, with Colonel Roelofs' com-

mand post just west of Pongam-ni in a dry stream-
bed. As darkness fell, the colonel climbed under the
trailer attached to his jeep and fell asleep.

That night Colonel Ordway was ordered to move
the regimental train through the pass. He argued
that the area ahead was teeming with enemy, but
General Kean back at his headquarters did not
believe so. Also, General Kean was just then under
considerable pressure from General Walker to get
cracking on the road to Chinju so the Marines
could be relieved and moved elsewhere to stop up
another hole in the dike.

Kean promised Ordway that a battalion of the
24th Infantry would come up on the right to protect
the flank.

So that night the 2nd Battalion of the 5th Regimental Combat Team moved out through the pass.
Once across they were out of communication with
the regimental command post. Lieutenant Colonel
John L. Throckmorton believed that the rest of the
regiment was coming along behind, but they were
not. The 2nd Battalion was out there all alone,
because after Throckmorton had his orders, new
orders had come from Kean to hold the rest of the
troops.

In the very early hours of August 12, Colonel
Roelofs was rolled out from under his jeep trailer by
Captain Claude Baker, his executive officer. Baker
had some bad news. For some time he had been
hearing shots around the C Company position on
the ridge north of the village, and now the battalion

had lost contact with the company. Roelofs jumped up and tried to reach the company by telephone and by radio. He had no luck. He sent runners and a wire crew out. He also informed Colonel Ordway of this development and urged him to move the supply train and the artillery out through the pass in a hurry. But Ordway had his orders from division, and apparently was reluctant to wake anybody up. He decided to wait until daylight.

Colonel Roelofs got into his jeep and went around the area. All the artillery and the supply trucks were ready to move. Returning to the command post, Roelofs learned that C Company still had not been heard from, but where it had been on the ridge there were lights signaling someone. They were not signaling Colonel Roelofs, so he figured they were for the enemy. Once more he told Colonel Ordway it was time to get the train out of that valley.

This time Ordway listened. He tried to get in touch with the division and failed. The promised battalion from the 24th Infantry had not arrived. Still, he decided to move. It was about four o'clock in the morning.

The supply train would move first, then the artillery, and the 1st Battalion would cover and follow.

The move began.

But the medical company tried to horn into the column from the side, an ambulance caught in a ditch, and the whole column was stopped until it could be pulled out. No vehicle moved more than 20 feet in the first hour.

Then came dawn. With it the enemy began to fire down on the column from the heights.

Colonel Roelofs went out ahead in his jeep, found Colonel Throckmorton's battalion on the other side of the pass, and asked them to move on west so the regimental train would have use of the road. Meanwhile, the North Koreans were systematically firing on the vehicles stuck down in the valley. They cut up the artillery, and some of the artillerymen fled into the mountains. The platoon that Roelofs left to guard the rear deserted its post, and the commander told Roelofs he had been ordered to do so. He never said by whom. Roelofs had no time to argue. He told Colonel Ordway he would send the platoon back, but Ordway said the road was so jammed he had better not.

BY THIS TIME the North Korean infantry had surrounded the artillery back in the valley and was butchering it. The North Koreans attacked from three sides. They brought in tanks and self-propelled guns. (So much for General Kean's belief that the North Koreans did not have much strength here.) The withdrawal of that platoon back at the flat had let the enemy into the area down the valley road. At point-blank range the North Korean tanks and guns began to destroy the American artillery at Pongam-ni village and the concrete bridge. The U.S. 105mm and 155mm howitzers could not depress far enough to engage the tanks. The only effective opposition to the enemy at this point was the heavy-weapons company, which was dug in and began raking the enemy with heavy machine-gun fire.

Colonel Roelofs headed back toward the village. On the way he met an artillery officer who said that the enemy had wrecked all the artillery. Roelofs ordered the 4.2-inch-mortar platoon to come out through the pass and then the heavy-machine-gun platoon to follow. The wounded were brought along. The many dead were left behind. There were not enough trucks left to carry them.

As Roelofs waited at the pass, three tanks came up from Pongam-ni. What they had been doing all this time no one knew. Roelofs ordered the tanks to stand by at the pass. The tankers said everyone back there was dead. Roelofs went down to check. He encountered a chaplain with a jeep full of wounded men. The chaplain confirmed that all behind were dead. Back at the pass, Roelofs found what was left of his C Company, twenty-three of one hundred eighty men. He sent these survivors up front to join A Company and then called B Company from its position on the hills. The company came down in orderly fashion in platoons, covered by the tanks. The tanks were the rear guard as the Americans disappeared westward over the pass. The enemy now lay between the column and its main line of supply. Behind were more artillery and service troops.

That morning, Colonel Throckmorton was ordered by Colonel Ordway to return to the pass. He did so, but only a handful of stragglers came up. Throckmorton then moved toward the regimental command post in the east.

Various units tried to clear the road around Pongam-ni but failed. Finally General Kean ordered the 3rd Battalion of the 5th Marines up, and also the 3rd Battalion of the 24th Infantry to attack through the hills to Pongam-ni.

FROM THE MARINE position on the southern road to Chinju, the battle seemed to be going splendidly. Colonel Taplett's battalion was only a day's march from Sachon.

Early on the morning of August 12 Colonel Newton's 1st Battalion moved on through the line, given the mission that day of taking Sachon. The Marines moved carefully, scenting trouble ahead. First came a fifteen-man patrol of the reconnaissance company, followed by the three platoons of B Company, with tanks between the platoons and tanks following the 3rd Platoon. The remainder of the battalion moved on behind.

The column moved on without opposition until noon, when the advance unit reached the tiny village of Changchon, about four miles from Sachon. There the reconnaissance patrol came under fire from hills on both sides of the road. It was a trap—but one that had sprung prematurely.

Captain John Tobin sent his 1st and 2nd platoons and three tanks forward to help Captain Kenneth Houghton and the reconnaissance patrol. They had to stay on the road because the land on both sides was paddy field, soft and sticky.

Meanwhile, more North Koreans moved along the hills above the fields toward the rear of the column and put the 3rd Platoon under fire from the hill the Marines called Hill 250. Captain Tobin called for an air strike. The strike came in, but the North Koreans still caught the 3rd Platoon in crossfire and stopped their attempts to move to one of the hills. A Company took another hill; this helped relieve the pressure. It took one more air strike to knock out the enemy machine guns on Hill 250. Then the Marine flanks were secure, and the rifle platoons could fan out and clear the enemy out of the area. They did so by advance and ambush. One platoon of B Company spotted enemy troops moving up the reverse slope of Hill 202. The platoon commander sent a squad to trap them as they neared the top. Technical Sergeant F. J. Lischeski placed his men at the top, with orders to wait until the enemy came up to seventy-five feet from the position, then open fire. The Marines waited, the North Koreans came up, and the Marines fired. They killed all thirty-nine North Korean troops trying to make that advance.

The Marine column stalled that day since the North Koreans were waging a tough fight to protect the battered column that had retreated from Kosong. They bivouacked near the area of the fighting. The next morning, Lieutenant Colonel Newton expected to go on into Sachon. But before then he had new orders. His battalion was to move the next morning by truck—but not to Sachon. There were new holes in the Eighth Army dike. The Marines had to give up their successful advance and plug the holes.

ON THAT MORNING of August 12, when General Kean learned that his 5th Regimental Combat Team column had been ambushed at Pongam-ni, he demanded one reinforced Marine battalion to come and save the day. This meant General Craig's brigade would lose a third of its strength. Craig had the message at eleven-thirty that morning. Moving around by helicopter, he organized a trucklift and at 1:00 P.M. had the 3rd Battalion of the 5th Marines on the way to try to retake all the artillery that had been abandoned in the valley.

That afternoon Craig was ordered to Masan to confer with General Kean. Craig got there by helicopter at six-thirty in the evening, having first stopped off at the Pongam-ni area to see how his Marines were doing in rescuing the Army.

The Marines did not seem to be having trouble. They had arrived three miles east of Pongam-ni at four o'clock in the afternoon. By nightfall they had secured the high ground north of the road and east of the village.

When General Craig arrived at General Kean's headquarters at Masan, Craig was told he had to withdraw from the Sachon assault. The reason, although no one said it that way, was that the Army had failed in the middle-prong offensive. The 5th Regimental Combat Team was in no condition to go on without its artillery and many of its supplies, although its 3rd Battalion had met the 35th Regiment to the north, and both were ready to continue. There was also another reason: The North Koreans had crossed the Naktong River farther east and threatened the whole line. Like firemen, the Marine brigade had to be rushed to the scene. The Chinju offensive was abandoned, and the Marines moved back around Masan.

On the morning of August 13 Colonel Taplett's 3rd Battalion attacked westward to rescue the men and vehicles of the 555th Field Artillery, who had been the principal victims of the Pongam-ni ambush. But the Army no longer called it an ambush; now it had become the Battle of Bloody Gulch. The unit had lost all eight of its 105mm howitzers, and the 90th Field Artillery Battalion had lost all six 155mm howitzers of its A Battery. As for equipment, perhaps one hundred vehicles were destroyed or captured in addition to the guns. The North Koreans claimed one hundred fifty-seven vehicles and thirteen tanks. The casualties had been very high—about 80 percent. When the area was recaptured, about one hundred bodies, all shot through the head, were found in two houses; this indicated that those shot had surrendered and been murdered.

All of this was because the 5th Regimental Combat Team commander had refused to take the advice of Colonel Roelofs and get the artillery and the supply train across the pass when the North Koreans first launched their attack.

ON AUGUST 13 the Marines reached the top of the hill overlooking Pongam-ni and could see the enemy troops on the flat below them. They were ready to go down and take them on, but then new orders came: They were to abandon the rescue attempt and rejoin the Marine brigade at Masan.

As for the 555th ("Triple Nickel") Field Artillery, it had to be completely rebuilt in terms of personnel and weapons and equipment. Guns and trucks scheduled for the ROK forces were diverted, and Lieutenant Colonel Clarence E. Stuart, who had just arrived from the United States, took over the battalion on August 13. Two days later, Colonel Throckmorton took over command of the 5th Regimental Combat Team from Colonel Ordway. On August 16 the highly publicized Task Force Kean was dissolved. The Chinju offensive might have been a victory; as far as the Marines were concerned, it *was* a victory. But Chinju was never taken, and the 5th Regimental Combat Team's wounds were so great that the Eighth Army could not possibly make any such claim. Furthermore, the reason that the 24th Infantry battalion promised to Colonel Ordway on that fateful night of August 12 did not come up is that the troops ran away from the fighting. Two companies were engaged on the evening of the 12th, but the soldiers disappeared in the face of very little enemy fire. By noon of August 13 the strength of the two companies together was down to fifty-five men, and they had suffered only ten casualties, three of these officers. The 24th Infantry Regiment epitomized General Walker's greatest single problem: the combat unreliability of his Army force.

With this imperfect weapon, plus the Marines, General Walker had to try to stop troops who were being pressed with fanatical insistence by the North Korean high command to take Pusan in the next few days even if whole divisions had to be lost.

12.

The Naktong Bulge

THE 1ST BATTALION of the 5th Marines had one last encounter with the enemy on the Chinju road. General Craig's orders were for them to move out early on the morning of August 13; in the middle of the night, however, the North Koreans staged another of their now famous night attacks. These North Korean 6th Division troops were mostly veterans of the Chinese Communist war against the Nationalists, and they were expert at night fighting. They managed to crawl up to the edges of the Marine positions, even though there was no breach of Marine security, and then launch two attacks bent on splitting the Marine force in two. They captured two Marine machine guns and turned them against the battalion. They fought with grenades and Chinese burp guns. But in the end they suffered very heavy casualties and withdrew. The Marine casualties were not light: twenty men killed and eighteen wounded. There was no time to try to get a count of the enemy dead, for the battalion was moving out to Miryang on the Taegu-Pusan road for a little rest before the next operation.

They reached Miryang on August 15 and had their first hot meal since leaving ship at Pusan. Their camp was located in a grove of trees, and they could swim in the Miryang River. They had a pleasant if brief break from action while General Craig conferred with General Church about the next operation.

General Walker's declaration that here the Eighth Army would stand and fight was now the key to the defense of South Korea. If the enemy took Yongsan, then Pusan would be in immediate and mortal danger.

THE NEXT MOVE had to be on the Naktong, because the North Koreans on the night of August 5 began their crossing.

First of all they fooled General Church. He had been expecting an attempt to cross the river near Hyopch'on (see the map "The Front Moves South") because the North Koreans had massed three regiments there. Opposite this area was the U.S. 21st Regiment. Instead of crossing there, the North Koreans made their major effort to the south, against the U.S. 34th Infantry. The troops undressed, rolled their weapons into their clothes, and carried them across. Some made rafts and floated machine guns, ammunition, and supplies across.

In this crossing, no heavy weapons were brought along. The infantry would have to make do with the simplest. These were crude but effective methods. The commander of the North Korean 4th Division, Major General Lee Kwon-mu, had learned them during the war against the Japanese, when he fought in the Chinese Communist Eighth Route Army.

He had also learned the value of timely intelligence. The North Koreans chose as a point of crossing a gap that existed between I and L companies of the U.S. 34th Infantry. How they discovered that gap is not hard to imagine. Just recently General Church had ordered all civilians in the 24th Division zone of defense out of the area from the river to a point five miles to the east. "If we are going to hold here," he said, "we cannot have any enemy behind us." So many times had the Americans been betrayed by North Korean soldiers or guerrillas masquerading as refugees that they had finally gotten the message: Civilians were not to be trusted. But the American lines were abutted by the ROK Army lines, and there it was more difficult to keep out Korean civilians or to identify possible spies. It seemed almost impossible to destroy the constant and effective North Korean spying on American positions.

Once across the river, the North Koreans dressed, formed up in a column, and began to march toward Yongsan. Another unit crossing farther up the river ran into an American minefield and was promptly shelled by American artillery. That force abandoned the attack and fell back across the river. The force that did get across headed directly for the 34th Infantry's 3rd Battalion command post and the mortar platoon position. Soon they overran the 4.2-inch mortars, and this action brought the battalion command post to the alert. Most of the troops fled to the rear. Lieutenant Colonel Gines Perez, commander of the 3rd Battalion, found Colonel Ayres of the 1st Battalion and gave him word of the crossing.

When Colonel Beauchamp had the word, he ordered Ayres to counterattack and reported to General Church that he was moving to stop the incursion. But the North Koreans were playing this game carefully. They did not attack the line companies but moved between them to penetrate behind the American positions along the river and take high ground. By dawn the North Koreans on the American side of the Naktong numbered nearly a battalion.

After moving through the abandoned 3rd Battalion command post, they found B Battery of the 13th Field Artillery in their path. The battery was situated at the northern base of Obong-ni ridge. The artillerymen retreated, leaving four howitzers and nine vehicles to the enemy.

Colonel Ayres and two of his officers set off in a jeep toward the river to reconnoiter the situation. When they reached the old 3rd Battalion command post, they came under fire from the hills around it.

C Company came up by truck and was also taken under fire. The soldiers got out of their trucks and were ordered to take the high ground where the firing was coming from. But the enemy was too strong, and C Company was cut to ribbons without achieving the high ground. Only about forty men survived.

A and B companies came up on foot and drove the North Koreans back to the point where the 3rd Battalion command post had been. It took all day, but by dark A Company reached the river and found part of L Company still there. B Company dug in on a part of the high ground the Army called Cloverleaf Hill. By this time the North Koreans had penetrated to Cloverleaf Hill but had not yet crossed the road to take control of Obong-ni ridge.

They had struck in the heart of "the Naktong Bulge"—that area west of Yongsan where the Naktong bends (see the map "The Pusan Perimeter") and the land forms a thumblike protuberance surrounded on three sides by the river. This was where the North Koreans continued to cross this second night, wading through neck-deep water, pulling rafts loaded with vehicles, heavy weapons, ammunition, and supplies.

They moved into this long valley surrounded by river and mountains, with Hill 311 as the principal height. On the east side the Yongsan road winds around the hill to the tip of the thumb, where a ferry then linked the road with the other side. Two key high points guard the eastern side of the thumb:

Finger Ridge lies on the north. Beyond it to the east lies a deep gully, and at the bottom of the gully is the village of Tugok. Hill 207 lies on the south of the road, and east of the hill is Obong-ni Ridge, which is directly south of Tugok.

As seemed to happen so often in these days, on August 6 the 3rd Battalion's I Company abandoned its key position at the base of the thumb of the bulge without authorization, although it was never under attack during the day. Other troops of the battalion's heavy-weapons company, a mortar platoon, and an anti-aircraft unit joined them in this withdrawal, thus leaving the American right flank wide open. General Church ordered the units back into position, and the commanders were relieved immediately.

During the day General Church committed the 19th Infantry to an attack that stopped part of the pressure. But as the first day ended, the enemy was securely across the river on high ground.

All night long the American artillery fired on the points that seemed most likely to be used by the North Koreans for crossing the river, but the North Koreans simply moved the scene of their operations and came on. On the morning of August 7 the 19th Infantry staged an attack and so did elements of the 34th Infantry, but they failed. The North Koreans pressed forward and occupied most of Cloverleaf Hill and part of Obong-ni ridge. At this point they gained domination of the east-west road that led into the bulge from Yongsan, five miles away. This was the road the Americans had to use to bring up vehicles. From their heights the North Koreans could see all the way to Yongsan.

That morning of August 7, the U.S. 9th Infantry Regiment of the 2nd Division was attached to General Church's command and ordered into the line to replace the 34th Infantry on Cloverleaf Hill. Colonel John G. Hill was told to attack as soon as possible, on the hill and across the road against Obong-ni Ridge. Hill put his 1st Battalion on the left side of the road and the 2nd Battalion on the right side. Behind them were 105mm and 155 mm howitzers.

On the night of August 7 the North Koreans moved more troops and heavier equipment across the river. They also had artillery and mortars captured from the 34th Infantry in the past two days.

At four o'clock on the afternoon of August 7, Colonel Hill's regiment attacked. They captured part of Cloverleaf Hill and part of Obong-ni Ridge. But during the night the North Koreans attacked and recaptured all this ground.

On August 9 the battle continued back and forth, but with the Americans consistently giving up ground. A Company of the 34th Infantry occupied high ground on the river. It was driven off.

On August 10 the North Koreans launched an attack against the 9th Infantry that won them all the ground the Americans had gained on Cloverleaf Hill. The Americans did capture Ohang Hill and other prominent points along the Naktong. That evening General Church gave Colonel Hill command of the Naktong Bulge and designated all the units in that area as parts of Task Force Hill. The main reason for this was to try to coordinate the efforts of the mixture of understrength units at Colonel Hill's disposal. He had his own 9th Regimental Combat Team, but the 3rd Battalion was missing. He had the 34th and 19th Infantry regiments of the 24th Division and the supporting 24th Division artillery, but the 34th Infantry was down to fewer than eleven hundred men, the 19th Infantry to seventeen hundred, and the combat strength of the regimental support units was about 40 percent of normal. With this collection of units he was to attack the next day.

On the night of August 10 the North Koreans sent still more force across the river. They had used another technique learned from the Soviets and from the Chinese Communist campaign against the Japanese: the underwater bridge. These structures were not properly bridges but fords, which could be built across broad but relatively shallow streams. Rocks, timbers, wreckage, and sandbags were piled by the engineers into a narrow roadway across the water, about a foot below the surface. Vehicles could pass, but from the air the "underwater bridge" was unlikely to be spotted by an observer. A bridge at the Paekchin ferry site brought in tanks, trucks, mortars, and artillery. By morning most of the North Korean 4th Division had crossed the river and was in position to advance.

Task Force Hill's attempt on August 11 to drive the enemy from the Naktong Bulge was to be a general attack, with protection on both flanks and a major drive down the middle by the 9th Regimental Combat Team and the 19th Regiment. It failed. The North Koreans had brought up enough heavy weapons to make the difference. Their artillery behind Cloverleaf Hill and Obong-ni Ridge stopped the American advance cold. That night the North Korean 4th Division brought the rest of the troops across the Naktong. That night also, the North Koreans began an enveloping movement, with troops marching around behind Task Force Hill against the roads south and east of Yongsan. Some of them disguised themselves as refugees, as usual; it was so easy with the hundreds of refugees moving south out of Yongsan toward Pusan. In this case a cart overturned, and more than a dozen rifles and ammunition were exposed. The North Korean soldiers began to run, but infantrymen shot down most of them before they could escape into the hills. Still, for every cart that overturned, how many got through? On the morning of August 12, the North Koreans had a strong roadblock two miles east of the town. They ambushed a convoy of ambulances and trucks. Another North Korean force threatened the Yongsan-Miryang road. Colonel Hill sent F Company of the 9th Infantry with extra mortars to dislodge the eastern road-block. He had no other riflemen to send south—his whole force was now trying to hold against what was developing into a broad attack by the North Korean 4th Division. So he assembled a rump force of about one hundred thirty clerks, cooks, truck drivers, and MPs and assigned them to the direction of Captain George B. Hafeman, commander of the I and R company. This unlikely attack unit moved into a position on the southern road at a pass near Simgong-ni. It was promptly attacked by the North Korean infiltrators, but it held. It held all day, although its only communication with Task Force Hill was by armored cars, which brought up supplies and ammunition several times.

The eastern roadblock posed a more serious problem. On August 12 General Walker's intelligence assessment indicated that the North Koreans had most of two battalions east of Yongsan. That threat was so great that Walker assigned the 27th Infantry Regiment to General Church to handle it. The 2nd Battalion (which had encountered the overturned cart) battled the North Koreans to a standstill that day. On August 13 the 3rd Battalion of the 27th Infantry came up to help, and by midafternoon the regiment had reached its objective, high ground north and east of Yongsan. These Americans had captured four pieces of artillery—two of them 105mm American howitzers.

Thus, for a change, one of the best American fighting units in Korea had held and recaptured territory, and service troops had blocked an enemy attempt to cut the Yongsan-Miryang road.

Meanwhile, the 9th Infantry was making a stand

at Cloverleaf and Obong-ni, and its example seemed to put new starch into even such over-stretched units as the remains of the 34th Infantry. The North Koreans had expected to have taken Yongsan by this time and to be marching down the road to Pusan. Instead they were held at Cloverleaf and at Obong-ni Ridge.

With the fires put out behind him on August 13, Colonel Hill planned a major attack on those hill positions. The assault against the pocket was scheduled for August 14 and 15. The latter was the most important day since the North Korean crossing of the 38th parallel. This was the day on which Premier Kim Il-sung of the North Korean People's Republic had promised to deliver to his followers all of Korea. It was the fifth anniversary of the Japanese surrender in World War II and the symbolic liberation of Korea from the Japanese yoke. The Americans had to expect that anything might happen on this day, including a general assault on all fronts. A powerful U.S. Air strike of one hundred planes was to precede the attack, followed by an artillery barrage. But the day dawned with heavy overcast and rain, so the air strike was scotched. The artillery barrage lasted only ten minutes. The infantry attack was carried out with enthusiasm but little success. The American units had lost a lot of men in the past few days, and they did not have the power to dislodge the enemy and hold the high ground at Cloverleaf and Obong-ni. The North Korean night counterattack more than made up for any ground they had lost during the day. Stubbornly, Colonel Hill continued to attack on August 15. But once again the weather was too bad for air support. Troops of the 34th Infantry distinguished themselves that day in hand-to-hand fighting, showing a ferocity rare at this time among the Americans. A black soldier, PFC Edward O. Cleaborn of A Company, was one of a platoon that assaulted a ridgeline and got into a hand-to-hand fight with the enemy. Thirty-five men had made this dash; in an hour, twenty-five of them were killed or wounded. The others withdrew except Cleaborn, who wanted "one more shot" at the enemy. If he got it, no one knew. He was killed there.

At the end of the day, Colonel Hill and General Church met and decided that they did not have the power to attack. They would have to go into defense. When General Walker learned this, he was not happy. General Church said (as was later shown to be true) that the entire North Korean 4th Division was facing them on the east side of the Naktong. General Walker did not believe it. Church and Hill both said they had to have more strength if they were to drive the enemy out of the bulge, and finally Walker had to accept that verdict. He had one more weapon: the Marine brigade.

The 24th Infantry Division had tried but failed to dislodge the enemy, even when given fresh troops. Colonel John G. Hill's 9th Infantry Regiment had been detached from the 2nd Division and attached to the 24th Division. Task Force Hill had launched an assault on the pocket and tried for two days to break it but had failed.

By August 14 the North Koreans had occupied the Naktong Bulge and had pushed along the road toward Yongsan, taking Hill 207, Tugok village, Cloverleaf Hill, Finger Ridge, and Obong-ni Ridge. The enemy position was sound and extremely strong. Three North Korean regiments were consolidating these positions, digging in, and preparing to attack toward Yongsan, only a few miles to the east.

Already the North Koreans had one hundred machine guns in place, plus a number of artillery pieces, including several of those captured at Taejon. They also had managed to bring several T-34 tanks across the river. If this bridgehead could hold and the armor, artillery, and main assault force of three divisions could be brought up, then it was goodbye, Pusan. The task of the reinforced 24th Division was to keep that from happening.

ON AUGUST 15 Colonel Collier of General Walker's staff flew down to Miryang to tell General Craig what was happening up north. A great deal had to be said. Above Taegu the North Koreans had crossed the Naktong and were driving south. To the east the North Korean 5th Division had fought through the ROK forces to reach P'ohang-dong, and their obvious next move would be down the Kyongju corridor to Pusan. And that was not all of it. Following the urgings of the government in

Pyongyang, the North Korean troops everywhere around the perimeter were pressing; they had already failed to deliver Pusan on August 15, but they were ordered to do so within the next few days. But of all the threats General Walker considered that at the Naktong Bulge to be the most menacing, and thus he was committing the Marines to that sector.

After Colonel Collier had explained the situation, General Craig ordered the brigade to break off its rest and recreation and prepare to move out to Yongsan. Craig then hastened to General Church's headquarters to confer on the use of his troops. At their conference it was decided that the entire reinforced 24th Division would attack on August 17.

On August 16, one hundred forty Army trucks were ordered down to Miryang to pick up the Marine brigade. General Craig flew back and forth in his helicopter from Miryang to Church's command post, and late in the day he visited the 9th Regimental Combat Team command post for a talk with Colonel Hill. He was not impressed with the fighting potential of what he saw: The soldiers had the look of weary men, and there were not as many of them on the line as he might have expected. The 9th Regimental Combat Team had been having a bad time these past few days. Colonel Hill was optimistic, but the Marine officers were concerned. They were to join the 9th Regimental Combat Team in a frontal assault on the North Korean positions, and the keys to the attack were positions on Hill 125 and Observation Hill, both held by 9th Regimental Combat Team units. Half a mile behind, the 34th Infantry occupied part of Cloverleaf Hill. The Marines were to relieve the 34th Infantry there. Then at H-Hour, the Marines would attack from Observation Hill toward their first objective, Obong-ni Ridge. The 9th Regimental Combat Team would head for Tugok and Finger Ridge. The 19th and 34th Infantry would cover the right flank, and the 21st Infantry would cover the left flank.

Lieutenant Colonel Murray came up to confer with Colonel Hill, too, and he was even more impressed with the poor condition of the 9th Regimental Combat Team troops. General Church had indicated a general assault, but Murray suggested that the Marines take off first to Obong-ni Ridge while the Army troops covered them with fire from Hill 125. After capturing the ridge the Marines would then cover the Army troops as they moved into Tugok and Finger Ridge. This plan would minimize the danger of the 9th Regimental Combat Team breaking down during a dual assault and opening a hole for the North Koreans to flank the Marines, although Murray did not say that at the meeting. Nor did he inform General Craig of the change in the tactics.

While this refined planning was going on, the troops were having difficulties. The Army sent fewer than a third of the promised trucks to Miryang. That meant most of the 5th Marines had to march a long way on the night before the attack. The available trucks had to be used to move Colonel Taplett's 3rd Battalion to Cloverleaf Hill to relieve the 34th Infantry there. It was one-thirty on the morning of August 17 before the 2nd Marine Battalion marched into its assembly area at the base of Cloverleaf Hill. The 1st Battalion was equally late in arriving in position for the assault, and few of the men got much sleep.

As morning neared, the Marines were ready. The 2nd Battalion would seize Obong-ni Ridge. When that was accomplished, the 1st Battalion would take Hill 207. When that was done, the 3rd Battalion would move down off Cloverleaf and take Hill 311. All this planning was dependent on intelligence received from the Army; the Marines had not had time to do any patrolling or observation of their own. No one in the brigade really knew the disposition of the enemy troops. But while the Marines were moving, so were the North Koreans. On the night of August 16 they attacked the 9th Infantry on Cloverleaf Hill and occupied some American positions. They also threatened other high points. Up north, in the sector of the Pusan Perimeter held by the 1st Cavalry Division, a new threat developed in the shape of another crossing of the Naktong. These were not troops of the North Korean 4th Division but of the North Korean 10th Division, a fresh unit brought in to make sure the assault on the Naktong Bulge succeeded. To meet this move,

General Walker committed troops of the newly arrived U.S. 23rd Infantry.

Obong-ni, which towered above the land, was a rugged series of steep hills and sharp gullies that ran down into the rice paddies on the flatland below. Those hills were the key: Hill 102, Hill 109, Hill 117, Hill 143, Hill 147, Hill 153 rising ever up the ridgeline. Halfway up was a red gash in the brown surface of the hills, where a landslide had exposed the clay. The Marines called it Red Slash Hill.

As dawn approached, Lieutenant Colonel Roise's 2nd Battalion moved up to its line of departure on the east side of the valley in front of Obong-ni. At seven twenty-five the artillery was to open fire on Obong-ni. At the same time Marine Corsair aircraft were scheduled to begin strafing runs on the ridgeline. But the best-laid plans . . . The artillery barrage was ten minutes late, and when it came the observers discovered that the artillery pieces had been improperly registered and the shells all fell behind the ridgeline. The air strike was so late that the Corsairs had time for only one pass at the ridge before the troops were moving out.

The assault was begun by E and D companies of the 5th Marines, by platoons. They crossed the valley rice paddies and started up the slope. The only sounds they heard were their own; ahead of them the enemy was eerily silent. From his observation post on Hill 125, Captain Zimmer observed the progress of D Company's 1st and 3rd platoons. He held the 2nd Platoon in reserve on the hill. Behind the riflemen came the bazooka section; off to their left came the platoons of E Company. They moved ahead, and still the silence held. It was suddenly broken, but not by firing against the assault troops. The 2nd Platoon of D Company on Hill 125 was hit by fire from Hills 117 and 143 on Obong-ni. Two men were wounded. Down below, the assaulting Marines moved up the ridgelines, the 1st Platoon up the gully toward Hill 102, and the 3rd Platoon moved on the left in the next gully. They were about halfway up when the North Koreans suddenly unleashed a hail of machine-gun and rifle fire from Hills 117 and 143. Marines began to drop. They were unable to get out of the gully and onto the slope of Hill 109. They fought for two hours, taking heavy casualties, but made no progress. Captain Zimmer committed the 2nd Platoon, which tried to move up the draw in which the 1st Platoon was pinned down but came under heavy fire from three hills. Most telling was the fire coming from the hillside north of Tugok on the Marine rear. Zimmer discovered this position and asked for artillery support, but it could not be delivered without hitting the men of the 9th Regimental Combat Team, because the North Koreans had infiltrated their positions. Zimmer's own 60mm mortars could not reach these enemy positions either.

The North Koreans tried to bring a heavy machine gun into position on the north side. A 75mm recoilless rifle scored a direct hit on it. The battalion called for air strikes in support of the forward line; by this time Second Lieutenant Michael J. Shinka's 3rd Platoon of D Company was reduced to 15 men, but when the air strike ended, he assaulted Hill 109 and took the top. On the far side a North Korean squad tried to counterattack. The Marine marksmen shot them down. At 11:00 A.M. the Marines held this first gain, but not very comfortably. Shinka's platoon was taking heavy fire from Hill 143 and Hill 207. He complained to Captain Zimmer, and Zimmer turned his mortars on Hill 143, but there must have been fire from other hill points, because it did not stop. By this time Shinka's force was down to six effective riflemen. When his ammunition resupply party did not appear he decided to withdraw and wait until some of the fire on his left could be stopped. The men took the wounded back down the hill and stopped three quarters of the way down and dug in. Shinka went back to see if there were more wounded left behind. While rescuing one marine, Shinka was shot in the chin. He saw a North Korean soldier, hurled a grenade at him, and bleeding profusely, hauled the wounded Marine down the hill. He was wounded again and spun around and rolled down the hill. He walked back to the Marine lines and was sent on to the regimental aid station. Before he went he made sure that ammunition had gotten forward to the remnant of his platoon.

E Company's 1st and 2nd platoons crossed the

rice paddy toward Hills 143 and 147. They crossed under a spatter of rifle fire, but when they started up the slope, machine guns from Obong-ni village began firing on them. The 1st Platoon charged through the village, but the 2nd Platoon faltered under machine-gun fire from Hills 147 and 153. Lieutenant William E. Sweeney, the company commander, saw what was happening from his observation post, but he could not raise the artillery or the mortar company to get support. He committed his 3rd Platoon, which moved up to fire on the hills and keep the enemy down. Sweeney went forward and found the 2nd Platoon disorganized; the 1st Platoon fought its way up the hill but was pushed back by "friendly fire" from U.S. artillery and by strafing by U.S. planes. The 3rd Platoon slipped back and allowed the North Koreans to open up with enfilading fire. This punishment stopped the Marine forward movement. By noon they had to admit they did not have the strength to conquer the ridge. The battalion had taken one hundred forty-two casualties, twenty-three of them dead. At one o'clock in the afternoon General Craig committed the 1st Battalion of the 5th Marines to move through the 2nd Battalion and resume the attack on Obong-ni. He also tried to get in touch with Colonel Hill to find out why the Marines had not received any of the covering fire that was supposed to accompany their attack, but he could not reach Hill.

Against heavy enemy fire, B Company moved

through D Company, and that unit retired. The new company followed the same route as the old, and halfway up the slope between Hills 102 and 109 was pinned down. The men of D Company had warned them, however, of the enfilading fire from Tugok, and they managed to call in 81mm mortar fire on the village, which quieted the machine guns so that the Marines could move. Just after 5:00 P.M. they captured Hill 102.

Meanwhile, A Company followed the route taken by E Company earlier. This time the Marines had the advantage of heavy artillery and air support, but once again the enemy fire was too strong and the company was cut to pieces. Several remarkable instances of heroism came out of this action, but the result was the same as before: A Company was hard hit and had to fall back down Observation Hill. They had not taken the ground they called No Name Ridge, but they had a strong foothold, and they had dealt the North Korean 4th Division a much harder blow that day than anyone realized, for in driving ahead despite heavy casualties they had inflicted even heavier casualties on the enemy.

THE ARMY THAT day had been more successful than the Marines. The Army's objectives were much easier. Late in the afternoon the artillery put a heavy barrage onto Cloverleaf Hill, and afterward the 2nd Battalion of the 9th Infantry took Cloverleaf without much opposition. That same afternoon the right flank force, the 34th and 19th Infantry regiments, took Ohang Hill. By nightfall the North Koreans in the bulge had taken an enormous amount of punishment and were short of food and ammunition. A radio message from a line unit was intercepted that night by 24th Division intelligence; it called on the corps commander to allow the North Korean 6th Division to fall back behind the Naktong.

The Marine M-26 tanks that morning had finished off the overblown reputation of the enemy T-34 tanks for good. During the day the American tanks had supported the infantry fighting at Obong-ni Ridge and had helped quell enemy activity in Tugok village. That evening, after the assault on Obong-ni Ridge had failed, the infantrymen of B Company on Hills 102 and 109 saw four North Korean T-34 tanks approaching the brigade lines along the east-west road. They were followed by a column of infantry. At 8:00 P.M. an air strike was called up and found the column. Marine planes destroyed the fourth tank and scattered the North Korean infantry along the road. But the first three tanks lumbered on, passed Finger Ridge and then Obong-ni Ridge, and approached the bend in the road at Hill 125.

The Marine tankers were just then refueling the M-26 tanks and replenishing ammunition after a busy day, but they jumped into action, moved down to the road, and prepared to face the enemy waiting behind the bend in the road. The guns of the M-26 tanks were loaded with 90mm armor-piercing shells. At the same time the crews of the recoilless 75mm rifles on Observation Hill and the bazooka men of the 1st Battalion's antitank platoon were waiting with their weapons ready. As the first T-34 approached the bend, it was hit by a 3.5-inch rocket, which knocked its right track askew. The tank crew began firing wildly as the driver tried to operate the vehicle in a line. Then the recoilless rifles smashed the left track and tore away the front armor. The T-34 wobbled around the bend firing its 85mm gun and machine guns in all directions, to come up against Technical Sergeant Cecil R. Fullerton's M-26, sitting, waiting. Two 90 mm armor-piercing shells from the M-26 caused the enemy tank to explode. One crewman got out of the flaming tank but was shot down.

Seeing what had happened to the first tank, the second T-34 sped toward the bend in the road. One 3.5-inch bazooka shell knocked the right tread askew; the tank began to weave around the curve, took another rocket in the gasoline tank, which caused an explosion, and then ran into 75mm projectiles from the recoilless rifles. It skidded to a stop off the road behind the first tank, and the 85mm gun kept firing across the valley. No one got out. A second M-26 tank came up, and the two U.S. tanks poured thirteen rounds of 90mm armor-piercing shells into the tank. The hull exploded. A North Korean tanker opened the hatch, and a bazookaman obliged with a white phosphorus shell, which turned the interior of the tank into a flaming pit.

The third T-34 came rushing around the bend and met the same fate as the other two.

THAT NIGHT THE Marines regrouped. Casualties were hustled off by ambulance and helicopter to medical facilities. The east-west road had collapsed in one area and had to be rebuilt during the night. The struggle for Obong-ni Ridge was about to begin again, and the Marines were reminded of the presence of the enemy there by sporadic firing from the ridge. Part of A Company was up on the saddle between Hills 109 and 117. Everyone was expecting some sort of North Korean assault, particularly after the tank foray of the early evening. General Craig was not much worried by the prospect; he had noticed during the day a weakening of the enemy. Even though the Marines had taken heavy casualties, they were in place all along the line, and their spirits were high. General Craig sent out a general warning to all units to be ready for counterattack, and the Marines dug in for the night, with A Company's command post at the top of the draw between Hill 109 and Hill 117. The company's 60mm mortars were set up in the gully.

Just before 11 o'clock that night the enemy began with a mortar attack that hit squarely in the Marine mortar position and knocked it out. Nearly every man was wounded. The mortar rounds also fell around A Company riflemen, but they were dug in on the height. Then, at two-thirty in the morning, the North Korean infantry came. A Company men heard noise on Hill 117, then machine guns on the peak began firing and grenades began coming in. A North Korean platoon charged into the position held by the handful of Marines of the 2nd Platoon. Meanwhile, two other North Korean platoons assaulted B Company on Hill 109. The attack was covered by constant enemy machine-gun fire from Hill 117. Grenadiers came first, hurling their charges. They were followed by troops firing burp guns. Behind the Marine lines the 81mm mortars of the 1st Battalion fired illuminating shells, which helped the Marine riflemen pick off the North Koreans one by one. A squad of North Koreans tried to make a flanking movement but was decimated.

A Company's 2nd Platoon held despite the fact that the odds were three to one against them. They were led by Technical Sergeant Frank Lawson, who was wounded three times that night. Finally, however, there were too many enemy and too few Marines, and the 2nd Platoon was overrun. The enemy penetrated the line of the brigade.

Apparently no responsible North Korean officer knew that a squad had squeezed through the line, because reinforcements did not come along. The North Korean squad came down on the A Company command post and forced it down the ridgeline, but the main strength of the attack remained on the crest and joined another group attacking Hill 109.

When Colonel Newton learned that A Company's lines had been breached, he ordered up a

constant artillery barrage on the enemy approaches
to the ridge. The 1st Battalion's 81mm mortars fired
all their ammunition, then borrowed all of the 2nd
Battalion's ammunition. The riflemen of the two
companies fought briskly, whether holding or
retreating on the ridge. By dawn, the North Korean
attack had run its course, the enemy casualties had
been extremely heavy, and B Company of the 1st
Battalion of the 5th Marines still held Hills 102 and
109.

Now it was the Marines' turn. General Craig had
ordered an attack at seven o'clock, covered by
Marine air support. A Company led the way to Hill
117. A machine gun on the hill started firing. Captain Stevens spotted the gun and called for an air
strike; a Marine fighter plane swooped down and
dropped a five hundred-pound bomb directly on
the machine gun. The action was so close to the
Marines that the concussion killed one Marine
BAR man, but the others were immediately on their
feet, and they rushed forward to take Hill 117. The
North Koreans fled down the reverse slope. The
Marines fired into the retreating groups and killed
dozens of North Koreans. A Company then turned
south along the ridgecrest and took Hill 143. The
3rd Platoon took Hill 147 against a handful of
hard-fighting North Koreans; most of the enemy on
this hill chose to turn around and run away. These
troops were obviously suffering a serious reverse in
the high morale that had carried them all the way
from the 38th parallel. As the Marines hit the crest

of the hill, they saw a company of enemy troops below, marching to the rear in orderly retreat. When the Marine machine guns began sweeping toward them, the formation broke up into a panic-stricken crowd.

Hill 153 was the highest eminence on Obong-ni Ridge, and this position was taken last. The Marines had expected it to be the most stoutly defended, but the reverse was true: When they came to the top they found nothing but abandoned equipment and weapons and a few enemy dead. The blasted foxholes gave evidence of the impressive success of Colonel Newton's long artillery barrage of the night before.

While the Marines of the 1st Battalion were taking Obong-ni Ridge, Colonel Taplett's 3rd Battalion was moving against the second objective, Hill 207. They came in front of Finger Ridge, and H Company attacked up the eastern spur, while G Company went to the right and attacked on the west. The companies were separated by a deep gulley. As they moved, down below on the road the tankmen saw a platoon of North Koreans trying to outflank H Company. The M-26 tanks began firing their 90mm guns and machine guns at a range of three hundred yards. That was the end of one organized North Korean platoon.

Soon H Company had gained the crest of Hill 207, and not far behind was G Company on the other side. The North Koreans fought with grenades, but the Marines took cover as the grenades came down, then rose and rushed forward, and the enemy fled.

Suddenly, from the reverse slope of Hill 207, hundreds of North Koreans began a panic-stricken flight to reach the Naktong and cross. The Marine planes overhead found scores of targets. They knocked out the command post of the North Korean 18th Regiment and made one strafing run after another along the banks of the rivers until observers swore that the Naktong River that day ran red with blood. The artillerymen behind the Marines zeroed in on the approaches to the river and destroyed whole concentrations of troops. By 10 o'clock that morning the Marine attack had ceased to be a fight. It was not even a rout of the enemy, it was a slaughter. At three-thirty in the afternoon the Marines were on the move to their third objective, Hill 311. An enemy platoon held that position stubbornly, in complete contrast to what was happening at the river, and it took all the rest of the afternoon and two companies of Marines to dislodge them. The position was finally declared secure the next morning.

So the Marines had done the job that General Walker had asked them to do: They had repelled the North Korean assault that was intended to isolate Taegu and make use of Pusan untenable to the U.N. forces. The Marines had suffered three hundred forty-five casualties, but unlike the Army casualty figures of the past in this war, the Marine figures showed a different sort of strength and determination: Only one marine was "missing," sixty-six were dead, and two hundred seventy-eight were wounded. The Marines stood and fought, and they took care of their own.

And if any among them had any squeamish feelings about slaughtering the North Korean soldiers as they tried to escape back across the river, then they only had to talk with the surgeon of the 3rd Battalion of the 5th Marines, Navy Lieutenant (j.g.) Robert J. Harvey. He had been assigned to examine an abandoned Army aid station that had been overrun by the enemy during the early stages of the enemy incursion into the Naktong Bulge. He found the bodies of thirty wounded men and medical personnel who had been murdered by the North Koreans.

For the first time during the Korean War the enemy had suffered a decisive defeat. The North Korean 4th Division had lost virtually all its equipment and weapons; the Marines recovered thirty-four enemy artillery pieces. As for casualties, prisoners indicated that the three rifle regiments of the 4th Division were reduced to about three hundred men each as they regrouped on the other side of the Naktong. The division reportedly was reduced to thirty-five hundred men.

The intelligence men also made some interesting discoveries when they looked through the booty left behind by the enemy. A large number of American weapons were found in the North Korean positions, many of them captured from Army troops during the early days of the fighting. And an SCR300 radio, of the sort used regularly by the Americans, was found at one command post, tuned in to the frequency of the 1st Battalion of the 5th Marines.

THE BATTLE ENDED, the Marines were released and assembled in a bivouac south of Masan in an area they promptly christened the Bean Patch. Officially the brigade was in Eighth Army reserve, but immediately the artillery was moved along to join General Kean's 25th Division, which was having trouble holding its sector of the Pusan Perimeter around Chindong-ni. And the brigade was put on warning that it might have to move at any moment to counterattack in the 25th Division sector. The brigade had won a battle, but there still was a war to be fought.

13.

Threat in the East

THE MAULING OF the North Korean 4th Division in the Battle of the Naktong Bulge had relieved the immediate threat to Pusan, but it had not solved the problem of defending the Pusan Perimeter. Five fresh North Korean divisions were sitting in a semi-circle around Taegu, only twenty miles from the town. Three divisions and some lesser units were off to the east. The disorganized North Korean 4th Division and the hard-hit North Korean 6th Division were licking their wounds in the Southwest. Only from that direction did it seem unlikely that a major attack might be launched.

The main North Korean buildup in this part of the peninsula was above Waegwan, northwest of Taegu. (See the map "The Front Moves South.") It was enough to make General Walker nervous, but it was not the only problem that bedeviled him as the Marines fought the victorious Battle of Obong-ni Ridge.

The threat along the eastern coast of Korea seemed to have been contained late in July with the series of setbacks dealt the North Koreans by the ROK 3rd and Capital divisions. But what apparently was not sufficiently appreciated was that much of the reason for that success had been the massive effort of the Allied naval forces and their effective bombardment of enemy shore positions, plus the air attacks by Allied planes. Early in August, urged in the strongest terms by the leaders in Pyongyang, the North Korean divisional commanders renewed the drive south along the eastern side of the peninsula. The warning was given late in July, but General Walker had more immediate threats on his hands, and the South Koreans seemed to be holding, so he made no effort to replace them in the line. If he had wanted to, it would have taken a Herculean effort, given his reserves. Instead, he counted on the optimistic reports of the American advisers with the Koreans, and he hoped.

The North Koreans were not blind to the thinking of the Americans. They perceived that the U.S. major effort was concentrated in the Southwest and along the Naktong. All the while, three North Korean divisions were in place to attack down the eastern side of the peninsula where two major roads led to Pusan. (See the map "The Front Moves South.") These were the North Korean 5th Division, supported by the 766th Independent Regiment, on the shore road; the North Korean 12th Division on the inner road to P'ohang-dong; and the North Korean 8th Division poised above Uisong on the road to Yongch'on, which lies astride a lateral road leading from Taegu to P'ohang-dong. In all cases, the forces these highly trained and highly motivated troops faced were ROK soldiers supported by American artillery, planes, and ships, but still ROK soldiers. Their morale had never recovered from the series of defeats suffered in the early days of the war.

Concurrent with the North Korean drive into the Naktong Bulge, the three divisions and independent regiment in the east geared up for a charge south to meet that August 15 deadline set by Kim Il-sung for the capture of Pusan. At the end of the first week of August they were in motion.

On the coast, the North Korean 5th Division had been fighting the seesaw battle for Yongdok against the ROK 3rd Division. The American and British warships that had proved so valuable in earlier encounters were otherwise occupied in the first week of August. The cruiser *Toledo* was available, but her skipper had gotten tired of firing eight-inch guns at troops and was itching to go off north to knock out bridges and bombard railroad tunnels.

On August 5 the North Koreans captured Yongdok again and pushed the ROK troops back southwest to Hill 181. The North Koreans now threatened Konggu-dong, the next town down the coastal road.

General Walker had the word, and he sent a message to Lieutenant Colonel Rollins Emmerich, the chief American military adviser to the ROK 3rd Division, that Yongdok *must* be retaken. The ROK commander set up a night attack. Just before dark the American fighters came in with rockets, napalm, and bombs to hit the enemy. After a fifteen-minute air attack, the *Toledo* fired her guns on selected targets, and the artillery joined in for another fifteen minutes. Then the ROK troops moved. They retook Hill 181, which they had lost during the day, and they held it. On August 7, with another air and artillery preparation, they drove north to the edge of Yongdok. But then the skipper of the *Toledo* perceived that the danger was over and went off north to bust bridges. That night the North Koreans harried the ROK troops with artillery barrages. Mortar shells fell into the ROK 3rd Division command post, and the brass panicked. They fled to a hillside dugout from which they had to be routed out by Colonel Emmerich after he found them with the use of flashlights. Apparently the South Korean commander, General Lee, was so frightened he was heedless of his responsibilities and indifferent to the confusion he was causing among the officers who were seeking orders. Next morning Colonel Emmerich advised that General Lee ought to be removed, and he was. He was replaced by Brigadier General Kim Suk-won. At about the time General Walker warned Colonel Emmerich that the five hundred twenty-foot bridge across the Osip-ch'on estuary at Konggu-dong must be held. For some time the bridge had been held by American engineer troops, but they were called away to other duty, and the South Koreans took over. They were told that they were not to blow that bridge except on specific orders from the American advisers. General Walker wanted the bridge intact in case a counteroffensive could be started.

On the night of August 8 the North Koreans threatened. They drove back the troops of the ROK 22nd Regiment, and many crossed the bridge. About three hundred fifty were still on the other side when the commander of the ROK regiment ordered the bridge blown without consulting anyone. So at about five-thirty on the morning of August 9 a violent explosion shook the countryside. Down went the Osip-ch'on bridge, and most of the three hundred and fifty troops on the north side were lost either to the enemy or to the waters of the deep estuary. Colonel Emmerich and General Walker were furious, and the new commander of the ROK 3rd Division was so angry that he threatened to court-martial and shoot the offending regimental commander. The officer was summarily removed from his command by the ROK Army chief.

This, however, could do very little to help a bad situation. The ROK 3rd Division moved down to Changsa-dong. The North Korean 5th Division outflanked the ROK troops and cut the road at Hunghae, only five miles from P'ohang-dong. The ROK 3rd Division was surrounded. The situation was so serious that General Walker flew down to Yonil Airfield for a conference with Brigadier General Francis W. Farrell, chief of the Korean Military Advisory Group, Colonel Emmerich, and General Partridge of the Fifth Air Force.

The question was: Could they hold? The military advisers thought they could. So General Walker told Colonel Emmerich to be sure that General Kim held around Changsa-dong. His job was to prevent enemy armor and artillery from coming down the road to P'ohang-dong. Then Walker flew back to Taegu to make one of his lightning shifts of American troops. He ordered the major part of the U.S. 9th Infantry Regiment to Yonil Airfield, south of P'ohang-dong and a major base for tactical American aircraft. He established Task Force Bradley because Brigadier General Joseph Bradley was to command this task force. Its mission was to protect the airfield.

The North Koreans were moving fast. That night of August 10 they ambushed part of the 9th Regiment on its way to the airfield. The troops had reached a point a few miles north of Kyongju on the lateral road from Taegu. General Bradley sent a relief force; this too was ambushed. Most of the troops of both units were rescued, but the speed and efficiency of the North Koreans was a matter to give the general pause. Troops of the North Korean 766th Independent Regiment had come around by mountain trail to the lateral road, and the ROK Army forces had known nothing about their movements. This again underlined the vast difference in the two armies: The North Korean Army's

Intelligence was superb; the South Korean Army's Intelligence was almost nonexistent. The problem of this particular roadblock was momentarily solved when Captain Darrigo (he who had first met the enemy at Kaesong), who was still a military adviser to the ROK forces, led an armored patrol of five tanks through the roadblock area. Simultaneously an air strike was called. The P-51s flushed the enemy troops out of the roadblock positions as the tanks came up and their guns and machine guns blasted the North Koreans again, then moved down to Yonil to help defend the airfield.

THE TROUBLES AROUND Yonil were just beginning. Meanwhile, in the center of the ROK line, the North Korean 8th Division moved toward Uisong. On August 9 the ROK 8th Division caught one battalion in a trap and nearly annihilated it. The North Koreans recovered and won back the lost ground, but they suffered losses that slowed them down for a few days. The South Korean success was largely due to a minefield planted along the road, and the efforts of P-51 fighter planes.

Then the North Korean 12th Division did just what General Walker had not expected: The division moved into the "impenetrable" mountains where there was no major road. General Walker had been quite right in his assessment that a modern division with artillery and heavy equipment could not manage that sort of terrain. What he did not know was that the division had virtually run out of artillery ammunition and sent most of its guns to the rear. With a few pack guns and machine guns it was no great trick for the soldiers to move onto the mountain trails. By August 9 they were just north of Kigye, on the P'ohang-dong road, and that day they defeated a ROK force just south of the town of Kigye.

General Walker hurriedly set up Task Force P'ohang, but it was unlike any other he had established. It consisted of three regiments, an antiguerrilla battalion, and a Marine battalion, all ROK, and a battery of the U.S. 18th Field Artillery. Of the ROK force, only one regiment had any battle experience. The rest were products of the reorganization of the ROK forces and consisted largely of pretty raw recruits. Task Force P'ohang was hardly even a second-class fighting force.

Whatever one might say about the North Koreans, at this point the soldiers of their 12th Division were fighting like demons. In order to make the trek through the mountains they had divested themselves of most of their equipment, but in spite of that, using automatic weapons and small arms, they drove the ROK Capital Division and Task Force P'ohang back to the south and east. The North Koreans suffered heavy casualties (almost a battalion), but they forged ahead. On the night of August 11 the future of Yonil Airfield looked so grim that the fighter planes were flown off to an air base farther south for protection. They returned the next morning, but no one knew how long they would stay. On August 11 the North Koreans entered P'ohang-dong and occupied the railroad station. It was the beginning of a battle in which first one side and then the other entered the city, only to be driven out a few hours later. P'ohang-dong became a no-man's-land for a few days.

Back in Tokyo, General Partridge was more than a little worried about the fate of his planes at Yonil Airfield. He had very little faith in the ability of the infantry to hold the position, because already the North Koreans had occupied the mountaintops and ridges all around the base. On August 13 he decided to withdraw the planes, and at noon that day he issued the orders without consulting General MacArthur. MacArthur let the Air Force know that he intended to hold the airfield; nevertheless, the P-51 squadrons were moved back from Yonil to Kyushu, which increased their flying time to target immeasurably and decreased their effectiveness in support of the troops just at the time they were needed most.

By August 14 the whole eastern side of the Pusan Perimeter was in danger. Most precarious at the moment was the position of the ROK 3rd Division, which had been cut off by the North Koreans and surrounded since August 10. The commander of the North Korean 5th Division knew the situation he had created and set out to exploit it with a series of punishing attacks. Day by day the perimeter of the ROK 3rd Division had to be contracted; the command post was moved to the coast at Toksong-ni. At the moment there was no way the division could be relieved by other land forces. The Air Force had deserted the scene. If the ROK 3rd Division was to be saved, the U.S. Navy would have to save it even if it meant a Dunkerque sort of operation, using rafts towed out to sea by American whaleboats.

On August 15, General Walker communicated this problem to the naval authorities in Japan, and they set the stage for an evacuation. The cruiser *Helena* came up to deliver fire support against the North Koreans surrounding Toksong-ni. The carriers *Valley Forge* and *Philippine Sea* sent their planes up in close support of the ROK forces. On the evening of August 16 four LSTs led by the destroyer *Wiltsie* moved into the beach. Jeeps and trucks were brought down to the shore to shine their lights on the evacuation operation. Outside, the support ships of Task Force 77 maintained a steady fire on North Korean troop positions to keep them quiet. At four-fifteen on the morning of August 17 the LSTs began moving out to sea. By eight o'clock they were all offshore, carrying fifty-eight hundred soldiers of the ROK Army, the American liaison group, twelve hundred civilian refugees, and one hundred vehicles. The ROK 3rd Division had lost most of its equipment, but the troops were saved to fight again. They were landed a few hours later at Kuryongp'o, and the next day the division was ordered into battle again.

While this was happening, other troops were fighting for the control of P'ohang-dong. On August 13 the North Koreans claimed to have "liberated" the city. The claim was premature, for the North Korean 1st Regiment troops who came in stayed only about three hours and then retreated under heavy bombardment from the U.S. Naval vessels offshore and carrier plane strikes. But it was certainly true that the North Koreans were all around the town. The North Korean 5th Division held the area to the north, the North Korean 12th Division held the high ground to the southwest, and it appeared that the fate of P'ohang-dong and Yonil was to be captured.

In their rush, however, the North Koreans had left the lines of communication on their sides open, and the ROK Capital Division and the ROK 8th Division now moved in the Angang-ni area, supported by American tanks and artillery. After two days of fighting, on August 17 the ROK troops pushed the North Koreans back above Angang-ni, and the Kyongju corridor to Pusan, which a few hours earlier had looked wide open, was suddenly closed off to the North Koreans. They had gambled on rushing down through the mountain passes and taking the ROK forces by surprise. To do so they had sacrificed their heavy weapons, knowing that the ROK forces had virtually none of their own. But they had not assessed the naval strength that the U.S. Navy now could employ along the shore and in the air. The American ships, planes, tanks, and artillery had changed the balance, and suddenly the North Koreans found themselves without ammunition, without supplies, with time running out, and

ever more ROK troops moving up on this front. On
the night of August 17 the North Korean 12th Division began to withdraw from the hills around
P'ohang-dong, harried by American artillery, naval
gunfire, and later by air strikes, all of which cut
deeply into the division as it moved up through
Kigye. On August 19 in the mountains north of
Kigye the division was reorganized as best as possible, amalgamating the troops of the 766th Independent Regiment, which had been cut to battalion
strength in the recent fighting. Two thousand
replacements were brought down from the North,
but the North Korean 12th Division even then
could mount only half strength. The demands
made by Pyongyang in the past two weeks had been
enormous, and the casualty rate showed it: Of one
battalion that went into action early in August with
more than six hundred men, only twenty survived
by the end of the last exhausted dash of the division
for Pusan on August 18. They had gambled on
driving straight through, although short of provi-
sions, ammunition, and food. They had lost. From
Pyongyang came a revised timetable: The Americans had to be driven out of Korea and Pusan captured by the end of the month.

14.

Taegu

AS THE DAYS went by and still the North Koreans had not been able to drive to Pusan, the authorities in Pyongyang began to realize that they might soon be in serious trouble. Whatever they might claim for propaganda purposes, they knew that the industrial power of the United States could produce an enormous amount of war material, given the time, and the American military establishment, having been caught napping, could be expected eventually to recover. Premier Kim Il-sung warned his generals that the longer they delayed in capturing Pusan, the more difficult it would become.

Still, the United States needed more time. Back in Japan General MacArthur was planning for an attack—an amphibious landing at Inchon, the port of Seoul, and a drive to the capital that would cut off the ten divisions of North Korean troops in the South from their supplies. But to make such a landing he had to have the troops and the supplies and the ships, and these were being untangled and assembled with agonizing slowness. It was an enormous job, given the virtual disassembly of the American military establishment that had taken place in the Truman administration. For example, MacArthur wanted a division of Marines. To provide it, the Marine Corps had to raid individual units, including the guard forces at American embassies abroad. It was hard going, but it was being done. The forces were gathering and moving toward Japan.

While this was happening, General Walker was trying to move his forces from a purely defensive role to a more active stance. He wanted them to make raids into the enemy positions, to attack, withdraw, and attack again to keep the North Koreans off balance. It was all part of his strategy of buying time with his limited forces.

The North Koreans were equally determined that they would have Pusan by the end of the month. They had tried the West and they had tried the East. Now they would try the center of the Pusan Perimeter at Taegu. Actually, the Taegu attack had begun at the same time as the other two—August 5—but it simply had bogged down, while the Naktong Bulge drive had failed, as had the Kyongju Corridor attack. But all three movements were part of the same whole, and the Taegu attack had to be dealt with by General Walker at the same time that he was shoring up the Naktong Bulge and the two eastern roads to Pusan.

Five North Korean divisions lay in the semicircle centered north of the city. The first to move was the North Korean 1st Division, which consisted of about five thousand troops at the time. The division crossed the Naktong far north of the Pusan Perimeter so was virtually unopposed until it came up against the ROK 6th Division. Then the fighting began, and the North Korean 1st Division was twelve days getting down to the Taegu area.

At the same time that the North Korean 1st Division was moving in the North, a little south of that unit the North Korean 13th Division began crossing the Naktong at Naktong-ni, in the defense area held by the ROK 1st Division. By August 7 the North Korean 13th Division had brought up some of its artillery, but then the ROK 1st Division attacked and forced the North Koreans to move up into the mountains. The ROK victory was only temporary; the commander of the North Korean 13th Division rallied his forces, attacked in strength, and by August 13 had reached a point only 15 miles from Taegu.

On August 6, the North Korean 15th Division was the next south on the perimeter. This division began crossing on August 6, and by August 8 it had tanks across (on an underwater bridge) and was advancing on Taegu. All this activity so far had been conducted against ROK sectors, and General

Walker had no great confidence that the ROK Army
would hold, so he prepared to shuffle American
troops around again in case of a North Korean
break through the ROK lines. But he also had the
North Korean 3rd and 10th divisions to worry about
in the Waegwan area. The 3rd Division, highly
experienced in the drive south from Seoul and now
rested, began crossing the river south of Waegwan
on August 9. The crossing was discovered by the
U.S. 5th Cavalry Regiment, and mortar, machine-
gun, and artillery fire was concentrated on it. The
casualties were serious for the North Koreans, but
most of the soldiers made it across and into the hills
on the east bank of the river.

On the morning of August 9, Major General
Hobart Gay, commander of the 1st Cavalry Division, ordered an attack to drive the enemy back
across the river. It was to be carried out by the 1st
Battalion of the 7th Cavalry Regiment, whose CO
was told that he faced a reinforced battalion of
North Korean shock troops armed with automatic
weapons and burp guns. The enemy had occupied
an eminence called Hill 268, just ten miles northwest of Taegu.

Lieutenant Colonel Peter D. Clainos, commander of the 1st Battalion, would also have the
assistance of five tanks and the 61st Field Artillery
Battalion. The tanks and troops moved up to the
base of the hill that morning. At noon the artillery
fired a barrage on the hill. It was hard to tell the
results, because unlike most Korean heights the hill

was covered with thick brush and trees. When the barrage was lifted the infantry started up the hill, but the day was hot and the low brush held the heat on the ground. American soldiers began dropping from heat exhaustion, and the attack lost its momentum and failed. The Americans dropped back to the base and dug in for the night. The next morning, the artillery resumed its attentions to the hill with more care and fervor. The results were far better; the Americans did not then know it, but the accuracy of the artillery bombardment had decimated the North Korean regiment that held the hill. But that was only one regiment of three in the North Korean 3rd Division. Other troops were moving around on their usual missions: cutting the roads and trying to encircle American units. Several officers and men from the divisional headquarters were wounded in an ambush on the Waegwan road that morning. In the afternoon General Gay had a narrow escape when he came up to the line and stopped to talk to officers of the 1st Battalion near Hill 268. An enemy mortar shell came in and killed or wounded everyone except the general and his aide. With such an example before him, the general personally ordered the five tanks to move up the road until they could take the reverse slope of Hill 268 under fire. They did. The enemy mortars were then caught between the U.S. artillery on the one side and the tanks on the other, and they retreated off the hill and across the valley. The 1st Battalion had no further trouble taking Hill 268. The retreating North Koreans were tracked by the U.S. artillery, which caught a large number as they formed up in a village to the west of the hill. The shells killed several hundred North Koreans. Documents found later indicated that about one thousand men of the North Korean 7th Regiment had crossed the river, and about seven hundred of them had been killed on or around Hill 268. The others retreated back across the river.

Nor did the other regiments of the North Korean 3rd Division fare a lot better. They also ran into American counterattack. As of August 12 the North Korean 3rd Division had been so hard hit that the chief of the Army corps relegated it to reserve until it could be rebuilt. So, as of that date, the two most effective North Korean divisions, the 3rd and the 4th, had been shattered in the drive on Pusan and withdrawn from action. However, the North Koreans still had fresh troops in their 10th Division.

The North Korean 10th Division's mission in this August all-out drive for Pusan was to cut the Taegu-Pusan road so that the Eighth Army troops could not escape, nor could supplies be brought up to them. Then, when the North Korean 3rd Division assaulted Taegu from the west and north, the North Korean 10th Division would come up from the south to complete the destruction of the enemy. On August 11 the North Korean 10th Division assembled at Koryong for the river crossing, which was to be made on the northeast road to Taegu. The road bridged the Naktong, but the bridge had been damaged seriously enough to prevent the passage of heavy equipment. Foot soldiers still could cross. General Walker had checked the bridge and decided to leave it that way as a trap. The American troops on the eastern side of the river had the bridge zeroed in for mortar and artillery fire. American troops of the 21st Infantry regiment occupied strategic positions on the hills and had set up fields of fire to focus on the crossing. But for the first crossing the North Koreans moved elsewhere, over shallow fords. It was midsummer, the year was very dry, and the Naktong River had dropped three feet below its usual depth. That meant men could wade the river at many places, carrying their rifles and ammunition overhead. A whole regiment came across that night, unopposed, and took Hill 409 and set up machine-gun positions. The Americans still had not learned to deal with North Korean night actions, that heritage from the Chinese Communists.

On the morning of August 12 the second regiment of the division crossed near the bridge shortly before dawn. Again, it managed to put about four hundred men across before the Americans knew what was happening. These North Koreans attacked the advance positions of the 7th Cavalry and overran them. But in proper light, the U.S. artillery and the American Air Force moved into action and with the help of the 2nd Battalion of the 7th Cavalry broke the attack and drove the North Koreans back toward the bridge. All was quiet then for two days on this front, but on the night of August 13 the North Koreans made another crossing and early in the morning penetrated a mile inside the American lines. Fighting broke out between this unit and the 2nd Battalion. General Gay ordered Colonel Clainos' 1st Battalion into action then, and they moved up the road by truck toward the area of the blown-up bridge. Here another crossing was in motion, the largest of all. It was supported by North Korean artillery and tanks firing from the west bank of the river. At last the opportunity the Americans had been waiting for had come. The 77th Field Artillery Battalion's howitzers fired nineteen hundred rounds of ammunition against the troops crossing and the enemy artillery supporting them. All along the line artillery and air strikes were extremely damaging to the enemy, and early in the afternoon the attack was broken and the disorganized battalions were moving as swiftly as they could back toward the river. In its most distinguished action thus far in the war, the artillery had broken the back of the attack. The North Korean 10th Division, fresh from the North, had been blooded—and bloodied. Some units had lost more than half their men, and altogether about a third of the division was lost to action until replacements came in.

This August drive gave everyone a bad fright. The North Koreans were attacking everywhere and were dangerously close to Taegu. General MacArthur believed the major concentration of enemy troops lay on the western side of the Naktong between Waegwan and Naktong-ni. He ordered a carpet bombing of the sort that had proved so effective in the Normandy battle of World War II. It was carried out on August 16 by nearly one hundred B-29s, which dropped one thousand tons of bombs. But the "troop concentration" supposed to exist in this area seven miles long and three miles wide had already been dissipated by moves of various divisions up and down the front to make the Naktong crossings, so the bombing basically accomplished nothing. It did not even knock out the enemy artillery. The best that anyone could say about it was that the artillery fire from the enemy in the area seemed to be less after the bombing. The greatest value for the Americans was to disperse another of the many myths about air power that had been generated in the battle of the Air Force for power in the post World War II service reorganization. That was the last experiment in carpet bombing along the Pusan Perimeter.

The serious threat to Taegu was generally perceived on August 16 as the North Korean 13th Division broke through the ROK lines in the North and descended toward Taegu, reaching the road that led down from Sangju to Taegu. Concurrently the North Korean 15th Division was moving down toward the P'ohang-dong-Taegu road, and when it reached that point it was to turn right and attack Taegu from the east. Also on August 16, the North Korean 13th Division received resupply of artillery and tanks from the North. At this point the North

Korean 13th Division was moving along the Sang-ju-Taegu road and reached Tabu-dong, just thir-teen miles northwest of Taegu. On August 18 North Korean artillery shelled Taegu, which was the immediate reason the Republic of Korea gov-ernment fled south to Pusan. The whole town of Taegu was in panic, and that included some four hundred thousand refugees whose presence had more than doubled the city population. The refugees then tried to flee south to Pusan and clogged the roads so badly that military traffic was nearly brought to a standstill. The ROK Army had to stop the evacuation. Even so, trickles of refugees began moving south on the back roads as Taegu was shelled two more times in the next two days.

Something had to be done to save Taegu, and General Walker ordered the U.S. 27th Infantry to do it. The ROK 1st Division was in contact with the enemy 13th Division but was steadily losing ground. The 27th Infantry was to conduct one of General Walker's "limited-objective attacks" to drive the North Koreans back to Sokchok, a little village four miles north of Tabu-dong. The infan-trymen came up by truck to the point where they could see the opposing Korean armies fighting in the hills above the road. The infantrymen dis-mounted then and began to move into action. The 1st Battalion moved up the left side of the road; the 2nd Battalion came up the right. The tanks came up the road, firing on the North Koreans on the hillside. The infantry swept the lower hillside on both sides of the road, and thus they moved rapidly for about three miles. Then they stopped because they learned that the ROK forces on both sides of the road had been stopped by the North Koreans and the American advance was doing nothing but putting a hole up the middle that the ROK Army was unable to fill. The regiment then took up a defensive position, with the tanks up front and the artillery at the rear. The ROK 1st Division was holding the high ground on both sides of the U.S. regiment. This stretch of the road was christened the Bowling Alley because of the terrain: high mountains on both sides of the narrow valley, with the road running straight almost north-south, and a stream meandering along the base of the hills beside it. The mountains were formidable: Yuhak-san on the west was twenty-seven hundred feet high, and Ka-san on the east was twenty-nine hundred feet high. Both these high points gave a fine view of the Taegu basin spread out to the south. The enemy was north, not far away, behind a row of hills at the fork of the road, where the main road turned off left to Sangju on the west, and where the lesser road forked to the right toward Kunwi.

Darkness and quiet descended on the long valley that night of August 18. But an hour later, the quiet of the night was disturbed by the sounds of tank tracks coming up the road. Two North Korean tanks followed by a self-propelled gun were making a reconnaissance in force. They were preceded by an artillery and mortar barrage from behind the hills at the fork, which fell on the American positions before the tanks and infantry arrived. But for once the North Koreans did not seem to have the right intelligence; they did not know what they were facing. The tanks came forward, and the bazooka-men of the 27th Infantry knocked out the second, and hit the first badly enough that the crew aban-doned it. The guns of the 8th Field Artillery de-stroyed the self-propelled gun. The artillery shot up a number of trucks and killed about one hundred infantrymen. Three more tanks came up the road but turned around and went back to the enemy lines without trying to attack. Thus began the Battle of the Bowling Alley.

That first attack of the night of August 18 was followed by another, much weaker one. Perhaps it was weaker because the Americans were stronger in several ways. They had artillery and mortars in position. They also had learned something about North Korean battle tactics in recent weeks, includ-ing the fact that like the Japanese in World War II, they were fond of using flares to signal the infantry. The Americans had some North Korean flares, and they used them to disinform the enemy troops; an attack was launched, and then a green flare above a certain spot in the line showed the North Koreans where they were to go, and they went—to find themselves up against American machine guns.

The next morning, August 19, the ROK troops on the right and the left tried to come up on both sides of the road. They made some gains, but they did not succeed in closing the gaps. General Walker perceived this North Korean move down the Sangju-Taegu road as the most important threat yet against Taegu, and ROK reinforcements were brought up, and so were American: The U.S. 23rd Infantry was brought in to protect the American artillery. During the day the Air Force made a number of close-support strafing attacks on North Korean positions, or what they thought were North Korean positions in the hills and along the road north of the 27th Infantry's defense line. For once they had plenty of time and the weapons to do the job. General Walker came up on one of his roving inspection tours of the front and announced his satisfaction. "Taegu is saved," he said that day. The North Koreans did not attack along the road that day, nor the next day, August 20, until late in the afternoon. Then, at about 5:00 P.M., the North Korean guns and mortars behind the northern hills began firing a barrage, and after darkness was complete it was not long before the sound of T-34 tanks was heard again. Five of them were coming, supported by a company of infantry. The North Korean 13th Division had its order: Attack, no matter the cost.

The attack came against well-entrenched defenders. American mortar and artillery fire stopped the tanks. The troops of the 27th Infantry held their fire until the infantry came to within one hundred fifty yards and then let go. The North Koreans suffered heavy casualties and retreated. The next morning the troops in the line reported seeing white flags, and an American patrol led by three tanks went up the road. About half a mile forward the patrol ran into evidence of the night's fighting: five disabled tanks (which were destroyed with grenades, two self-propelled guns, an antitank gun, and a 120mm mortar). The Americans were fired on several times, but by what obviously were small groups of soldiers in outposts. The Americans penetrated about a mile and a half, found more destroyed equipment, a number of enemy bodies, and another tank, and then came back. They did not discover any groups of North Koreans who wanted to surrender, but that was not unusual: The North Korean Army was modeled on the Soviet, with the political officers playing a major role. One of the jobs of the political officers was to prevent surrender, and those troops who had shown white flags had been brought under control by daylight. Throughout the conflict it was difficult for the North Koreans to give up; on one occasion an American infantryman was tackled by an enemy soldier who came charging across the field, into his position. The American thought he was about to be involved in hand-to-hand combat. But all that North Korean wanted to do was give up, and this staging of a one-man attack was the only way he knew to escape his political officer.

On the afternoon of August 21, the engineers laid mines along the road and streamed in front of the

American positions. That night the infantry had reason to thank them; as darkness fell, the North Koreans behind the hills began the longest and most powerful artillery barrage yet involved by either side. It lasted until nearly midnight, when the North Korean 13th Division launched its major attack against the Americans on the road and the South Koreans on both sides. The first indication of the nature of the attack came from 27th Regiment troops on high ground on the left side of the road. They reported hearing tanks, and the artillery behind fired star shells that lighted up the valley. There they came: The infantrymen counted about 20 armored vehicles coming down the road, with the shadows of enemy infantrymen around them. The vehicles were tanks and self-propelled guns, and they were firing as they came, but most of their shells were going off into the rear areas. The American mortars and artillery began firing on the column, but the infantry in the line and the U.S. Sherman tanks up front held their fire until the North Koreans got to the minefields. Then the machine guns and the American tanks spoke up. The Sherman tank gunners, the mortarmen, the artillery, the bazookamen, and the mines took their toll. So did automatic-weapons fire and rifle fire. The fighting lasted until dawn; then the North Koreans withdrew back along the corridor. In the light the Americans counted the wreckage of nine tanks, four self-propelled guns, and several armored personnel carriers and trucks. The enemy infantry casualties were enormous; prisoners taken late in the fight reported that their units had been cut to ribbons, and the Americans estimated enemy casualties at about thirteen hundred. General Walker had certainly not erred in assessing the threat; since the North Korean 13th Division had been unable to force the Taegu basin alone, now the North Korean high command had also sent in the 1st Division, and its troops showed up that night for the first time, attacking the ROK forces anew on the hills along the road. The North Korean 1st Regiment had forced its way around the fighting to a high point above the road to Taegu and had brought American vehicles and troops under fire.

In this action the growing resentments between American and ROK Army officers broke loose. Colonel Michaelis, upset by the North Korean 1st Regiment's incursion behind his lines, accused the ROK 1st Division of laying down on the job and not fighting. Major General Paik Sun-yup retorted that he would be pleased if his men had so easy a job as the Americans, sitting down in the valley with heavy artillery, mortars, bazookas, and tanks and waiting for the enemy to come up while his troops fought hand to hand with little more than rifles. The ROK 1st Division was fighting, he said, fighting as hard as it could.

For once an ROK officer was right: The 1st Division was fighting hard. But the Americans had been disappointed so many times that Colonel Michaelis's outburst was predictable and understandable.

If the ROK troops did not have heavy weapons, it was because they had lost so many of them in the retreat south and because, generally speaking, they had not shown any particular ability to use them. But in this war so far there was plenty of opportunity for finger-pointing about failures in fighting on the American side as well as on the South Korean. It all went back to the original problem: The United States had virtually disarmed itself and had neglected the arming of the South Koreans, even refused them arms, while the Soviets had moved apace with arming the North Koreans; so when the crunch came in the summer of 1950, Americans and South Koreans both were ill prepared to meet it. The problem as of August was to hang on until better days could come. Little by little, by such draconian measures as those advocated by Colonel Emmerich on the east coast, the fighting quality of the South Korean Army was being improved. So was the caliber of the Americans fighting in Korea. The deepening suspicion between American and South Korean fighting men was coming at the wrong time.

Colonel Michaelis' outburst, however, was caused by a real difficulty. The North Korean 1st Division had posed an important new threat. On the afternoon of August 22, troops and artillery of that division managed to get between the 27th Infantry and the 23rd Infantry and to make an artillery attack on the U.S. 8th Artillery that knocked out the fire direction center and threatened the whole line of communications of the 27th Infantry up front. But the threat had come a little late. That night General Walker sent the 1st Cavalry and the 23rd Infantry to clean up those hills overlooking the main route of supply. Also on the night of the 22nd, the North Koreans attacked again along the Bowling Alley and suffered the usual results. A colonel of North Korean artillery surrendered that day, piqued because he had been roasted by his divisional commander for failing to shell Tabu-dong and thus win the war. That surrender was significant as an indication of the state of morale at the top of the enemy field command: The constant demands on the divisions were wearing them down. The North Korean colonel gave information about the placement of his guns that enabled the Americans to conduct an air strike the next day on an orchard a few miles up the road and destroy about 20 guns that were supporting the North Korean attacks on the Bowling Alley. On August 23 the U.S. 23rd Infantry cleared the mountains, forcing the North Korean 1st Regiment back northward, but not before a number of small units had erupted on the sides of the road to assault the American rear, particularly the artillery. Several vicious fire fights developed, but by this time the Americans had learned to deal with such violent action without panic; the North Koreans did some damage, but they were driven off with heavy casualties and then moved north.

On the evening of August 24 the 13th Division

staged the nightly attack down the Bowling Alley just after midnight. Again it was tanks and infantry; again several tanks and self-propelled guns were destroyed and the North Korean assault was repulsed. It was the last. The next day the North Korean 13th Division's commander ordered a withdrawal; the troops mined the roads and moved back northwest, giving up the assault on Taegu. Instead of quarreling, the officers of the ROK 1st Division and the American 27th Infantry Regiment should have been congratulating each other, for another enemy thrust had been thrown back, and from all indications it had been the most powerful launched by any enemy division since the Marines had crippled the North Korean 3rd Division at Obong-ni. The North Korean 13th Division had been hard hit, and the North Korean 1st Division's 1st Regiment had lost all its artillery. The ROK Army and the American Army had for once covered themselves with glory.

15.

Summer Offensive

THE FAILURE OF the North Korean Army to break
through the U.S. and ROK lines in the first three
weeks of August created an atmosphere of despera-
tion in the North Korean camps. Every general
knew that his career was on the line, and several had
already been sacrificed because of their "failures."
The fact was that the easy victories of the early days
had made the politicians in Pyongyang overconfi-
dent, but how was a general in the field going to
convince a politician back in the capital of the facts?
General Chai Ung-jun, commander of the field
armies, had already been replaced by General Kim
Chaik, and several divisional commanders had also
fallen by the wayside. In mid-July from Pyongyang
came reinforcements and a renewal of the demand
that the Americans and ROK forces be driven into
the sea and Pusan captured by September 1.

It was not going to be that easy. General Kim's

two Army corps numbered about one hundred thousand men, 10 percent greater than the original invasion command. The general also had been sent an infusion of new T-34 tanks from the USSR. But a third of his troops—the replacements—were young recruits who had barely finished basic training. For example, the North Korean 6th Division, which had been so badly battered by the U.S. Marines, was rebuilding at Chinju; that division was sent forty-five hundred young conscripts from the Seoul area. In a civil war this was a dangerous move at best, since there was no way the conscripting authorities could guarantee the loyalty of men drafted by conquest. Even if every man was a convert to the North Korean cause, these were hardly effective soldiers; they arrived without weapons, were issued grenades, and were told to pick up rifles on their first battlefield. These untried men comprised half the rebuilt North Korean 6th Division's force of eighty-five hundred men. Another three thousand men, conscripts rounded up locally in Southwest Korea, were on their way to the 6th Division. These conscripts were totally untrained and suitable only as a labor force. For the North Koreans there was no more ready reserve—it had been gobbled up in the fighting of the past two months. A more serious problem from General Kim's point of view was that as of mid-August the North Koreans had lost their greatest advantage: preponderant strength in weapons and trained soldiers. A new division had come southwest to back up the

North Korean 6th Division; it was the North Korean 7th Division. Its formation indicated the difficulties of Pyongyang these days. As nucleus the Army had drawn on the North Korean 7th Border Constabulary Brigade, organized as a border patrol for the 38th parallel. To this unit had been added four thousand recruits, half of them from South Korea, half from North Korea, and a newly organized artillery regiment, to bring divisional strength up to about ten thousand men. But there was very little military experience in the ranks of the North Korean 7th Division.

Despite all the sea and air power turned against North Korea in the past two months, the North Korean Army continued to resupply the forces in the South with remarkable skill. There is no question that the bombardment of ports and factories and the B-29 air attacks on strategic targets were taking their toll in the North. But ammunition and food and replacements of guns and tanks were still coming south. Much of the movement was done at night to avoid the fighters and bombers that ranged up from Japan. Little by little the supply line was weakening, but by the end of August that deterioration was not very apparent.

The ROK Army was up to ninety-one thousand men, and the weeding-out process was ridding the command of most of its inferior officers. To take a share of the ground war, Great Britain had sent a fifteen-hundred-man brigade drawn largely from the Middlesex Regiment. To be sure, this was not a large force, but it was a very brave one. The major British participation continued to be naval; without it, in the beginning, affairs would have gone much more badly than they had. The coming of the British land force was already attracting promises from other U.N. countries to participate in some way in the struggle, thus showing their opposition to "aggression."

THE MAJOR MILITARY effort was being carried by the Americans. In two months they had rebuilt several military units, and the unfit officers had quietly been removed to other parts. General Walker now had five ROK divisions and four American Army divisions that were being built up to full strength. In the 24th Division, the 34th Infantry Regiment was virtually disbanded, and all its personnel were assigned to the 19th and 21st regiments to make up the three battalions that had existed prior to the military cutback. There wasn't much unit loyalty to worry about; of the two thousand men who had originally come to Korea with the 34th in June, only one hundred eighty-four were left; all the rest were dead, wounded, or missing in action. The 5th Regimental combat team was now assigned to the 24th Division as the 3rd Regiment, bringing that division up to unit strength, although it still needed some four thousand replacements to bring the various units up to strength. The same sort of strengthening was done to the other divisions, so at the end of August General Walker's four divisions were all up to strength on paper.

The 63rd Field Artillery also was reduced to a paper unit, with the personnel and equipment transferred to three other field artillery battalions to provide the three batteries that brought these units up to the standards of the days before the cutback. Walker had the British brigade and the 1st Marine Brigade. The Eighth Army had more than five hundred medium tanks; about thirty light tanks suitable for scouting; and one battalion of the heavy Patton tanks, which were superior to the T-34. (A tank battalion numbered about seventy tanks.) Supplies were coming in to Pusan at the rate of one thousand tons a day. The Air Force was burgeoning in Japan and South Korea; the naval force had grown to one hundred fifty ships. And, with the Battles of Sach'on, Obong-ni Ridge, P'ohang-dong, and the Bowling Alley, the North Korean drive had lost its zing. The odds, in other words, seemed to have changed to favor the defenders. If General Kim was to achieve Pyongyang's objective, it would have to be done with a lightning thrust that would drive to Pusan, destroy the port facilities and then take the town, cut off the Americans from resupply, and then cut up the units piecemeal. Even now, with a two-to-one preponderance of U.N. troops over North Korean it might be done, because in some ways the numbers were misleading. The

ROK Army left much to be desired. In mid-July the ROK had opened a replacement training center at Taegu. But the products of this center were young men given ten days' training and then sent to fight. Another such center was opened a month later, and a center to train second lieutenants was opened at about the same time. Five new divisions were organized, one to come into existence each month beginning in September, each division to number ten thousand men.

The Americans started another program, too. They began the incorporation of ROK recruits into the four American divisions in Korea. This was done because of sheer necessity—there simply were not enough American recruits to fill the companies. Thus was invented "the buddy system," in which each ROK soldier in an American unit was supposed to pair with an American soldier and learn the ropes from him. Sometimes it worked that way, sometimes it did not. Most of the trained American fighting men found the ROK soldiers a nuisance. Officers sent them into battle with a silent prayer, knowing the unit ran a constant danger that the ROK soldiers would panic under fire and perhaps cause consternation among the Americans as well. It was obvious that these drastic measures were prompted by emergency, but their effect on the fighting capacity of the American units is not so obvious. Certainly after the Koreans joined, the units lost their homogeneity. By the middle of September the experiment was seen to be a failure, but as the month began it was in full flower and it affected most of the Army units.

Such organizational changes were occurring in August in the midst of the fighting in all sectors. The North Koreans had failed to break through in the East, the North, and the West, but the fighting continued in all these areas on an outpost basis.

In the Haman area, the front of the U.S. 24th Regiment was more or less static after the Marines left for the Taegu front. But since this southwestern front represented the greatest penetration of the North Koreans toward Pusan, the North Korean 6th Division had to keep the pressure on just in case there was some development that would let them slip through. So the 24th Infantry Regiment fought a long battle in August for possession of several heights, especially Battle Mountain at Sobuk-san. From this attenuated struggle came the names Bloody Knob, Old Baldy, the Rocky Crags, Engineer Road, and Green Peak. These bits of territory changed hands so often during August that no one could remember exactly how many times. Finally they were taken and held by the Americans as the month came to an end. Once again the Americans had held, although not without extreme difficulty. The long struggle of the 24th Infantry produced a number of acts of heroism and superior leadership, but against great odds. For example, on August 22 the enemy held Battle Mountain, and the Americans were attacking. Lieutenant Gerald N. Alex-

ander was in command of a platoon of L Company,
which was exhibiting a reluctance to move into
enemy fire. Alexander pushed and cajoled and got
the men forward two hundred yards in one hour.
Then when they reached their objective, North
Korean troops lobbed a handful of grenades at
them, wounding half a dozen men. The platoon
panicked and ran down the hill. The lieutenant
chased them and caught them after one hundred
yards. He ordered them back up the hill. The men
refused to go. Alexander and a BAR man went up
alone and found no enemy on the crest of the mountain. Reluctantly the platoon came back up then.

But it was not just Alexander's platoon; the
whole company was equally rotten. Other junior
officers also reported it was almost impossible to
move their men under fire. Lieutenant Colonel
John W. Corley, commander of the 3rd Battalion of
the 24th Infantry, complained disgustedly about
the quality of the U.S. troops under his command:

"Companies of my battalion dwindle to platoon
size when engaged with the enemy. My chain of
command stops at company level. If this unit is to
continue to fight as a battalion it is recommended
that the Table of Organization of officers be
doubled. One officer must lead and another must
drive. . . ."

These were the troops from the soft life of the
Japanese occupation, and they never had been
trained for or gotten used to combat. General
Walker distrusted the 25th Division in general and

the 24th Regiment in particular. The continuing problem of the American divisions brought in early in the campaign was combat discipline. Time after time American soldiers fled the field of battle under fire. So did the ROK troops who were serving alongside the 24th Infantry.

By August, of course, thousands of replacements had been brought in from Japan and from America. The 25th Division's strength had risen to fifteen thousand men. The 24th Division, still not sent back to Japan for rebuilding, as had previously been decided, was up to fourteen thousand troops. The U.S. forces were suffering from more than just the softness of "occupationitis"; the whole military establishment had gone soft.

Thus, while the numbers had changed and the U.N. forces could be shown on paper to overpower the North Koreans, the fighting qualities of the armies were not nearly so disparate. The Americans had learned. It still was a horse race for Pusan— only, however, if the North Korean Army massed its force rather than trying to attack on three fronts at once.

There was no indication that the North Koreans had such an intention. Indeed, although the North Korean 6th Division was rebuilt and resupplied in August, in addition to what ought to have been patrolling action around Battle Mountain it was also involved in fighting against the U.S. 35th Infantry in the last days of the summer assault. The North Koreans mounted an attack on August 17, on the northern road from Chinju to Masan. They tried for six days, lost many men, and gave up. The Americans were the veteran soldiers now, and the North Koreans were the ones making many of the mistakes. Even so, it is obvious how enormous was the pressure exerted from Pyongyang on Lieutenant General Kim Ung, commander of the I Corps, to make him send a reorganizing division into action. What would happen next would depend largely on the skill of the North Korean high command and on General Walker's ability to bring up troops against them, troops who would fight.

All this was recognized in Washington. The Department of the Army sent Major General Leven C. Allen to Korea to become General Walker's chief of staff. Hitherto, Walker had been depending on two very competent colonels to handle staff affairs, but there was no comparison between the clout General Allen had in dealing with other commands and that which the colonels had.

AS SEPTEMBER BEGAN, General Walker's intention was still to hold the perimeter until General MacArthur could stage his amphibious landing at Inchon, scheduled for September 15. Walker was worried about that operation, particularly since MacArthur seemed about to take the Eighth Army's ace in the hole—the 1st Marine Brigade—away from him. The 5th Marine Brigade was part of the 1st Marine Division, along with the 1st Marine Brigade and the 7th Marine Brigade. The division was scheduled for

the Inchon operation, and that meant the 1st
Marine Brigade would have to return to Tokyo to
get ready. General Walker asked that the brigade be
transferred to his command, but the 1st Marine
Division commander, Major General Oliver P.
Smith emphatically declined. But it was not that
simple; the decision would depend on the tactical
situation in Korea. As of the last few days of August
the situation seemed reasonably secure, so General
MacArthur ordered the brigade restored to the 1st
Marine Division as of September 4. The Marines
got busy packing and sent most of their heavy
equipment down to Pusan for shipment to Japan.
But then North Korean General Kim took a hand in
affairs. Late in August he launched the greatest
offensive yet laid on by the North Korean Army.

If all that North Korean strength had been
assembled at one point—the southwestern end of
the Pusan Perimeter, for example—General Kim
might have broken through. But his plan was to
continue the assault on all fronts; it seems to have
been made without reference to the changed situation of the American and ROK armies. Now that
the perimeter had stabilized in a relatively small
area, General Kim's Intelligence network was not
so effective. The Americans had adopted a new
policy of shooting on sight any Korean civilians
who moved around at night. This change, plus a
new security consciousness by the ROK forces, cut
down effective espionage remarkably.

From his headquarters in Kumch'on, northwest

of Taegu, General Kim directed the great assault that was to be launched simultaneously against all sectors. Thirteen infantry divisions, one armored division, two armored brigades, and miscellaneous independent units all would move on the same day with the same objective: Pusan. The North Korean 6th and 7th divisions would break through the U.S. 25th Division around Masan. The North Korean 9th, 2nd, 4th, and 10th divisions would break through to Miryang against the U.S. 2nd Division and then follow the Taegu-Pusan rail line down to Pusan. The North Korean 3rd, 1st, and 13th divisions would move through the U.S. 1st Cavalry Division to Taegu and then turn south. The North Korean 8th and 15th divisions would move through the ROK 6th and 8th divisions on the lateral road east of Taegu to P'ohang-dong, then follow down to Miryang and Pusan. The North Korean 12th and 5th divisions would defeat the ROK Capital and 3rd divisions at P'ohang-dong and then take Yonil Airfield and march south to Pusan. The battle order called for the assault to begin in the Southwest half an hour before midnight on August 31, but the North Korean 12th Division changed the timing, perhaps by accident. At four o'clock on the morning of August 27 a North Korean force overran a company of the ROK 17th Regiment north of Kigye. (See the map "The North Korean Attacks in the East.") What may have been a testing action then turned into something far more formidable: The whole regiment collapsed and gave way; the

18th Regiment, which was on the right flank, also gave way; Kigye was captured with ease by the North Koreans, and the whole Capital Division fell back onto the south side of Kigye Valley. Thus what began as a local action turned in a matter of hours into a major defeat of the Capital Division and a new threat to the Pusan Perimeter. General Walker arrived at his Eighth Army headquarters that morning to find a large hole in his perimeter. He dispatched Major General John B. Coulter, his deputy commander, to the scene to discover what was happening and to stop it. To give Coulter the clout he needed he appointed the general to command a new task force: Task Force Jackson would include the ROK I Corps, the U.S. 21st Infantry, and parts of other U.S. units. Coulter hurried down to Kyongju, headquarters of the ROK I Corps, and found that the I Corps was falling apart. He began trying to raise the morale of these Korean officers while he planned a counterattack to regain the ground lost. The 27th Infantry was already on its way and arrived at Kyongju that afternoon. Coulter sent the 3rd Battalion up behind the ROK Capital Division.

Soon enough he recognized the extent of his problem: When advised of an attack planned for the next day, the I Corps commander refused to comply. His troops were too tired, he said, and they faced too many enemy and had taken too many casualties. As if this were not enough, when the North Korean 5th Division above P'ohang-dong learned of the easy victory of the North Korean 12th

Division, the 5th Division too began to move south against the ROK 3rd Division. Colonel Emmerich asked the 3rd Division to attack, and its commander also refused. He said he was going to retreat out of P'ohang-dong, and the only way Emmerich persuaded him to stay was to announce that come what may the American advisory group would stay there. The 3rd Division commander, Major General Kim Suk-won, very nearly broke down at this announcement but agreed to stay on temporarily to save face. The truth was that the South Korean Army was at the end of its rope, and the I Corps was at that moment worth virtually nothing to the defense line. That night of August 27 the ROK 17th Regiment again abandoned its position in hills north of the command post, and Coulter had to cancel the morning attack. The ROK forces regained the hills that day but lost them again that night of August 28. Elements of the 21st Infantry had to be sent to help the ROK 3rd Division, which was being overrun by the North Korean 5th Division around P'ohang-dong. Seeing what was happening on the eastern front, General Walker tried to shore up the South Koreans by telling them that help was on the way. The enemy was making a "last gasp" fight, he said. He called on the South Koreans to stand up and fight at this vital moment. The call did not rouse much of a response. On August 29 the U.S. 21st Infantry had to take over the defensive positions of the ROK 3rd Division around P'ohang-dong.

Generals Walker and Coulter had a difficult nut to crack. The South Koreans were extremely sensitive to criticism of their military skills, but the fact was that they were not very effective at this point. Had it not been for U.S. air power, the North Korean 12th Division might have kept right on moving, but as it was, the carriers sent help. With U.S. tanks and artillery the ROK Capital Division managed to hold itself together, but it was not pushing the North Koreans back. On the east coast the American naval vessels were bombarding enemy troop concentrations to help the defense. By September 1 the threat was serious: The North Korean 5th Division had taken many hill positions around P'ohang-dong, and the North Korean 12th Division had slipped about three thousand troops between the ROK 17th and 18th regiments above Kyongju. General Walker was correct in his assumption that the North Korean troops were tired and undersupplied, but they were fighting vigorously, and the South Koreans were not. The burden fell on the Americans. On September 2 Colonel Stephens's 21st Infantry attacked alone northwest of P'ohang-dong where the North Koreans had captured an eminence called Hill 99. From their positions above the hill they fed a constant stream of reinforcements onto the hill, and several attacks by the ROK 3rd Division had failed. With tanks and mortars, the Americans tried to take the hill—and failed. They lost two tanks, one to a North Korean minefield and the other to an operational accident.

And the next morning the situation grew worse because the North Korean 12th Division began moving in its part of the general attack. The ROK 17th and 18th regiments were thrown back farther in the hills south of Kigye. On the night of September 2 the North Koreans reached the lateral road from Taegu to P'ohang-dong at a point three miles east of An'gang-ni. The ROK Capital Division had virtually collapsed. Thus General Coulter had to pull his 21st Infantry back from the P'ohang-dong area to save Kyongju. Lieutenant Colonel Perez's 3rd Battalion took up a horseshoe-shaped position around An'gang-ni and on high ground overlooking the lateral road. Coulter also sent the untried ROK 7th Division toward the enemy area of penetration. The division marched up to the enemy, and the enemy threw them back in a rout. With that disaster the ROK Capital Division withdrew from An'gang-ni. The whole I Corps front collapsed.

The speed with which the ROK I Corps fell apart left no time for General Coulter to shore up the defenses of An-gang-ni. The American troops and tanks in the town could not fire on the North Koreans coming up because they were all mixed up with fleeing South Korean units. The American forces withdrew, and Colonel Perez moved his battalion back to friendly ground. He had to fight his way through an enemy roadblock. When he reached the regiment north of Kongju he discovered that G Company was missing. He struggled back to rescue the company, then fought through the roadblock again to get to the regiment. In the course of these engagements Perez lost three tanks to enemy fire.

That night of September 3, the North Koreans moved all around An-gang-ni and toward Kyong-ju. They cut the road at several spots. General Coulter expected an attack on Kyongju momentarily, particularly since there was a ten-mile gap northwest of the city between the ROK Capital Division and the ROK 8th Division. He moved the 21st Infantry into the gap.

The South Koreans were suffering from a bad case of panic. On September 3 Colonel Emmerich reported that the ROK 3rd Division commander was preparing to withdraw from P'ohang-dong. Coulter went to the ROK I Corps and secured an order to the 3rd Division commander to hold. But from that time on, Coulter checked every hour or so to be sure the South Koreans had not done what they had done before—simply pulled out, telling no one. The next crisis came on September 4, when the ROK I Corps commander announced that he was pulling out of Kyongju. Coulter told him he was not, and he put four tanks around the I Corps headquarters to make sure. He also sent American Korean Military Advisory Group (KMAG) officers out to stop ROK Army units from fleeing the town. They did stop the ROK troops, at gunpoint. That night he prepared for the coming attack, but it did not materialize. The North Korean 12th Division had different orders: They were to take Yonil Airfield, so they turned southeast that night.

Meanwhile, at P'ohang-dong, the situation was growing more critical as the ROK 3rd Division proved virtually useless. On September 5, Colonel Emmerich hurried down to Yonil Airfield, where the U.S. 9th Infantry was located, and borrowed a platoon of tanks. He got back to P'ohang-dong and moved the tanks into position for defense of the city just as the ROK 22nd Regiment collapsed in the face of the enemy. Five North Korean self-propelled guns were moved toward the city; the accompanying troops were confident that they would be unopposed. Then they ran into Colonel Emmerich's tanks. The tanks knocked out the first gun, and the other four were withdrawn. Emmerich then called up air strikes, and the U.S. planes destroyed the other four guns. The enemy was stymied, held off by one determined officer—not even a commander but an "adviser"—using all the resources at his call. But one officer, no matter how determined, could not win here. In midafternoon came an order to evacuate everything from Yonil Airfield. That night the ROK 3rd Division commander gave up entirely and "took sick." On September 6 the North Koreans captured P'ohang-dong.

The total failure of the ROK I Corps created a serious problem for General Walker. The I Corps commander and the commander of the 3rd Division both were removed, but that did not solve the problem. General Walker had to move more U.S. troops east to counter the gains made by the North Koreans. He moved up General Church's 24th Division to Kyongju and removed General Coulter from command. Perhaps Coulter's handling of the South Koreans had not been the most tactful, but he was not fooling himself about the quality of the ROK effort. He returned at this point to Taegu to staff work. Church moved out of Kyongju to open ground south that he felt was more defensible, and he prepared to resist the assault he expected from the North Korean 15th Division. He also found himself facing the North Korean 5th Division around P'ohang-dong, and this is where the major action developed. The North Koreans had cut off the lateral road to P'ohang-dong and all the other roads in the North and were driving on Yonil Airfield. General Church formed a new task force under Brigadier General Garrison H. Davidson and sent it on a circuitous road south to Yonil. The long column included two battalions of the U.S. 19th Infantry, one battalion of the 9th Infantry, several artillery units, a tank company, a combat engineer company, and several automatic-weapons units. It arrived south of Yonil Airfield in midevening of September 10. General Davidson had gone on ahead by plane, and he and Colonel Emmerich conferred on the best method of operations. In this area the ROK troops had again been giving ground steadily, but Emmerich said they could fight if they wanted to, and Davidson assigned the new commander of the ROK 3rd Division to retake Hill 131, a commanding piece of ground between two ROK regiments, which they had lost a few hours earlier.

Prompted by Colonel Emmerich, they did attack and did regain the hill, and the next day the 19th Infantry passed through that position and launched an attack of its own, which brought them over the hills and down into the valley near Yongdok. The threat to Yonil Airfield had been ended. Another fire had been extinguished, and on September 13 the task force returned to Kyongju. The fighting in that area had been fierce; the 19th Infantry's 3rd Battalion had been engaged for a week in a struggle for a high piece of ground north of Kyongju called Hill 300 along with another regiment of the ROK 3rd Division. They took the hill finally but at great cost; the U.S. battalion lost nine second lieutenants in the struggle. But the North Koreans had lost very heavily; on the afternoon that the hill fell, the Americans counted two hundred fifty-seven dead enemy troops on the hill itself, plus the abandoned weapons and equipment of a battalion. The combination of ROK effort (which could be enormous when the troops were adequately led) plus the American infantry, the tanks, the artillery, the air strikes, and the sea strikes by ships offshore had decimated two North Korean divisions—the 12th and the 5th—and had brought the great September offensive to a shuddering halt on the east coast. The ROK forces pursued the enemy now, and the Americans were brought back to Taegu and Kyongju. Crisis had followed crisis, but somehow General Walker had kept the South Korean I Corps in the war and pushed it into victory. The North Koreans also had suffered seriously from a program begun much earlier that only now was beginning to show results: the American strategic attack on enemy lines of supply. For two months the Navy and the Air Force had been blasting North Korean lines of communication along the mountains of the east coast. There was no way that the North Koreans could bring adequate supplies down the coastline in the face of this effort, and in the end the strategic smashing of the supply route told the story. The North Koreans ran out of everything, and they had to quit the offensive in this sector.

16.

Down the Center

COINCIDENT TO THE attack of the North Korean forces in the East came the drive from the North down the center of the Pusan Perimeter in the sector defended by the ROK 6th and 8th divisions. The North Korean 8th Division headed for Hayang, and the North Korean 15th Division moved toward Yongch'on.

The ROK forces defended spottily. The ROK 6th Division, supported by U.S. artillery and air strikes, did a fine job of holding the North Korean Eighth Division. In ten days that North Korean division was reduced to military rubble in a succession of battles around Hwajong-dong, fourteen miles short of its first objective. As of September 1, the division's strength was about sixty-five hundred men. By September 10 it was about a third of that. On September 1 the division had twenty-one brand-new T-34 tanks. On September 10 it had one. But

the story of the North Korean 15th Division as
opposed to the ROK 8th Division was entirely different. As of September 1 the ROK 8th Division
comprised ninety-one hundred men; the North
Korean 15th Division numbered seven thousand.
Yet in four days the North Korean 15th Division
penetrated to the lateral road near Yongch'on. A
T-34 tank got behind the South Korean forces and
they panicked; they had still not learned the discipline of antitank warfare. Even the KMAG advisers
could not hold them in place; units and parts of
units scattered all across the countryside. On September 6 North Korean troops entered the town of
Yongch'on and then took up positions on the high
ground around it. From that point they cut the
roads and attacked south. So easy had been the early
advance that the divisional commander got fool-
hardy and sent his artillery out ahead of the infantry
along the southern road. The artillery came to grief
when two new ROK regiments—the 5th and 11th—
appeared to back up the demoralized ROK 8th Division. That fortuitous arrival of reinforcements was
no miracle but a result of action taken by General
Walker. During this whole period of crisis, Walker
kept in almost hourly touch with the situation of
his troops on half a dozen fronts. At the moment
that he learned the ROK 8th Division was cracking,
he dispatched those other two regiments to save the
day. Meanwhile, the KMAG officers had been
scouring the area, rounding up the elements of the
ROK 8th Division, and bringing them back to-

gether again. The new regiments sparked an attack
that smashed the North Korean 15th Division.
They captured two tanks, a dozen field guns, a
self-propelled gun, and many small arms. That
booty was an indication of the condition of the
North Korean 15th Division. It had lost its chief of
artillery, its chief of staff, and many of its line
officers. The ROK 8th Division's morale was
improved by the KMAG officers, who told the soldiers what a great job they had done. Believing that,
they went on to do better. Again sparked by the 5th
Regiment, they chased the North Korean survivors
north and captured more guns, more equipment,
and more supplies. So on the eastern shore of the
Korean peninsula and along the right center of the
line, the U.N. forces had held during the September
offensive. But these were not the major points of
North Korean attack; Taegu and the Southwest
were the focal areas. Above Taegu, twenty-one
thousand North Korean troops of three divisions
massed for the drive against that key city. The
North Korean 3rd Division would attack in the
Waegwan sector, the North Korean 1st Division
would move down the mountain ridges to the east
of the Sangju-Taegu road, and the North Korean
13th Division would go down the ridges on the west
side of the road. This area was held by the U.S. 1st
Cavalry Division, which on September 1 numbered
nearly fifteen thousand officers and men. General
Gay also had the British 27th Brigade, which held
the southwestern corner of his line.

The action in the Taegu sector began on September 1 with an American attack ordered by General Walker. The purpose was to draw enemy strength away from the southwestern corner of the Pusan Perimeter, where the North Korean I Corps was making the major attack of the campaign. General Gay planned an attack on Hill 518, five miles northeast of Waegwan. It was launched on September 2 after an air strike and an artillery barrage. But the hill was a big, sprawling mass of ridges, and at least twelve hundred North Koreans were entrenched around it, with machine guns, 82mm and 120mm mortars, and plenty of ammunition. The attack was slipshod, the three battalions of the 7th Cavalry Regiment had just been brought together and had not operated in concert before, and the result was an attack that lost all the force of regimental power and deteriorated into a series of platoon advances. It failed. During the next two days the Americans attacked several times without success. (See the map "The N.K. Attacks on Taegu.")

On the right, the 5th Cavalry staged another attack against Hill 303 and captured the height but had extreme difficulty holding it. The reason was that the North Korean 3rd Division was itself attacking, feeding more men and more ammunition into the hills and moving troops around behind the American positions.

During the next two nights the North Koreans infiltrated troops around the units of the 7th

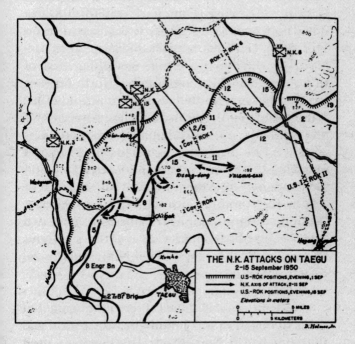

THE N.K. ATTACKS ON TAEGU
2–15 September 1950

xxxxxxxxxx U.S.-ROK POSITIONS, EVENING, 1 SEP
━━━━━━━━► N.K. AXIS OF ATTACK, 2–11 SEP
━━━━━━━━ U.S.-ROK POSITIONS, EVENING, 15 SEP

Elevations in meters

0 — — — — 5 MILES
0 — — — — 5 KILOMETERS

D. Holmes, Jr.

Cavalry until it was hard to tell where lines of communication lay. The Americans were in touch then only with units to the west. To the east, the North Koreans had moved between them and Taegu. On September 5 Generals Walker and Gay agreed that it was time to withdraw the whole 1st Cavalry to defensive positions. It was not as easy as it had been to move up. The new position included Hill 465 and Hill 380, both of which were alive with North Koreans. So to retreat to new defensive positions, the regiment would have to attack and drive the North Koreans off those positions. The 2nd Battalion of the 7th Cavalry was chosen to take Hill 465, while the other two battalions marched west toward the no-man's-land of Waegwan. The job of attacking was given to Captain Herman L. West's G Company, while the rest of the battalion was to take up high ground south of the hill. Action was to begin on receipt of a prearranged code word that would come by telephone. Captain West briefed his officers and NCOs. They were to move out immediately when the word came, and they were to take all the supplies they could carry.

The weather was dreadful, pouring rain that made the valleys a sea of mud. Because of it the 2nd Battalion had to abandon a tank that was stuck fast in the mud. Captain West's eighty men of G Company stood in the rain, waiting for the order to move out. It was three o'clock on the morning of September 6 when the word came. The column began to move with the 1st Platoon at the point and the 3rd as rear guard. Every man knew that enemy soldiers were all around him. The column approached Hill 465, and the men began to slip on the muddy slope, weighed down by their heavy loads of ammunition. But by eight o'clock that morning they neared the crest of the hill. Captain West stopped the column for a rest while he and the lieutenant of the 1st Platoon went forward to take a look. They had gone only a few yards when they ran across three North Korean soldiers who were apparently just getting ready to eat breakfast. West waved the leading platoon on, and they shot down all three. With the 1st Platoon ready to open fire on the crest, Captain West ordered Lieutenant Larry Ogden's 2nd Platoon to circle around to the south and then take the crest of the hill under the covering fire of the others. Ogden's platoon began to move, and it reached a point fifty yards from the crest when the North Koreans opened fire. He stopped the platoon and waited while the 1st Platoon covered, then brought the men back out of the line of fire. He then took four men to reconnoiter for an unguarded approach to the top. He could not find such an approach, for there were plenty of North Korean soldiers up there, and they had every avenue blocked. Each time a man raised his head, he drew fire.

At two o'clock in the afternoon the sky cleared and the sun was soon steaming up everything in sight. The heat created a new obstacle. Captain West called up battalion headquarters by radio, asking for help to dislodge the enemy. But all the other companies were having the same sort of problem: too many North Koreans. The impasse forced battalion headquarters to come up with a new plan of attack. G Company was to wait until nightfall, then move around to the east side of the hill. The 1st and 2nd battalions would form a new line on the east and support G Company as it drove for the crest.

So G Company waited out the heat of the day on the hillside, and after dark it began the march. The hillside was rocky, and the rocks slid out from under the men's feet. The radio stopped working. Seven men had been killed during the day's fighting, and their bodies were left on the hillside for the moment, but five men had been wounded, and they had to be carried along. It was very slow going, not helped a bit by a volley of artillery shells—"friendly fire"—that fell very near. Everybody dropped. More fire came in. One shell landed between Captain West and First Sergeant William Williams, who was about twenty-five yards away. The shell knocked a loose rock against Captain West's back and knocked him down. At first he thought he was paralyzed, but soon feeling came back. He got up and signaled everyone to go on. Sergeant First Class Alvin W. Link was lying next to Sergeant Williams. Link shouted at Williams to come along, but Williams did not move, and when Link rolled him over, he was dead.

Captain West cautioned the men against firing

their weapons. "The North Koreans are all around," he said. "By moving without firing they probably will mistake us for their own troops."

So the column moved along through the darkness, silently. They reached the bottom of the hill and then turned southeast along a trail. At an intersection of the trail the weapons platoon, which was leading the company, turned right instead of left and got lost. The trail they took led them back toward Hill 465. It was some time before Captain West learned that his company was split up. He stopped then and set up a perimeter defense for the night.

Lieutenant Harold R. Anderegg, commander of the weapons platoon, stopped when he realized they were separated from the main body, but then he went on following this trail, which seemed to lead to high ground. They stopped frequently to rest because they were carrying three of the wounded plus a light machine gun and a mortar. They also had a ROK soldier with them. They passed a number of North Koreans in the dark, and once Master Sergeant Jimmy Reed came up against one North Korean face to face. Sergeant Reed was a small man, the North Korean took a long look at him, then both stepped to the right and went their own ways. At about three o'clock the lieutenant realized that five men were missing. Sergeant Link and Corporal Harold Tobodo crept back and found them; they had fallen asleep during a rest break. The column moved on until it reached a small, flat area where Lieutenant Anderegg stopped for another rest. The men pulled their ponchos overhead, lit cigarettes, and soon were asleep.

An hour later light began to show in the east. The lieutenant sent Sergeant Reed to the top of the hill they were on with most of the platoon while he stayed behind with the wounded and the men carrying them. Reed and Link went off as scouts, and the rest of the men followed in a skirmish line. The sergeants reached the top of the hill just as the sun peeped over. About three quarters of a mile off to the east they could see Hill 465. At the top of the hill Reed found foxholes that had been dug by the North Koreans. He put two men in each of four of the holes. Sergeant Link put Corporal Tobodo and PFC John Harper in another hole with the light machine gun and told them to get it ready to fire. They did so. Then Tobodo got up to take a look at another hole about five yards away; it was covered with pine boughs. He stopped and looked hard at the hole. Something inside moved. Then he yelled at Sergeant Link:

"I think there's somebody in this hole."

Link came up.

"Hey," he shouted, "GIs in this hole?"

The only answer was a cough.

Sergeant Link left Tobodo to cover the hole and moved up to Sergeant Reed's hole.

"I think there are gooks over there."

Just then Lieutenant Anderegg came up.

"Well, clean them off," the lieutenant said.

Just then they all heard firing at the bottom of the hill. Anderegg sent four men down to investigate. Reed formed the rest up into a skirmish line. Corporal Tobodo stood with his rifle in hand, guarding the hole with the brush on top. Harper, holding the light machine gun, stood nearby. Reed walked up to the hole and pulled off the brush. There sat four North Koreans, rifles between their legs. Reed gestured to them.

"Come on out."

No one moved.

Reed reached down and grabbed one man by the shirt collar and pulled him out of the hole. His insignia indicated he was an officer. He twisted loose and ran. Harper shot him down with the machine gun. Others of the platoon shot the other three men in the hole, and fired into another hole that was covered with brush, and when they moved the brush they found two more bodies.

While this was going on, Sergeant Link was looking around the hill. He spotted five other North Koreans in holes from 25 to 75 yards away.

"More gooks!" he shouted, and he pointed them out to Sergeant Reed. The sergeant took five men and set out in a skirmish line. They killed two more North Koreans, and then came to another hole where a very young soldier was sitting, paralyzed. Reed grabbed the North Korean's rifle and wrested it away. He motioned for the North Korean to come out. He looked too young to kill (Reed was an ancient nineteen years old, himself). The North

Korean would not budge from the hole. Reed shouted for someone to send up their ROK soldier. He came to the edge of the hole and began talking to the North Korean boy. Finally the North Korean came out of the hole and surrendered.

Continuing across the top of the hill, Reed's men killed seven more North Koreans and took two more prisoners. Were these the raw recruits, most of them with virtually no training, who had been sent into action in this desperate all-out assault on Taegu of the North Korean 13th and 1st divisions? Not at all. From papers found on the bodies, they discovered that this was a regimental command post, and the man who had twisted away and run to his death was the regimental commander. Two others were his staff officers.

Lieutenant Anderegg then went down the hill to find out what was going on. He ran into Captain West and the remainder of the company. The firing that Anderegg had heard had come about when Captain West's men were surprised by three soldiers who approached West's defense perimeter just after daybreak. These men had been wearing U.S. uniforms, so the Americans let them in, but then someone challenged, and the three men turned and ran. G Company opened fire and killed them. Then firing began from other weapons all around them, and Captain West realized his sixty men were surrounded. Up on the hill he heard firing and assumed that came from Lieutenant Anderegg's men. So he started the company up the hill, and they ran into the four men Anderegg had sent down to look for them. At eight o'clock that morning the company was assembled and moved off to its objective, half a mile to the east. There the battalion was astounded to see them, since they had been out of touch for twenty hours and surrounded by North Koreans all that while.

The 2nd Battalion fought all the next day but never did reach the top of Hill 465 and finally was ordered to stop trying and to assemble on the eastern edge of the hill. Then the battalion withdrew, covered from Hill 303 by the 2nd Battalion of the 5th Cavalry. Both regiments continued to withdraw under heavy enemy fire until they reached points astride the Seoul-Taegu highway. Only near the end did they learn from captured documents that they had begun their "limited offensive" in the teeth of the North Korean 3rd Division's attempt to move south toward Taegu and that Hill 518 was a central gathering point for a number of large units.

For the next four days the 1st Cavalry Division fought a fierce battle against the reinforced North Koreans, who were determined to take Taegu this time. They pushed toward Waegwan, and they pushed east. They reached several points less than ten miles from Taegu. The struggle seesawed on the hills: One moment the Americans held Hill 174, a few hours later it was in North Korean hands, then the Americans won it back. That hill changed hands seven times during the struggle.

The North Korean 1st and 13th divisions attacked at this same time down the Bowling Alley, which was held by the 8th Cavalry. The problem was that the 8th Cavalry's reserve was badly depleted. The North Koreans struck first along the Sangju-Taegu road at Hill 448 two miles north of Tabu-dong. They surrounded the 2nd Battalion, but that unit managed to fight its way back to the lines of the 3rd Battalion, which had put up a roadblock just north of Tabu-dong. Nevertheless, the North Koreans captured Tabu-dong on September 3, and another position, called Hill 902 by the Americans, and the fortress of Kasan by the South Koreans. This rocky crag was important in 1950 as it had been in history, because it gave observation and artillery direction in the valley that led down to Taegu. General Gay was fearfully short of reserves and had to employ a company of the 8th Engineer Combat Battalion as infantry to try to retake the hill. What he did not know is that the hill was held by a whole battalion of the North Korean 1st Division. D Company got stuck and dispersed on the hill, and E Company went up to help. The North Koreans pinned them down along a wall of the old "walled city." The plight and the behavior of PFC Melvin L. Brown, a BAR man, shows how the fighting went. Brown was dug in on a point of the wall where it was only about six feet high. The North Koreans kept trying to come over the wall and PFC Brown kept shooting them down. He exhausted his BAR ammunition and then his grenades, and he was wounded. Binding up the wound, he refused to leave his position even when he ran completely out of firepower. Each time a North Korean got up on the wall, Brown hit him on the head with his entrenching tool. Finally the company withdrew, but not PFC Brown. He was killed at his post (and posthumously awarded the Congressional Medal of Honor). Eventually all the engineers had to be brought back due to the force of the North Korean attack, and it was found that D Company had suffered 50 percent casualties. One officer was wounded, carried down the mountain, and left in a Korean house until a jeep could pick him up. But the North Koreans got there first, tied up the officer, built a fire under him, gouged out his eyes, and pulled off one of his thumbs before he died. Another officer was tied up, doused with gasoline, and then set afire. After that there was no sense talking to the men of the 8th Combat Engineer Battalion about taking prisoners of war or preventing atrocities. General MacArthur had already warned Kim Il-sung and the other political leaders of North Korea that they would be held responsible as war criminals for atrocities. The North Korean leaders had issued instructions that prisoners of war were to be taken and treated humanely, but the atrocities continued, and as the war went on, they often were met by equal treatment from the Americans and other forces whose men recalled the tortures and the murders.

As the 8th Combat Engineers withdrew they learned that a battalion of North Koreans was inside the walled city, and three more battalions were coming up to support it. There was no way that a company or two was going to take that position.

From that point the North Korean 1st and 13th divisions started their move against Taegu. General Gay ordered tanks up to the area to break up the attack. They put a crimp in it, but at about that time (September 9) the U.N. forces began to suffer from an ammunition shortage, and this gave the enemy an unexpected advantage. The 1st Cavalry was now concentrated north of Taegu, with the ROK 1st Division on its right. The ROK troops did very well. The North Koreans sent wave after wave of raw recruits up to attack (prodded by fire from burp guns in their rear), and the ROK riflemen and machine gunners massacred them.

On September 11 the fighting reached a climax. The U.S. 1st Cavalry Division was concentrated in the hills and astride the Tabu-dong road just six miles north of Taegu, and in the Kumho River Valley between the North Koreans and Taegu Airfield. The Americans were taking heavy casualties: C Company of the 7th Cavalry Regiment was down to fifty men.

The climax began when the 3rd Battalion of the U.S. 8th Cavalry attacked Hill 570 and failed to take it. The North Koreans that day assaulted and seized Hill 314, which was dangerously close to Taegu. Here was a case in which an ROK unit saved the day. The unit was the ROK 5th Training Battalion, which assaulted Hill 314 twice, and although thrown back, held the reverse slope until the 3rd Battalion of the 8th Cavalry could come up. Together these units prevented further North Korean advances. On September 12 the 3rd Battalion of the U.S. 7th Cavalry came up, too. That day General Walker ordered an attack all along the line. The key to the whole position was Hill 314, where the North Koreans had moved almost a battalion, and which they intended to use as the jump-off point for the final assault on Taegu. Lieutenant Colonel James H. Lynch's 3rd Battalion of the 7th Cavalry was at this point down to five hundred fifty men. They had come from the United States only two weeks earlier and had been in action for only nine days. The survivors had learned a great deal in that short period. This time they massed the riflemen on the ridgeline to secure maximum firepower. Unfortunately there could be no artillery support because of the ammunition shortage, but they did get an air strike before they set off from the point of departure on the bottom of the hill.

As the battalion started its attack the enemy responded with mortar fire. The men moved upward and out of the mortaring, against only sporadic small-arms and machine-gun fire. But after they had gone a quarter of a mile, they reached the point at which the North Koreans had registered their mortars and set up their machine-gun fields of fire. They ran into such intensive defense that they were forced to drop and seek cover. On their left they could see the North Koreans preparing to counter-attack. They called for an air strike, but no planes were then available. They called for artillery and mortar fire from the 3rd Battalion of the 8th Cavalry, which was behind them, and this they got. It made it possible for Colonel Lynch's battalion to repel the counterattack, and when it was nearly over the air strike appeared to plaster the top of the hill with napalm and strafing.

During this fighting the battalion suffered a sizable number of casualties, particularly among the officers. I Company commander Lieutenant Joseph Fields lost a quarter of his men very quickly. He reorganized the company under fire. Lieutenant Marvin Haynes led a small group of men to drive off a dangerous counterattack on L Company. Fields was killed. Haynes was wounded. But in contrast to previous actions of many American Army units, Colonel Lynch's men showed a high degree of battle discipline and initiative. Master Sergeant Roy E. McCullom, the weapons platoon leader of I Company, took over the company and led the riflemen until he had been wounded four times.

After the air strike, the battalion moved again upward toward the top of Hill 314. They gained the crest; the North Koreans launched a hand-to-hand counterattack and drove them down. They attacked again. Mortar and machine-gun fire held them off. They called for another air strike, and after it had come, Captain Robert Walker of L Company led men of both companies to the top, scratching up a sixty-degree slope for the last few yards. At the top they drove off the North Koreans and took over their positions. Captain Walker reorganized the men into one fighting unit; there were eighty of them left, half from L Company and half from I Company, which had lost every one of its officers. But the enemy soldiers on the hill had numbered seven hundred, and of those, two hundred lay dead on the slopes. Many of the others had been captured. As the Americans looked over the field they saw that most of the enemy dead wore American uniforms and had American weapons. They found more evidence of North Korean Army atrocities, more Americans murdered after capture.

The capture of Hill 314 relieved the enemy pressure north of Taegu. For the next six days Colonel Lynch's battalion held the hill. In its shadow the 2nd Battalion of the 8th Cavalry attacked and drove the North Koreans back from Hill 570 nearby. The ROK 1st Division advanced to the walled city on the night of September 14 and fought a hard battle there against about four thousand enemy troops on that night and the next day. The enemy was beginning to withdraw. The attack of the North Korean II Corps was blunted.

17.

The Greatest Threat

THE ATTACKS BY divisions of the North Korean II Corps were wearing and dangerous, but the greatest threat to the U.N. line came in its most vulnerable area, in the southwestern portion of the Pusan Perimeter, where the North Koreans were only thirty miles from Pusan.

Although the weather was extreme—the monsoon season seemed to be making up for its tardiness by extra-heavy rains—aerial reconnaissance in the last days of August indicated a North Korean buildup of major proportions along the southern part of the Pusan Perimeter, opposite the U.S. 2nd and 25th divisions. The pilots had learned to look for underwater bridges across the Naktong, and they found three of them. These were all bombed, but the engineers knew that the North Koreans could reconstruct them overnight. All this activity, the movement of thousands of troops into the area, new tanks and new artillery indicated a coming attack, and General Walker expected it as of August 28. He got an attack, as noted before, but not this one. General Kim was waiting until September 1. On the night of August 31 the North Korean I Corps moved. All the way along the line the North Korean troops began to cross the river on underwater bridges. The North Korean 6th Division moved toward Haman, north of the highway to Masan. Its objectives were Haman, Masan, and Chinhae. In three days the troops were supposed to to be on the outskirts of Pusan. The North Korean 7th Division marched toward Naktong, then wait for the 6th Division to come up on the right and the North Korean 9th Division to come up on the left. All three would then drive the last few miles into Pusan. That meant more than twenty-eight thousand North Korean troops in this assault in the South, aimed at the positions held by the U.S. 2nd Infantry Division (seventeen thousand men) and the U.S. 25th Division (fifteen thousand men).

The numbers would indicate that the Americans had an advantage, but the numbers did not show the caliber of the troops. The North Koreans, even with all their raw replacements, were led by junior officers and men who wanted to fight. Too often the opposite attitude was true of the Americans they faced.

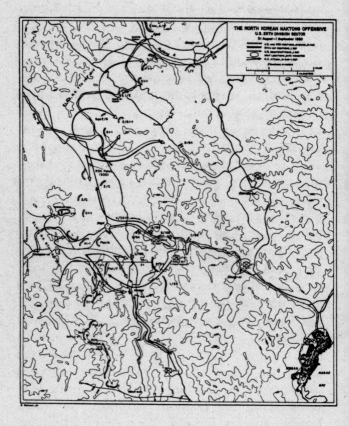

Just before midnight on August 31 the North Koreans hit the 24th Infantry Regiment's F Company on the Changam-ni-Haman road with spectacular success. (See the map "The North Korean Naktong Offensive, U.S. 25th Division Sector.") The North Korean high command had warned its divisions to fight at night, not in the daylight, when the Americans could bring the force of their artillery and air strikes to bear. And this first attack certainly bore out the wisdom of that advice. F Company broke under the pressure, and so did G Company behind it. The North Koreans captured an American 75mm recoilless rifle in the first flash of the action and then turned it successfully against American tanks, knocking out two of them in a few minutes. The North Korean overran a section of 81mm mortars and captured most of them. These were important matters, because the North Koreans were short of weapons, so every American rifle, every machine gun, every piece of artillery meant a great deal in the fighting. Four hours after the attacks began, the commander of one G Company platoon discovered he had only fifteen men with him, eight of his own and seven ROK soldiers. All others had fled, including the BAR man who was supposed to be guarding an opening in the wire surrounding the platoon position. The North Koreans attacked through that opening with burp guns and grenades and overran the position.

Colonel Champney's 24th Infantry certainly had not improved much nor learned combat discipline.

When enemy fire hit E Company farther up the hillside, the 3rd Platoon decided to go elsewhere. Lieutenant Charles Ellis, the company commander, discovered them just as they were moving. He ordered them back into position, and to emphasize his order, he fired a shot between the feet of the platoon leader and warned him that if he had to shoot again the platoon leader would never have to worry again about retreating. Lieutenant Ellis then went off to his right flank and found that platoon also deserting. Ellis steadied the men and went back to the center. But he could not be everywhere, and before the night was over nearly every man of E Company had deserted under fire and run down the hill. A number of them ran through the minefield the U.S. engineers had planted and were killed. As morning came, Ellis and eleven men held the line. Four of the men tried to run for it, and all were killed. Ellis and the others stayed on that hill fighting off enemy attacks. But seven brave men in one small sector were not going to affect the outcome much.

The behavior of E Company was not unique. Most of the men of the whole 2nd Battalion of the 24th Infantry deserted under fire that night. It was a useless battalion. By dawn its desertion had imperiled the regimental command post and opened the city of Haman to attack. Colonel Champney moved the command post from Haman to a point two miles to the northeast. The battle was not yet eight hours old, the Americans had suffered a serious setback, and the desertion of one battalion had created all sorts of trouble. A North Korean unit came down on C Battery of the 159th Field Artillery, whose men thought they were well behind the line. Fortunately two tanks were there, and they helped the artillerymen fight until the howitzers could be moved out and back through Haman to safety. They got out just in time; by dawn Haman was occupied by a battalion of North Koreans.

Colonel Champney sent his 1st Battalion to counterattack and restore the positions lost. Lieutenant Colonel Paul F. Roberts got ready for the move, and he organized about forty men from the remains of the 2nd Battalion to go with him. But as he moved the men up and they made contact with the enemy, they too fled to high ground east of Haman. The way was clear for the North Koreans, and two regiments moved swiftly through the Haman gap.

The same sort of problem was developing in the North, where the 35th Infantry's G Company was stationed on the riverline. Shortly after 11:00 P.M. on August 31 North Korean artillery began firing on the American positions along the riverline. Under the protection of that barrage a reinforced regiment of North Koreans crossed the Nam River on an underwater bridge and attacked. The regimental commander, Colonel Fisher, had assigned the ROK the task of defending low ground between his 1st and 2nd battalions at the crossing site, which was an old ferry post. But the ROK troops scattered with the first enemy fire, and the position was deserted. The Americans had expected some warning before the enemy came. The first they knew, North Koreans were swarming around their flanks in great force, with tanks, self-propelled guns, anti-tank guns, and machine guns. They tried to outflank the 2nd Battalion and to move toward Komam-ni. Luckily the 35th Regiment was not like the 24th. The engineers had prepared well: They had a minefield on the crest of the hill called Sibidang-san, and the North Koreans ran right over it, with disastrous results to several companies. But they just kept on coming. The Americans maintained discipline, fired, and kept firing even though ammunition grew short. They were reduced to stripping machine-gun belts for rifle ammunition before a platoon from the base of the hill came up with resupply.

Following their leaders' instructions, the North Koreans ended their attack just at dawn. The field of battle showed that it had failed; they had abandoned machine guns, mortars, and rifles, the commander of the North Korean 13th Regiment lay dead on the field. An American relief force led by tanks cleared the road to Sibidang-san just after dawn. The tanks still were there when the North Koreans tried another attack. That was the end of it for the moment; the 35th Infantry held all its positions but that of G Company, which had been outflanked after the ROK troops fled. The enemy,

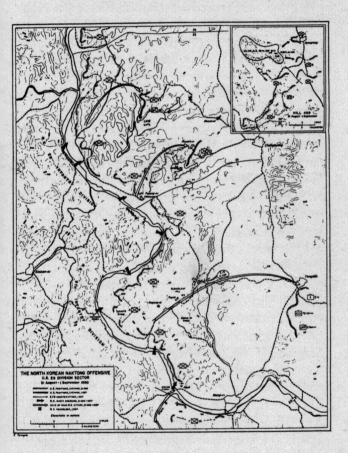

THE NORTH KOREAN NAKTONG OFFENSIVE
U.S. 2d DIVISION SECTOR
31 August - 1 September 1950

however, had pierced the line and moved through and was on both sides.

Farther north, around the junction of the Nam and Naktong rivers, the 2nd Division's 9th Infantry faced an attack that night of August 31. This came from the North Korean 9th Division, and it began just above the confluence of the rivers. The part of the perimeter assigned to the regiment was 11 miles long, so there was no hope of holding all the ground. The Americans took positions on the high ground along the river. The 1st Battalion's A Company held a long finger parallel to the Naktong at the Kihang ferry site, and here the enemy planned one of its assaults near the village of Agok. (See the map "The North Korean Naktong Offensive, U.S. 2nd Division Sector.") Two U.S. tanks, two anti-aircraft trucks that mounted 40mm and .50-caliber weapons, and two squads of riflemen held a roadblock not far from the ferry site. Sergeant Ernest R. Kouma was commanding one of the tanks on the west side of Agok about forty yards from the ferry. Close to him was the second tank, commanded by Sergeant First Class Oscar V. Berry. After nightfall on August 31, it was dark and so foggy Kouma could not see across the river. He heard dogs barking. Then mortar shells began coming in on the American positions. The North Korean assault across the river had begun. Half an hour before midnight the fog lifted and Sergeant Kouma could see an enemy pontoon bridge, two-thirds completed, directly in front of his position. He ordered the tank gunner to begin firing on the bridge with the 90mm gun, and he opened up with the .50-caliber machine gun. Soon the other tank and the anti-aircraft trucks joined the firing, and in a few moments the bridge collapsed and the pontoons broke loose and floated downstream. The Americans sank most of them with machine-gun fire. But other North Koreans had crossed the river farther down, and they turned up toward A Company. The company moved up to positions higher on the hill and informed the tankers that they were doing so. Just then seven men came running up to the tanks. They were Koreans in U.S. uniform, wearing the 2nd Division Indian head shoulder patch (which the ROK troops assigned to the division wore). They came up to Kouma's tank, and one of them told him in excellent English that the North Koreans had broken through and overrun A Company. Kouma was up top, checking over his .50-caliber machine gun. Suddenly the man gave a signal and all seven Koreans began throwing grenades at the tank. At the same time the tank came under fire from machine guns on a hill close by. The tankers began firing at them, and so did the anti-aircraft trucks. They also began throwing grenades at the Koreans. Then the tank came under fire from the rear. These strange Koreans knew the password and got into the anti-aircraft truck that had a .50-caliber weapon and killed all the crew save one. The second truck, a half-track, escaped, and the tanks were left to fight it out with the Koreans.

They repelled several attacks. After about an hour Sergeant Berry's tank engine began heating up, and he told Kouma he was going to withdraw. Kouma elected to stay on and fight there. A mile back, Berry's tank caught fire and he and the crew abandoned it. Sergeant Kouma stayed on at Agok through the night, and he was wounded twice. After dawn, Kouma headed back to friendly lines, firing on enemy positions as he went along the road.

Who were those Koreans who attacked the tanks? Were they North Korean soldiers? They may have been, but the evidence seems to point the other way—toward their being part of the ROK group assigned to the regiment. The shoulder patches, the familiarity with the regimental units, the knowledge of the armored force password all indicate this. It seems unlikely that North Koreans could have picked up the uniforms on the battlefield, and there was little time for them to capture ROK troops and force them to reveal the password. It seems apparent that once again the Americans were the victims of treachery.

Meanwhile, the North Korean 9th Division infantry had attacked across the river north of Agok and overrun the positions of C Company in a hurry. The men of C Company fought for a very short while and then tried to escape the enemy, who were around them on three sides. They escaped all the way to the area of the 25th Division south of the Naktong.

In conformity to General Walker's demand for limited-objective attacks, Colonel John G. Hill of the 9th Infantry had planned Operation Manchu for the night of August 31. His battalion-size task force was going to cross the Naktong River by assault boat at the Paekchin ferry, which served the road to Yongsan, and advance to a point where Intelligence indicated the enemy had a command post and communications center. The troops would destroy the post, capture prisoners, and return across the river in the darkness. The trouble was that their mission was interrupted by enemy troops who crossed the river and caught the heavy-weapons platoon by surprise as they were setting up their mortars in support of the American crossing. They also surprised the two infantry companies at the base of a hill overlooking the river. Most of Task Force Manchu was wiped out, and Colonel Hill narrowly escaped entrapment.

The American communications were not very good. The attack should have warned the troops of the 9th Infantry up and down the line, but it did not. The North Korean 9th Division's infantry crossed into the hills under an artillery barrage. By midnight they were ready to attack the American positions and soon overran them. By dawn the North Koreans had made mincemeat of the 9th Infantry and held those important, familiar landmarks, Obong-ni Ridge and Cloverleaf Hill. Three North Korean infantry regiments of the North Korean 9th Division crossed the river that night.

North of the U.S. 9th Infantry positions were those of the rest of the 2nd Division, the 38th Infantry and the 23rd Infantry regiments, both new to this terrain. Their task was principally to keep the enemy out of the town of Ch'angnyong on the Yongsan road. The enemy attacked the 23rd Infantry first and overwhelmed several companies, then drove through, splitting the 2nd Division. The 2nd Battalion of the 23rd Infantry held before Ch'angnyong, but the enemy 9th Division had penetrated to the road to Yongsan, and the North Korean 2nd Division was trying to take Ch'angnyong from the west. The North Korean 10th Division was crossing also to take part in the battle. The U.S. 2nd Division was in bad shape and threatened to become disorganized. The North Koreans had driven a wedge six miles wide and eight miles deep inside the division and had overrun several companies on the Pusan Perimeter firing line.

On the morning of September 1, General Walker appeared at the 2nd Division front in his special jeep built with support bars so that he could stand in the rear as the jeep sped along. General Walker saw that the threat in the middle of the 2nd Division was the greatest yet made by the North Koreans in this September offensive. If they could break through, roll up Taegu, and turn south, they could destroy the whole Eighth Army position. The general gave orders to the 2nd Division to conduct a "stand or die" defense of the Ch'angnyong-Yongsan road position to prevent the enemy from coming through. Then the general called on the Air Force and the Navy to work over the Naktong River line in that area as they had never done before. And finally the general called for the Marines.

18.

Back to Obong-ni

AS OF NOON, September 1, the North Koreans had made huge strides in their attack along the southwestern axis of the Pusan Perimeter, leaving isolated American units scattered on the hills behind them. The northernmost group of the North Korean 2nd Division was driving up around Lake U'P'o, a shallow body of water about five miles northwest of Ch'angnyong. (See the map "The North Korean Naktong Offensive, U.S. 2nd Division Sector.") The second major breakthrough came north of Lake Samor-ho, threatening Ponch'o-ri. The third line of attack, across the Paekchin ferry, was driving against Yongsan. And all along the line of attack, the North Koreans had been up to their old game of infiltrating well behind the American lines and setting up traps and roadblocks.

With all the other activity of September 1 it was

not easy to isolate the main enemy attack, but by noon General Walker had done so: It was once again the Naktong Bulge, and the North Koreans hoped to break through the Taegu-Pusan road and roll down that road to victory.

During the day Major General Lawrence B. Keiser, commander of the 2nd Division, had been assessing his situation and advising the Eighth Army of developments. He was in touch with General Craig of the 1st Marine Brigade, who now knew that, at least for the moment, he was not going to Pusan and to Japan to prepare for the Inchon landing. There was other work to be done. As of midday, September 1, however, General Walker still was not quite sure where he was going to put the Marines. General Craig moved his command post up to Miryang. That night he had his orders from General Walker: Move the Marines to positions south of Yongsan. That put them behind the 2nd Division's 9th Infantry Regiment. That night the Marines prepared to move out, and at six-thirty on the morning of September 2 the 2nd Battalion of the 5th Marines was in position, covering the Yongsan road.

That morning General Craig visited General Keiser and prepared to move the Marines through the 2nd Division lines. He spent much of the rest of the day reconnoitering by helicopter. At two-thirty in the afternoon he met General Keiser again at the 2nd Division command post. The 2nd Division staff was badly rattled. They had reason to be: The military situation of the 2nd Division was deteriorating steadily. The North Korean 1st and 2nd regiments of the 9th Division had advanced to the doors of Yongsan after penetrating the 2nd Division's line. They had with them three artillery battalions and two tank battalions. Behind them came the North Korean 4th Division. To be sure, that division had suffered greatly and was understrength, but it had troops and weapons. As of the morning of September 1, U.S. 2nd Division troops available to General Keiser to defend Yongsan consisted only of a handful of units of the 9th Infantry: the division reconnaissance company, the 72nd Tank Battalion, the 2nd Engineer Combat Battalion, and what remained of E Company, which had been knocked about severely in the night fighting.

A Company of the 2nd Engineers had been sent to the south side of the Yongsan-Naktong River road. D Company had taken the north side of the road. A Company met the enemy first, about two miles west of Yongsan, and fought them all day supported by three anti-aircraft vehicles, two quad .50-caliber machine-gun carriers, and one twin 40mm gun carrier. During this fighting D Company moved back to the southern edge of Yongsan, and at the end of the day A Company also moved back to high ground southeast of Yongsan. A platoon of infantry also was in position on these hills. They commanded the road from Yongsan to Miryang, the next town down the line. Meanwhile, the divisional reconnaissance company and the tanks of the 72nd Tank Battalion had met North Koreans farther south, the enemy obviously trying to encircle Yongsan. The Allies fought them off that afternoon. Sergeant First Class Charles W. Turner of the reconnaissance company mounted a tank, operated its turret machine gun, and directed the tank's fire. He and the tank knocked out seven enemy machine guns before Turner was killed. But neither defense group could prevent the enemy from moving into Yongsan. After dark, the North Koreans moved into the low ground and entered the town from the south. By three o'clock on the morning of September 2 four enemy tanks led about a battalion of North Korean troops into Yongsan. They attacked the engineers who were holding the hills that commanded the road, but those soldiers fought briskly. They had no artillery support, but they improvised their own. They did have eighteen bazookas, and they turned these against the North Korean infantry with good effect. They also had four light machine guns and four heavy machine guns, and they had the help of two companies of tanks. With these weapons and rifles and carbines and grenades D Company of the 2nd Combat Engineers held the position above the Yongsan-Miryang road and kept the North Koreans from getting through.

During the afternoon, Colonel Hill managed to round up about eight hundred soldiers of the over-run companies of the 9th Infantry, and he counterattacked with the help of some tanks. These men fought their way into Yongsan and took control of the town again. Bazookamen and air strikes destroyed a number of North Korean T-34 tanks that day and drove the North Koreans up into the hills so that by evening the engineers and the 9th Infantry held the hills half a mile west of Yongsan and around the town. The immediate threat to Miryang was stopped, but until the gap in the lines could be sealed off, the danger continued.

That is why when General Craig met with General Keiser and the staff of the 2nd Division on the morning of September 2 they were nearly frantic. They called on the Marines to attack immediately on a broad front, to take back all the lost ground. General Craig rejected this wild plan: Many of his Marines had not even reached their assigned positions, and the Marine air control system had not been set up. If he attacked he would have no support from his own aircraft. He was not about to commit the Marines piecemeal to sticking their hands in the dike. He insisted that the attack must wait until the morning of September 3, and finally the Army officers agreed.

The point of attack was old familiar ground: the center of the Naktong Bulge. This time the Marines were to attack four miles east of Observation Hill, for the North Koreans were too close to Yongsan for comfort. The line of departure would be the ridgeline about a half mile west of Yongsan, south of Myong-ni. The high ground still was held that day by the 9th Infantry. When the Marines passed through, the 9th Infantry was then to swing to the right and cover the Marines' right flank. Farther north, the 23rd Infantry was to hold its positions. On the left, the Army would send tanks and the 2nd Engineer Battalion to attack southward and link the front with the right side of the 25th Division. This was the plan drawn on the evening of September 2. The Marines were to move at seven-fifteen the next morning. (See the map "The Second Naktong Counteroffensive.")

The only problem with the plan was that the North Koreans did not wait. They attacked the 2nd Engineers that night and held the high ground that was supposed to be the jump-off point.

The Marines' attack was to be carried out by the 1st and 2d battalions of the 5th Marines, moving astride the road. The 3rd Battalion would be in the rear, blocking the southern approaches to Yongsan. But when the Marines of the 2nd Battalion came up very early that morning and got out of their trucks about a half mile south of Yongsan, they ran into sniper fire as they marched through the town. This was a nuisance and slowed them down. It was six-thirty before the Marines reached the western end of Yongsan and the road junction where a minor road headed up to the village of Myong-ni, about a mile northwest of Yongsan.

When the Marines were one thousand yards from the line of departure, they suddenly discovered that the whole right side—the 9th Infantry position— had collapsed. Thus on their right flank the

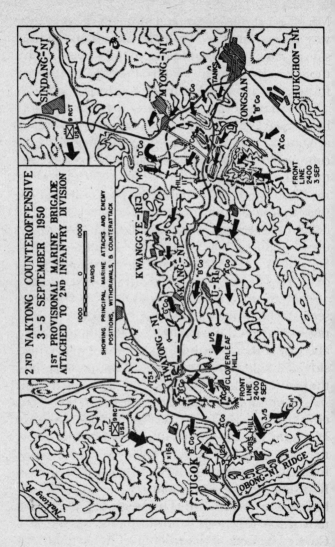

2ND NAKTONG COUNTEROFFENSIVE
3-5 SEPTEMBER 1950
1ST PROVISIONAL MARINE BRIGADE
ATTACHED TO 2ND INFANTRY DIVISION

SHOWING PRINCIPAL MARINE ATTACKS AND ENEMY
POSITIONS, WITHDRAWALS, & COUNTERATTACK

1000   0   1000
YARDS

Marines had the enemy, and ahead of them to the west lay the enemy. The 1st Battalion, on the left side of the road, found that Army troops ahead at the line of departure were retreating toward them, followed by North Koreans.

This confused situation was observed from above by General Craig in his helicopter. He landed back at Yongsan and came up by jeep to confer with his commanders. Some adjustment had to be made in the directions of approach of the 1st and 2d battalions, but that was all. The important thing was that the ridgeline that had been designated as the line of departure for the Marines' attack in the plan made on September 2 had become the first objective on September 3. This demanded some reorganization of activity.

Colonel Murray, commander of the 5th Marines, sent several Marine tanks up to help cover the retreat of the 9th Regiment soldiers from the ridge ahead of the 1st Battalion. As soon as the tank fire slowed the North Koreans down, the soldiers got off the hill. Lieutenant Colonel Roise called for an air strike and moved his 2nd Battalion troops out to clear the road and secure the Marines' right flank. When the air strike came in he directed it against that ridgeline and also plastered the ridge with tank fire, artillery, mortar rounds, and machine-gun fire. It was 8:00 A.M. before the Marines had cleared those hills below Myong-ni. Then the 2nd Battalion moved toward the hill northwest of the village. Covered by tank and artillery fire, all the Marine units moved ahead, going west on the road that led to Tugok, Obong-ni Ridge, and the Naktong beyond. All the way, both battalions called on air strikes, on the artillery, and on the mortar platoons for support, and they got it. The coordination of air, ground, and artillery made all the difference. They had Army tank help, too, and an Army tank destroyer gun. These weapons were particularly useful in knocking out enemy heavy-machine-gun positions. A and B companies had to cross a rice paddy to reach the bottom of the ridge they were to take. They did under a barrage, and at 11 o'clock they began the assault on the hill. The mortars plastered the hilltop; then the Marines got up and started forward in a skirmish line, making an enormous racket that frightened a whole North Korean company out of their positions on the forward slope of the ridge. The North Koreans turned and ran. The Marine riflemen came up behind them and shot them down.

So the 1st Battalion of the Marines secured the original "first objective" at about noon.

The next target of the 1st Battalion was a continuation of the ridge that ran parallel to the road. A and B companies did not stop long after the first victory but waited only for corpsmen to come up and take the wounded and for ammunition resupply. While they waited they came under attack from higher ground and called for an air strike. The Corsairs came in dropping napalm and strafing, and a large group of North Koreans fled down from their hill, crossed the road, and went up Hill 117, which was in the operational zone of the 2nd Battalion. The Marines saw them coming and plastered the hill with artillery and mortar fire, which left a trail of bodies and equipment up the hill. But many of the North Koreans made it to the hill, and soon troops of the 2nd Battalion were coming under fire from this high point. Lieutenant H. J. Smith, commander of D Company, said his men were getting heavy machine-gun fire. Colonel Roise ordered him to attack the hill, since the North Koreans there threatened the whole right side of the advance. D Company moved out across a rice paddy to assault the hill. They were supported by the men of E Company on high ground adjacent to the paddies and by a platoon of men with 75mm recoilless rifles who quickly destroyed an enemy artillery piece on the hill. But a T-34 tank's 85mm gun fired into the antitank company position, causing nine casualties. D Company gained a foothold on a spur of the ridge but then encountered the troops who had fled from Newton's advance—about two battalions. D Company marched up the hill into an enormous barrage of small-arms fire that was joined by artillery. The advance of D Company stopped abruptly as men began to fall.

Off to the left of their attack, tanks moved along the road westward, starting out about a quarter mile west of Yongsan. Very soon they ran into enemy armor, and the fight was fierce. Several tankers were shot as they came out of their M-26 turrets to make observations. The 2nd Tank Platoon moved up onto a low hill that overlooked the road and surprised three T-34 tanks, which they destroyed with their 90mm guns. They also caught a number of antitank guns and trucks on the road and did considerable damage to these. Two more enemy tanks were destroyed that afternoon.

In the afternoon the 1st Battalion advanced again, along the south side of the road, and more North Koreans fled across the road to the heights on the north, thus putting themselves in the way of the 2nd Battalion's advance. So the 1st Battalion made good progress, but the 2nd Battalion faced about twice as many troops as expected. As the day's fighting came to an end, the 1st Battalion had all its objectives, but the 2nd was bogged down on the edge of its second objective planned for September 3. The real difficulty was the exposed position of both battalions. The 2nd Battalion was sprawled along a front longer than a mile. The 1st Battalion was spread out along a mile front, with a right flank of one thousand yards on the road. Both battalion commanders knew the North Korean propensity for night attacks, and they took safety precautions. That evening the engineers sowed antipersonnel mines and rigged hand grenades and many other privately invented explosive devices, such as TNT blocks wrapped with spikes and set to trip wires. An antitank minefield was laid across the road near Hill 117, and at the same time when the engineers encountered an enemy minefield, they disarmed all

the mines. They came across only one enemy soldier, whom they killed, then went back to the
Marine lines to report success. They had scarcely
gotten inside the perimeter when the sky was laced
with flashes of lightning. The monsoon descended
with a vengeance, the wind began blowing hard
and cold, and the rain came pelting down into the
foxholes as Colonel Murray chewed over the reports
of his battalion commanders. The 2nd Battalion
had taken a beating that day, with D Company
suffering most of the Marine casualties. So Murray
decreed that on this second day of combat the 3rd
Battalion would pass through the 2nd Battalion
lines and make the attack on the north side of the
road. Then everyone waited for day's light.

Perhaps the rain had dampened the North
Korean spirits. In any event, there was no attack on
the Marine perimeters on the night of September 3.
At dawn on the next morning the engineers were
out removing the mines around the positions, and
when a group of enemy became visible on a hill
ahead of B Company, the artillery began firing on
them. The riflemen had an indication of a changed
atmosphere in the battle when scores of North
Koreans were seen throwing down their weapons
and running away from the bombardment. The 1st
Battalion assault began at 8:00 A.M. and proceeded
with a new ease, for resistance was very slight. Most
of the North Koreans they saw were running away.
Air strikes along the road and in the hills and
valleys accounted for many casualties among the

enemy. Marine tanks moved ahead rapidly and knocked out little pockets of resistance. The artillery fired when advised of targets. The North Koreans took a terrible beating as their advance lost all its vigor. At three o'clock in the afternoon the 1st Battalion reached its day's objective, the high ground south of the road at the village of Kang-ni, two miles from the jumping-off place of that morning.

At about the same time that the 1st Battalion attacked, the 3rd Battalion moved through the lines of the 2nd and against Hill 117. On the day before, this had been the core of the North Koreans' resistance. But on September 4, when the 3rd Battalion riflemen charged across the rice paddy to start up the hill, the only North Koreans they encountered were dead. The positions were unoccupied, the base of the hill had the feeling of emptiness. They took the southern half of the hill very quickly and killed only 15 North Koreans in doing it. H Company, which had swung around to the north in a flanking movement, ran into even less resistance. Forty minutes after the attack had begun, the hill, which had been alive with enemy troops the day before, was in Marine hands. The worst casualty of the morning came about when a personnel carrier struck an enemy mine on the secondary road east of Hill 117. Ten men inside were killed or wounded. By noon the engineers had cleared off this second minefield.

The 3rd Battalion moved on past Hill 117 to the hill north of Kang-ni, where it ran into machine-gun fire. But the machine guns were silenced by air strikes and artillery, and the North Koreans retreated. At three-fifteen that afternoon the hill was taken. The Marines had stopped the enemy's advance, saved Yongsan and the road beyond, and put the North Korean 9th Division into retreat. All this while air strikes, artillery, and mortars were blasting the road back to the Naktong River. Marines coming up the road toward the front line saw a scene of enemy disaster unequaled in this war. Hundreds of dead North Koreans lay along the road and on the hillsides. It was a whole column that had been coming to reinforce the enemy and had been caught by artillery and air power. A number of officers, among them a battalion commander, were among the dead. Tanks, vehicles, mortars, and guns were strewn about. The Marines recovered many American guns and vehicles, which they turned over to the Army's 2nd Division. They even came across a dead paymaster with a truck full of North Korean currency.

That same day Colonel Newton's 1st Battalion attacked the second objective, Cloverleaf Hill south of the road to the river. The North Koreans fought for a little while, mostly with machine guns, but air strikes took the starch out of them and by 6:00 P.M. Colonel Newton could report to Colonel Murray that Cloverleaf Hill was securely in Marine hands.

Once again, as night fell, the Marines were sprawled across the Korean countryside in thin lines. Once again the engineers spent much of the night laying mines and other explosive defenses. Somewhere ahead enemy artillery was fighting back, and the 3rd Battalion command post was shelled that night. But at two-thirty in the morning, night fighter planes from the American carriers took a hand, and the mortar position suspected of doing most of the shelling was hit. The night fighters brought something else new, they bombed the enemy troops trying to move along the roads. So the night no longer belonged to the North Koreans, nor could they expect, as General Kim had told them to expect, that at night they would be free from American air attack.

On the morning of September 5, the North Koreans did try to stage an attack on the 9th Infantry positions north of the Marine lines. They chose the moment when a rain squall struck the American soldiers' position and came charging in with burp guns rattling and grenades flying. G Company of the 9th Infantry bore the brunt of this attack. Shouting North Koreans came after the soldiers on the ridgeline. From their positions on Cloverleaf Hill, the Marines saw this attack develop and massed their machine-gun and rifle fire against the first wave, driving it back. But more North Koreans came on against the 9th Infantry. Sergeant First Class Loren R. Kaufman's platoon came up to help halt the attack. They ran into a platoon of North Koreans who were trying to encircle the ridgeline. Kaufman bayoneted the first North Korean he saw, who happened to be the point man for the attackers. Kaufman then threw some grenades, and the sergeant and his platoon engaged the other North Koreans with rifle fire. The North Koreans abandoned the encirclement, and Kaufman led his men to the rescue of G Company. On the line they fought hard. Sergeant Kaufman led several assaults against infiltrating enemy as the day wore on. He destroyed a machine-gun position and a mortar. (Later he was awarded the Congressional Medal of Honor for this engagement.) Although the fighting lasted into the night, and a large force of North Koreans was pitted against G Company, the infantrymen held their position.

THE MARINES OF the 1st Battalion led the Marine brigade's assault that day. First they had to survive an unexpected assault from a pair of Air Force P-51's that sliced in on Cloverleaf Hill and strafed along the ridgeline. The Air Force had not gotten the word that Cloverleaf was in American hands. One Marine was wounded and a lot more were swearing before the attack ended. The air strike delayed the marine attack for twenty minutes, but at 8:20 A.M. they moved out to strike Hill 125 and Observation Hill. This meant moving down from Cloverleaf into the rice paddy. Then B Company crossed the road that runs between the two hills. In an hour B Company had taken Hill 125 and A Company had seized Observation Hill. Next came the tough one: Obong-ni Ridge again. They could see it well from their new positions, and the opening of fire on both companies from Obong-ni indicated that it was not going to be so easy. Colonel Murray knew that, and he had ordered the 3rd Battalion to come up on the left, through the rice paddy south of Cloverleaf Hill, and prepare for a two-battalion assault on Obong-ni. But during the day the fighting was hard enough, and the enemy position was seen to be strong enough, that Colonel Murray canceled the plan and ordered the 3rd Battalion to join the 1st Battalion troops on Observation Hill. The tanks, which had been coming along the road, were warned to sit tight in the cut between the two hills held by the Marines. The main reason for the change was the weather, which prevented effective air operations. The P-51 attack was an indication; the Marine air groups were not going to risk any more attacks on their own men, but they were not operating against the enemy, either. Murray ordered his men to dig in on the slopes of the hills and wait.

A large enemy force was concentrated on Obong-ni Ridge, the village of Tugok, the northern base of Observation Hill, and on Finger Ridge, all in the area of the Marines' B Company. All morning these Marines on Hill 125 were soaked by rain squalls and occasionally harried by small-arms and machine-gun fire from positions across the way. But just after two o'clock in the afternoon, the firing began to take on a new tempo. The sporadic machine-gun fire became intense. Mortar rounds began to come in. An enemy antitank gun on Fin-

ger Ridge began firing at the infantry positions.
Captain Francis Fenton saw all the signs of an
impending attack. He got on the radio to report
back to Colonel Newton at the battalion command
post. Just then the radio went dead, probably from
the effects of the constant soaking rain of the past
few hours. At the same time, the battalion command post's radios went out. So there was no warning put out over the air. Nor could Captain Fenton
do anything when he saw enemy tanks and infantry
moving down the road toward the pass between
Observation Hill and Hill 125. He could watch, but
there was no way to warn the Marine tanks down
there. But he could watch only for a moment,
because then a company of North Koreans attacked
B Company's hillside under heavy covering fire
while another unit swung around to the company's
right. The Marines moved up to the crest of Hill 125
and began firing. Fenton did send a bazooka squad
down to the road at the base of the hill to help the
tanks, but they came too late for the first of them.
The Marine M-26 tanks were concentrating on the
machine guns on Obong-ni Ridge, with their
90mm guns pointed to the left, when the enemy
tanks swung around the corner straight at them and
opened fire with their 85mm guns. In a few seconds
the first two American tanks were destroyed. Both
crews managed to escape the tanks, but the American tanks behind were blocked from fighting by the
dead tanks in front. It was now that B Company's
assault squad arrived with their bazookas and

smashed the first T-34. The 1st Battalion's assault platoon arrived with more 3.5-inch bazookas and knocked out the second enemy tank and an armored personnel carrier that was moving in its wake. The North Korean armored assault down the road was brought to a sudden halt.

Up on the side of Hill 125 the Marines engaged in hand-to-hand fighting with the North Koreans who were coming up the slope. Grenades were flying like baseballs at a training camp. The company's mortars soon exhausted their supply of ammunition, and the company was low on grenades and rifle ammunition, too. The North Koreans kept on coming, and finally Captain Fenton sent out two runners. One went to the 9th Infantry position on the ridge north of Hill 125, asking that they get Army artillery to drop some shells on the Marine front. The request was soon answered, and howitzer shells began blowing up the North Korean advance. At the same time the second runner reached Colonel Newton at the battalion command post and asked for mortar support, so the battalion's 81mm mortars began firing on the enemy side of the hill. Colonel Murray sent A Company to help in the fight, and the 3rd Battalion took over Observation Hill. The artillery fire, the mortars, and the reinforcements did the job. The enemy had penetrated to within fifty yards of the B Company positions but was turned back by four o'clock in the afternoon and retreated down the hill to Tugok. No more North Koreans came up either against the 9th Infantry or the Marine positions. The drive of the North Korean 9th Division and the North Korean 4th Division had been stopped. It was not started again. The exhausted Marines moved out that night to Pusan, to board ship and go to Japan, then to board other ships and head for a new battle. The Army forces around Obong-ni had nothing more to worry about that night, and although they did not then know it, the North Koreans would not be able to renew their offensive in the area.

19.

The Ultimate Effort

NORTH OF THE fighting around the Naktong Bulge, troops of the North Korean 2nd Division advanced on September 1 against the U.S. 23rd Regiment around Changnyong. By dawn they had isolated the 1st Battalion and overrun the regimental command post five miles northwest of Changnyong. On the evening of September 2 the North Koreans entered the town, and the 23rd Infantry was cut off.

Early the next morning General Haynes sent three tanks down the road to Yongsan to link up with the 9th Infantry Regiment. Only one got through. The 38th Infantry still was farther north than the 23rd, and General Keiser sent his 2nd Battalion to link up from the north with the 23rd, but they found the North Koreans in full possession of the heights along the road. For three days the battalion, aided by air strikes, fought the North Koreans before the U.N. forces captured the vital

Hill 284. On the slopes they found about 150 dead North Koreans. When they reached the top and could command the ground around, they saw North Koreans retreating into a village below the hill and called on the artillery, which systematically destroyed the village. Going down into the destruction, a patrol found a large stockpile of American small arms, ammunition, radios, and grenades, which the enemy had captured along the line. The fact that they prized them so much as to store them carefully was an indication of the desperate supply situation of the North Korean 2nd Division in early September.

The 1st Battalion of the 23rd Infantry still was cut off, but it remained intact three miles west of the Naktong, on a height from which it could harry the North Korean movement of supplies and troops down the road to Changnyong. For three days the battalion fought from that position, completely surrounded and supplied by air drop.

The rest of the 23rd linked up finally and consolidated its position in the hills next to the 38th Infantry. The next step was to wipe out units of the North Korean 2nd Division who were all around them and to interdict their supply routes along the roads. The fighting continued through September 8. On that day the North Koreans began a new furious attempt to break through the American line to the east. They started with a night attack, fought until dawn, laid off until evening to avoid American air strikes, and attacked again on the evening of

September 9. This was a costly maneuver, but the orders from Pyongyang were specific enough: Attack, attack, attack. The North Korean 2nd Division did just that for those first nine days of September. At the end of the period, the 23rd Infantry was down to less than 40 percent effective fighters. The North Korean division had suffered about four thousand casualties. Even then, when the North Korean 2nd Division was no longer able to sustain an attack, its troops continued to harry the American rear areas around Changnyong by infiltration and road-blocks.

· Next to the North Korean 2nd Division on the northern part of the Pusan Perimeter, the North Korean 10th Division faced part of the U.S. 38th Infantry and the British 27th Brigade. This division was the North Korean reserve, waiting for the other troops to take Taegu and begin the drive on Pusan, whereupon it would speed down the line, move through the leading elements, and make the final rush. It never happened that way. The North Korean 10th Division fought a few skirmishes with Allied troops but made no concerted drive southward until after the second week in September, and then it was too late. The North Koreans' Naktong offensive had been nipped off by that time.

The final threat to the Pusan Perimeter was made by the North Korean 6th and 7th divisions along the southwestern segment of the defense line. On the night of August 31 troops of the North Korean 7th

Division broke through the ROK line south of the confluence of the Nam and Naktong rivers and by morning had infiltrated as far east as Chirwon-ni and Chung-ni. That put them just four miles northwest of Masan. The U.S. 24th Infantry had proved to be totally incapable of positive action, so the fate of Pusan really hung on the U.S. 35th Infantry and the 27th Infantry, the only other defense forces between the perimeter and Pusan.

On September 1 the North Koreans continued to cross the river in this same area northwest of Chirwon-ni. Artillery spotting planes sighted a force of nearly a battalion crossing between the 1st and 2nd battalions of the 35th Infantry and called down an artillery strike. The 64th Field Artillery responded nobly and destroyed most of the crossing force. Fighter planes helped, and later in the day artillery and fighters interdicted another crossing attempt with heavy casualties to the enemy. The artillery was particularly effective along this part of the Pusan Perimeter. The 159th Field Artillery Battalion was located in the northern sector. Its guns kept after the North Koreans crossing the river. The 90th Field Artillery Battalion's 155mm howitzers concentrated on the area back of Chungam-ni through which the North Korean 6th Division was moving its supplies and destroyed many troops, trucks, and artillery pieces.

But the North Koreans kept coming down the Komam-ni highway and the Chirwon road. By

evening the North Koreans had completely surrounded the 35th Infantry. The trouble for the
Americans was caused, as usual, by a large territory
being watched by too few men. The 1st Battalion's
F Company was located along the Naktong around
the Namji-ri bridge; E Company was south of that
as far as the Kuhe-ri ferry; G Company was south of
that point around the confluence of the Nam with a
smaller stream, and below that were the ROK
police who had fled during the night, leaving a
great gap in the middle of the U.N. line.

The major assault came against E Company that
day, but E Company was well dug in and put up a
good fight, mauling several enemy companies that
attacked. F Company did the same to enemy troops
assaulting around the Namji-ri bridge. G Company suffered most: The company lost its commander early in the day; the 3rd Platoon lost its
commander in the afternoon; the enemy climbed
the low hill on the Nam River, about five miles
from the Naktong junction, to attack the Americans on top, and in spite of a successful air strike
they got into the American positions, and hand-to-
hand and grenade fighting became the rule. By 6:00
P.M. Sergeant First Class Junius Poovey was in
command of the 3rd Platoon, and he had only a
dozen fighting men still on their feet and seventeen
wounded. At night he withdrew from the hill,
bringing the wounded down under cover from a
platoon of tanks. They moved to Hill 179, the
command post of G Company.

On the morning of September 2 the 2nd Battalion of the 27th Infantry attacked the North Koreans who had taken that low hill and by afternoon had reestablished the old defense line. About two thousand North Koreans, however, had infiltrated inside that line. So Lieutenant Colonel Gordon Murch was given orders that night to take his battalion of the 27th Infantry around again to attack to his rear to clear the lines of communication of North Koreans. G Company of the 35th Infantry took over all the old positions once more. Again the North Koreans attacked G Company, and the whole scenario was repeated: Colonel Murch turned around, retook the positions, and turned them back to G Company. This brought them to the night of September 3. On September 4, Colonel Murch once more headed down into the gap between the 1st and 2nd battalions of the 35th Infantry to try to clean it up. Almost immediately he came up against a strong force of North Koreans with a number of heavy machine guns.

The immediate problem was that the 1st Battalion of the 35th Infantry stuck out farther to the west than any other American unit; the North Koreans were around it on three sides and threatening also from the rear some distance back. The main supply route had fallen into enemy hands, and American vehicles could use the road only during the daylight hours, and then only if they moved in force. The 1st Battalion of the 35th Infantry, now consolidated on Sibidang-san height, had surrounded itself completely by wire with minefields, booby traps, and every other device the engineers could manage to install. Aided greatly by A Battery of the 64th Field Artillery Battalion, the defense had been successful for two days, and someone estimated that the enemy between the night of August 31 and the morning of September 3 had lost about three hundred fifty men trying to capture that position. On the night of September 2, the North Koreans made their most desperate attack yet. Shortly after midnight they came in force, surrounded the 1st Battalion command post, and attacked several batteries of the 64th Field Artillery. The heaviest attack was launched against A Battery.

A Battery was in position about three miles north of Haman on the Masan-Chinju road and the single-track rail line that ran between these towns. The battery command post was in the village of Saga, which was strung out along the main road. For three days and nights Captain Leroy Anderson, the battery commander, had warned his men that the enemy were all around them and they must be constantly on the alert. He had taken every possible advantage of the terrain, putting five of his six howitzers in a protected position formed by a low ridge. The sixth was on the north side of the railroad line, across a four-foot gulley. The fire direction center, on the other side of the railroad track, was situated in a tent erected in a four-foot-deep dugout. It was within voice distance of all the guns.

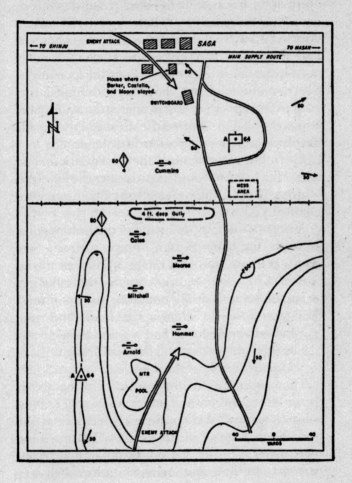

The wire section's switchboard was in a dugout north of the tracks amid the houses, which some of the men were using for shelter. Around the battery position stood ten defensive posts, which contained four .50-caliber machine guns, three .30-caliber machine guns, and two M-16 half-tracks, each of which mounted four .50-caliber machine guns. Four of the posts were on the ridge around the main gun position and connected by field telephone. All the others were within shouting distance.

The night of September 2 was very dark and so foggy that from one position to the next, forms were blurred. During the night all the howitzers were manned and were firing missions ordered by the infantry up front. At two forty-five on the following morning the battery's first sergeant, Master Sergeant William Parker, was standing near the switchboard when he saw several men moving along the main road. This was odd; his men should be at their posts. So Sergeant Parker shouted:

"Who's there?"

The men did not reply. They speeded up.

"Halt!" shouted the sergeant.

Then he made out three forms pulling something along the road. They were North Korean soldiers, and they were pulling a wheeled machine gun. They dropped off into the ditch, turned the machine gun on the battery position, and began firing. At the same time, machine-gun fire began to come in from several other points on the ridgeline around the five-howitzer position. Then another gun opened up from the village of Saga. The two elements of the battery divided by the railline were involved in two separate actions.

At approximately the same time as Sergeant Parker was challenging the North Koreans, Sergeant Herbert L. Rawls, Jr., the wire chief, recognized that something was wrong and ran to the nest of civilians' houses on the road to start waking up men. He awakened PFC Harold W. Barker, PFC Thomas A. Castello, and PFC Santford B. Moore. They got up groggily. Two Korean puppies they had recently adopted began to bark. Having given the alarm, Sergeant Rawls then ran to the switchboard to warn the men on duty there. Just as he came up, so did a North Korean with a burp gun in his hands. Sergeant Rawls was shouting to Sergeant Joseph R. Pursley when the North Korean opened fire. The North Korean then threw a grenade into the switchboard dugout. Both sergeants were killed, and so were two of the three men in the switchboard dugout. The survivor was Corporal John M. Pitcher, who continued to work the board.

As this racket began, Corporal Bobbie H. McQuitty ran to his three-quarter-ton truck, which mounted a machine gun. The North Koreans had pulled one of their guns directly opposite the truck. Corporal McQuitty got to his gun and tried to open fire. The gun would not fire. He leaped from the truck and ran across the rice paddy toward the front line of the 35th Infantry, where he had seen a tank earlier that day. He was going to try to get that tank to help.

At the same time, the men awakened by Sergeant Rawls began to move. Barker got out of the house first, running until he saw a North Korean machine gun dead ahead and turned to dash back to the house. A bullet hit him in the knee. Castello and Moore got him into the house and laid him on the floor. Then they stood in the corners, next to the walls. From the next room in the house another man rushed out, but as he stepped outside the house he ran into a group of about fifteen North Korean soldiers. One of them shot him in the mouth, and he was dead before his body hit the ground.

When the firing began, three North Korean machine guns at the south end of the battery opened fire against the howitzers. So did a half dozen enemy riflemen around the howitzer area. The three howitzers nearest the ridge were under heavy fire, and the crews jumped into the gun pits to take cover and figure out what was going on. Neither the quad .50's nor the two machine guns on the village side of the railroad could open fire without hitting Americans. One of the half-tracks moved and fired a few rounds, and then its traversing mechanism broke down. It could not be operated by hand, either, so the crew backed the vehicle to the gully by the railroad tracks. When the crews of the .50-caliber and .30-caliber machine guns realized that the battery position had been invaded, they pulled back north toward the other half-track.

Just about then the field telephone in the fire direction tent began to ring. The phone was picked up by Lieutenant Kincheon A. Bailey, the battery executive officer. What was wrong? battalion wanted to know. Why had the guns stopped firing?

Lieutenant Bailey had been hearing the machine-gun fire, but that was not unusual; often the sounds of small arms and machine guns could be heard in the battery position at night. But when battalion asked, he began calling up the gun crews to ask what they knew. They all replied that nothing was unusual except for the sixth section, commanded by Private First Class Ernest R. Arnold, which did not reply at all. At that moment the sixth section was under intense machine-gun fire, and nobody in the pit wanted to reach up to the edge where the field phone was located. Lieutenant Bailey then reported what he knew and left the fire direction tent to investigate PFC Arnold's situation.

On the left, an enemy soldier came up to the pit occupied by Master Sergeant Frederick J. Hammer's section. The enemy soldier threw several grenades into the pit, and one of them killed one man and wounded several others. Another grenade exploded in the ammunition storage and set fire to about one hundred 105mm shells. Sergeant Hammer, seeing the ammunition burning, told his men to make a dash for the gully down by the railroad tracks. At the same time the men of the Mitchell and Coles howitzers also made a run for safety. Just then Master Sergeant Germanus P. Kotzur realized what was happening and raced to the Cummins howitzer north of the railroad tracks and ordered the crew to begin laying down fire on the hill from which he believed the enemy had come.

Lieutenant Bailey approached Sergeant Hammer's howitzer position, and by the light of powder that was burning fiercely he could see a number of North Koreans moving around the howitzer. One of them was writing in Korean in chalk on the gun, "Hurrah for our company." Lieutenant Bailey assumed that everyone in the position was killed or captured, and he ran back. On the way he encountered Sergeant Kotzur, who told him what he knew and what he had done. Lieutenant Bailey then went to the howitzer commanded by Corporal Cecil W. Meares and ordered him also to start firing against the ridgeline. The two howitzers fired eighteen rounds. Bailey also ordered the gun crew to begin firing their small arms against the Hammer gunpit where the North Koreans were in control. Meares' men then began firing and throwing grenades at the North Koreans. Lieutenant Bailey and Sergeant Kotzur decided they had best get the men to the safety of the gully until they found out how bad the penetration had been. Sergeant Henry E. Baker ran to a 2.5-ton truck that carried a ring-mounted .50-caliber machine gun, and Private First Class Richard G. Haussler went with him to feed the gun while Baker operated it. They opened fire on the North Koreans to give the gun crews protection. They fired twelve hundred fifty rounds in about ten minutes. Under their fire Captain Anderson made a personal inspection of the gun positions to be sure none of his men had been left behind in the pits.

The battery defense was then organized in the gully, which had also become the battery aid station. All the living members of the battery were in the gully except three men in the fire direction tent, Corporal Pitcher at the switchboard, and Barker, Castello, and Moore, who were still in the house north of the railroad, listening to the puppies yap and worrying whether the North Koreans would come to investigate.

As soon as battalion headquarters learned what was going on at A Battery, the battalion commander, Lieutenant Colonel Arthur H. Hogan, began to help out. The artillery from other batteries was called in around the positions of the A Battery guns. C Battery of the 90th Field Artillery Battalion fired shells to within fifty yards of the gully and prevented the enemy from sending reinforcements. And then the tank that Corporal McQuitty had gone for showed up on the Masan road. From the gully the defenders fired light weapons at the North Koreans. By dawn the enemy activity was much reduced, and not long after that the men of A Battery reclaimed their guns. The North Koreans had killed seven men and wounded twelve, destroyed four trucks, and let the air out of the tires of one howitzer. They had written in chalk on three of the guns, but they had not damaged any of them; apparently they had been confident almost till the last that they would capture these guns. When Captain Anderson made a body count, he discovered twenty-one dead North Koreans around the positions.

THROUGHOUT THE FIGHTING the U.S. 24th Infantry Regiment, which was composed of black soldiers, proved to be almost totally useless. After the first collapse on the night of August 31, the regiment was moved back to Haman. General Kean was so concerned that he asked for part of the 27th Infantry to do the 24th Infantry's job and got Colonel Check's 1st Battalion to come up and protect Colonel Champney's 24th Infantry Command post, since his own soldiers could not be relied upon. When the men of the 27th arrived they found the roads clogged with milling American soldiers, most of them out of unit, out of uniform, out of weaponry. Neither the 1st nor the 2nd battalions of the 24th Infantry could be reassembled as units. Military policemen threatened the soldiers at gunpoint to get them off the road they were clogging, preventing trucks and fighting troops from coming up. Check finally got his men forward, and after an air strike and artillery barrage at four-thirty on the afternoon of September 1, the 1st Battalion of the 27th Infantry attacked westward into Haman and secured part of the ridge on the west side. Thus on September 1, the 25th Division was saved not by the 25th Division, but by a combination of air power from the carriers *Valley Force* and *Philippine Sea,* the Fifth Air Force, and Colonel Check's battalion. It was noon on September 2 before the troops retook the positions held by the 24th Infantry at the beginning of the North Korean offensive. For two days Check's men withstood successive counterattacks on the ridges and killed about one thousand North Koreans.

By this time most of the American officers were loath to use the 24th Infantry for any purpose whatsoever, but General Walker insisted that they had to fight. So on September 4 the 1st Battalion of the 24th Infantry and F Company, which was all that could be salvaged of the 2nd Battalion, took over their old positions, and the men of the 27th Infantry moved back east of Haman. Once again that night the North Koreans attacked, and once again the men of the 24th Infantry fled. A number of officers, black and white, and a number of noncommissioned blacks fought bravely, but the majority of the black troops ran away, and it took threats at gunpoint to drive them back into the line. Most of the soldiers vanished into the hills and reappeared far behind the lines. Colonel Check's 27th Infantry Battalion once again bailed them out. Check ordered 24th Infantry stragglers to follow his men into battle, but most of them refused unless pushed at gunpoint. By this time MPs and other infantrymen were perfectly willing to point their guns at the men of the 24th Infantry. Colonel Champney was wounded on September 6 and replaced by a tough young West Point lieutenant colonel named John Corley. General Kean recommended to General Walker that the 24th Infantry be disbanded.

"It is my considered opinion that the 24th Infantry has demonstrated in combat that it is untrustworthy and incapable of carrying out missions expected of an infantry regiment," he said. The general was simply repeating common knowledge and echoing the considered opinions of the 24th's officers and many of the black noncommissioned officers. But at the moment General Walker refused. The subject of black troops was a ticklish one in an army that had just begun to integrate. General Walker hoped that somehow Colonel Corley could make a fighting unit out of the 24th.

The opportunity came at Battle Mountain near Sobuk-san, in the mountain area that stretches southward to the coast. This was part of the 24th Infantry defensive area, but the troops had performed so badly that a company of the 5th Infantry was sent in to give the position backbone and to round up the 24th Infantry stragglers every night and send them back to their units every morning. On September 7 the North Korean 6th Division troops did attack Battle Mountain again. Rather than trust the 24th Infantry, General Kean sent troops of the 5th Infantry to resist the attack, and a part of the 27th Infantry to help. In a three-day battle they failed to take all the high ground, then were moved back to Masan to put out another fire, leaving the 24th Infantry on the edges of Battle Mountain. Colonel Corley decided not to try to attack, but to hold another height east of Battle Mountain and to surround the enemy position with minefields and barbed wire and hold them back with artillery. This system worked until September 14, when a North Korean unit made a frontal assault on I and L companies of the 24th Infantry, and once again most of the 24th Infantry riflemen fled the scene. Major Melvin R. Blair, who had just assumed command of the 3rd Battalion, tried desperately to hold the height but did not have enough men to do so and finally had to withdraw. By this time the North Korean drive had been stopped elsewhere along the line, and the North Korean troops around Battle Mountain went nowhere. In the middle of September it was as if two exhausted dogs were standing off after a long fight, growling at one another and making an occasional lunge but too tired to go for each other's throat.

IN JAPAN EVENTS were in progress that would make the Battle of the Pusan Perimeter worthwhile. The great strength of the North Korean military machine was committed here in the South of the Korean peninsula. Meanwhile, General MacArthur was preparing for a surprise invasion far to the north, and then a drive across the peninsula to cut off the North Korean troops from their supply lines

and their border. On September 7 the 1st Marine
Brigade was in Pusan. For the next six days the
Marines slept in the open on the docks, and ate their
meals aboard the transport ships that soon would
take them around the end of the peninsula and up
to join the amphibious landings. By day the
Marines trained, and they also trained three thousand troops of the Korean 1st Marine Regiment,
which had been attached to the U.S. Marines for the
coming landings.

The Marines did not know where they were
going. It had taken a while, but the Americans had
become aware of the nature of their enemy. Back on
the Pusan Perimeter the horror stories of the devil-
ish brutality of the North Koreans reached a new
peak in these days. A group of cooks and kitchen
police, bringing food up to the line, was captured in
the 35th Infantry area by soldiers of the North
Korean 7th Division. One messman escaped by hiding in a haystack, and then he listened to the
screams of the others as they were tortured. When
the bodies were found, one had been castrated and
his fingers cut off before he was shot. Others had
been tied up and their feet cut off before they were
murdered. Others had their tongues cut out. As the
North Korean offensive reached its most frenetic on
the night of September 3, a gang of the ever-present
guerrillas surprised a party operating a radio relay
station four miles from Masan. They tied up the
Americans, ransacked the station, and then shot

every one of the Americans. The murderer, who used a tommy gun, was a woman.

Yes, the Marines had learned. And they knew that every Korean town was a hotbed of spies. One of the officials of the Korea Press Association turned out to be a spy for the enemy. No Koreans outside the ROK government were to be trusted, and even in the government treason was a matter of great concern.

When the Marines sat in their bivouac and trained their Korean counterparts it was apparent that they were going somewhere in those transports at the dock. So one day they were lined up in formation and an officer read them a long lecture on the hydrographic aspects of the west coast port of Kunsan. Undoubtedly the word was flashed that night by radio to North Korea that the Americans were planning to invade Kunsan from the sea. But every U.S. Marine knew very well that wherever they might be going, it would not be Kunsan. And they were right. They were on their way to Inchon, one hundred miles north of the other port, the gateway to Seoul and the way across the peninsula.

20.

Perimeter Held

AS OF SEPTEMBER 15 the Pusan Perimeter was quiet.
The major Naktong offensive of the North Korean
People's Army had failed to break through and take
either Taegu or Pusan. The war was far from over,
but at last the Americans were in a position to take
offensive action. It had taken about three months
for the American military establishment to come to
this position—really a remarkably short time given
the state of American defenses in June 1950.

The responsibility for the dangerously weak state
of the American military establishment in the
spring of 1950 must be laid at the feet of the Truman
administration and the Congress; in other words,
the politicians. In the winter of 1945-46 it became
apparent that the United States and the Soviet
Union would not agree on the future of Korea. The
gap between the American and Soviet political sys-
tems was too great for that. The United States

insisted on Korean national unification through free elections. To the Soviets this insistence meant the probability that the government of a unified Korea would be American-oriented because the population of South Korea was about twice that of North Korea. Certainly the majority of Koreans were not Communist-oriented; as of 1983 nowhere in the world has a Communist government ever come to power through free election. Given the location of Korea, on the Soviet border, it should have been apparent to the U.S. government that the Soviets never would accept a pro-American government of Korea. That truth was certainly understood by members of the American military who were present in Asia. It was not understood in Washington, where in 1945 and 1946 the clamor was to "bring the boys home" at all costs. Because of this pressure from Congress, in November 1945 General Marshall told General MacArthur to raise a paramilitary force (national police) in South Korea so that more American troops could be relieved of occupation duty. The force was to have the characteristics of the old Philippine constabulary: equipped to keep civil peace but not to be construed an army. The main reason for so characterizing the force was again political; the diplomats did not wish to annoy the Soviet bear or the American isolationists by creating a purely military force. General MacArthur saw from the beginning that a "police force" would be inadequate and suggested the establishment of a South Korean army. But again the politicians had their way, and when in January 1946 the problem was given official attention, the joint chiefs of staff specified that the establishment of a Korean army should await Korean independence, which presupposed unification. This was just a year after the establishment of the United Nations, and many Americans believed that the U.N. could operate as an international police agency to prevent wars and settle international disputes. This belief was central to American foreign policy, and if nearly forty years later it seems incredibly naïve, well, the United States, for all its immense power, *was* incredibly naïve in those days. And when one blames the politicians for political and military bumbles, one really has to come back to the people of the United States. Most of them accepted the United Nations as the great hope for world peace. Most of them looked upon the world with an affability unknown outside U.S. borders. Most of them wanted to "bring the boys home" because they had done their duty, won the war, and now should be able to pick up or begin their normal lives and look forward to a life of peace. On a few occasions in American history politicians have actually provided leadership for the people, but for the most part they have been responsive to the will of the people. So, in essence, the amiability and naïveté of the American people was the basic cause of America's virtual disarmament and of a number of foolish political and military decisions in the late 1940s.

Given the order that an army was not to be formed in South Korea, General MacArthur settled upon a national police force of twenty-five thousand, aided by a state police force of twenty-five thousand and a small coast guard for inshore patrol. They would be armed with cast-off Japanese small arms. The first such unit was formed in January 1947, and Lieutenant General John R. Hodge, the military governor of Korea, assigned a handful of American officers to guide the birth and growth of the force.

General Hodge, however, had no faith in the idea, because South Korea was in political chaos. Having been occupied by the Japanese for nearly forty years and having been made part of the Japanese Empire, the people of South Korea had no modern political tradition except rebellion against Japan. One symbolic figure of this rebellion was Dr. Syngman Rhee, who had been living in mainland United States and Hawaii for the past twenty years. Rhee, however, was not popular with most of the Koreans who had been anti-Japanese activists in the last days of the war. They regarded him as old-fashioned and out of touch with affairs. These people were also more socialist by political leaning than capitalist, a factor that almost immediately dominated the political situation. With the capitulation of Japan, the People's Party had set up its own government in South Korea, and when General Hodge arrived with his occupation force they met him and told him they were in charge. But

General Hodge had his orders: *He* was in charge, and he had no authority to deal with any "government." Thus from the outset political tensions and confusions dominated the American occupation of South Korea. The end of 1945 and 1946 were marked by great political instability in South Korea and growing conflict between the South Koreans and the American occupiers. Dr. Rhee was brought back to Korea by the decision of President Truman. Dr. Rhee seemed to be the only figure who would respond to American interests as they were then seen in Washington.

Dr. Rhee appealed to many of the conservatives— largely people of some substance, and many of these were suspect because the only way one could prosper in Korea under the Japanese was to cooperate with the Japanese. Therefore in Korea in the 1940s wealth was a *prima facie* indication of collaboration with the old enemy. Revolutions have been fought on lesser grounds. Immediately the left and center forces began to complain that the Americans were preparing to set up a puppet government. In fact the American political leaders would have been wiser to do so than to leave a political vacuum for two years as they did. Their excuse, which grew lamer every month, was that the unification of Korea in terms of the Yalta agreement would solve the political problem and that the United States had no authority to set up an independent South Korean government. Given the modern history of the region and the actions occurring above the 38th parallel that divided the American and Soviet occupation areas this attitude surpassed the naïve and verged on the stupid. In extenuation, it must be remembered that aside from a handful of missionaries and smaller contingents of scholars and businessmen, virtually no one in the United States knew anything about Korea. When Korea was being gobbled up by Japan, Americans were still talking about Manifest Destiny. When the U.S. Army's XXIV Corps occupied South Korea in 1945, virtually the only Americans who spoke the Korean language or knew anything of the social, political, or economic history were the returned missionaries, and their political views tended to the traditional.

The schism between General Hodge's military government and the people of South Korea grew during 1946 and early 1947. From the American point of view the leftist political leaders proved totally unreliable, and the Communists were a constant problem, given to counterfeiting South Korean money to meet expenses. General Hodge's basic distrust of the Koreans continued. Thus the constabulary grew slowly. By the end of 1946 it numbered only about five thousand men. But then American policy suffered a basic change in direction. From the beginning General Hodge had indicated that with the shrinking forces and material at his disposal from the fall of 1945, he would be unable to defend South Korea against attack. In Washington politicians began to wonder if it was worth defending at all, and the questioning led to an attitude readily dispensed at middle levels in the State Department that Korea was not part of the American sphere of influence. The talk of moving Americans out altogether grew stronger. The pressures on General Hodge to speed up the formation of the defense force also grew, and by the end of 1947 the South Korean paramilitary organization had grown to about twenty thousand men. Washington asked Tokyo about building up a South Korean army, Tokyo asked General Hodge, and he said it could be done in a year or so if the wherewithal was made available. That would mean an army of one hundred thousand men. It would be better at two hundred thousand, but General Hodge was a realist, if sometimes misinformed. (He accepted, for instance, the view that major defections from the North Korean Army to South Korea could be expected. It turned out just the opposite in the months before the North Korean invasion.) When the Americans pulled out, which was now in the foreseeable future, he wanted to leave an army of one hundred thousand with small arms for another one hundred thousand.

The idea was rejected by General MacArthur, who took the woolly (and perhaps personally politically inspired) view that "unilateral action by the United States at this time would be inconsistent with the proposal submitted to the United Nations. . . ." MacArthur's political advisers obviously were not in touch with the course of events that had been shaping in North Korea since before the end of

World War II. Personally, MacArthur was already being talked up for the Republican presidential nomination in 1948.

During the Japanese occupation of Korea, many Korean patriots fled the country to escape what they regarded as tyranny. Until 1937 some of these Koreans made their way to China, and from there some, such as Dr. Rhee, came to the West. After the Japanese began invading East China, that avenue of escape was closed, and more Koreans escaped into Siberia and North China. Some became bandits. Many allied themselves with the Chinese Communists and joined the Chinese Communist armies. One of these was a youth named Kim Sung-chu. He joined the Chinese Communists in Manchuria and became a guerrilla leader. Later he joined the Soviet Army and rose to the rank of captain. Another was Choe Yong-gun. He fled to China in 1925 and attended the Whampoa Military School, which was the Chinese Republic's West Point. When Chiang Kai-shek and the Chinese Communists broke, Choe took the Long March with the Communists and ended up in Yenan, where he was trained at the Yenan Military School for service with the Communists. He became a Party member and served with the Eighth Route Army.

Mao Tse-tung and the other leaders of the Chinese Communists planned carefully for the future during those war years, when most Americans did not even know of the existence of a place called

Yenan. In 1939 the Chinese Communist leaders encouraged the establishment of the Korean Volunteer Army (KVA), whose ultimate purpose would be the establishment of a united and independent Korea. They armed this force, and Kim Sung-chu joined it in 1941. Under a general named Kim Muchong the Korean Volunteer Army fought alongside the Chinese Communists during war against Japan. At the Japanese capitulation, the Korean Volunteer Army was twenty thousand strong. General Kim marched them to Korea, but they were stopped at the border by the Soviet occupation troops. General Semyon K. Chistyakov, chief of the Soviet occupation of North Korea, shared all the fears about the reliability of the North Koreans that General Hodge had about the South Koreans. The Soviets wanted a North Korean government that would follow Soviet policy, not an independent government established by a Korean army of heroes. So the KVA was disarmed. But Chistyakov (who had far more authority in North Korea than General Hodge had in South Korea) made a very intelligent deal with General Kim. He gave back the arms in return for Kim's promise that the KVA would go back to Manchuria and fight with the Chinese Communists for victory over the Nationalists. When that was done, the KVA could come back to Korea.

Meanwhile, General Chistyakov set about creating a military and political force in North Korea that could take power. That young Soviet Army captain, Kim Sung-chu, came to Pyongyang with the occupation forces. He changed his name to Kim Il-sung (the name of a dead Korean resistance hero) and was quickly elevated by the Soviets to chief of the state they established in the Communist pattern. The Soviet intent was made very clear with the establishment of Pyongyang Military Academy in the fall of 1945. At first the fiction was broadcast that this institution was to train a police force, but inside Korea everyone knew better. Pyongyang was training a cadre of officers for the North Korean Army. After the Chinese Nationalists were scourged off the mainland, the KVA did return to Korea and was integrated into the growing North Korean Army.

In the South, General Hodge had recommended that the establishment of a South Korean army be done in secrecy to prevent the North Koreans from becoming restless. General MacArthur still snorted at the concept of a South Korean army but did authorize the buildup of the police force to fifty thousand men. Meanwhile, events took their course in South Korea. Syngman Rhee was elected President of the Republic of South Korea. He declared that a fifty-thousand-man force was totally inadequate to oppose what he knew to be the growing North Korean Army. At least, he said, if the United States was going to move out of South Korea, it must leave him a military advisory group. This was done. Under the tutelage of this group Rhee forged an army, and by March 1949 it was an army of more than one hundred thousand men, but it was woefully trained and woefully equipped. Most of the men had been recruited in a five-month period. By June the Americans had convinced themselves (officially, at least) that the South Korean defense capability was better than that of the North Koreans. How the officials of the Department of the Army came to that conclusion is a mystery. It could not have been more inaccurate. But it convinced the U.S. Congress and the State Department and it also convinced Dr. Rhee, who began flexing his polemical muscles and talking about invading North Korea. (This, of course was just the sort of ammunition the North Koreans needed to get moving.)

What is evident is that the Americans did not have any of the facts about what was occurring in North Korea. The truth was that by the spring of 1949 the Soviets had established in secrecy a North Korean army that was the second most powerful in Asia, more powerful than the American forces, more powerful than the Chinese Communist armies, second only to the Soviet armies in Siberia. Thus, from the beginning, there was no question about the intent of the Soviets; they wanted a unified Korea under the North Korean Communist government, and after he had considered the growing weakness of American policy, Soviet dictator Stalin believed he could get it by unleashing the North Korean Army. From early 1949, when a whole new group of Soviet military advisers arrived in Pyongyang to prepare the North Korean Army for an offensive war, the die was cast. After that it was just a question of timing.

From the outset, the establishment of the South Korean military force showed the disarray of the American military establishment in the late 1940s. Congress insisted that the military be reduced to a peacetime footing. The congressional leaders slashed military expenses to the point where weapons research was cut drastically and production of new weapons was virtually interdicted. The Army had no choice but to arm the South Koreans with cast-off World War II equipment—which would have been quite proper had not the Soviets been arming the North Koreans with the most modern weapons in their arsenal. By mid-1949 the United States had established a military bureaucracy in Korea, known as the American Mission in Korea, of about five hundred officers and men. The purpose was to develop and train a South Korean force capable of self-defense. But General MacArthur, whose influence was enormous although his authority over Korea was purely logistic, said then that he felt that the South Korean force should be capable of making only a token defense against an invasion from the north. The South Koreans wanted tanks, but Colonel William H. Sterling Wright of the advisory staff advised that the roads were too poor to support tanks. Meanwhile, the Soviets were supplying the North Koreans with modern T-34 tanks. The South Koreans did not get tanks and did not know how to fight against tanks, and when the tanks came down on them in the summer of 1950, they were terrified by them.

This disarray of the American military establishment was a part of the general confusion of the United States in the last years of the 1940s. Based on a complete misreading of the internal situation in China at the end of World War II President Truman had led the United States down precisely the wrong road. General Albert C. Wedemeyer and other sincere military officers argued that the Nationalist government of Chiang Kai-shek could be shored up and that Chiang could then win the civil war. So did many civil advisors, particularly businessmen, sons of businessmen, missionaries and their children, and those who had long been associated with China. For the Republic was such a political and social improvement over the Empire and the warlordism that had ruled China almost completely until 1925 that they were blinded by the past. Their views were mutually self-supporting and backed up by a large segment of the American press, led by Henry Luce's Time, Inc., publications. As the son of a missionary, Luce had a soft spot in his heart for China; he also remembered many truths from his school days that were no longer true.

One comparison suffices to differentiate between Nationalists and Communists: The ricksha was a Chinese institution, rickshas and palanquins had existed for thousands of years. The Nationalists accepted this form of inhuman drudgery in which a man is turned into an ox. The Communists rejected it. All a reader need ask himself is which idea is better? Millions of Chinese in all parts of the land began to believe their lives would be easier under the Communists than under the Nationalists. One can overstate the importance of popular support in a civil war of the sort that existed between the two Chinese factions. But in a negative sense, the communists had all the better of it. The villagers would hide them and claim ignorance of any of their activities. For the Nationalists in their dealings in the countryside it was too often as if they were foreigners in a strange land. That was the real truth of the revolution, but it was one that was more discernible at the village level than in the cities. Since virtually none of the American advisers in favor in Washington spoke the Chinese languages, it was not easy for them to get a living view of events and of the people as they changed. The China that existed in 1946 was not the China of even August 1945, certainly not the China of December 7, 1941. American failure to recognize the change set up the American disaster. The Communists in the Northwest moved into the Northeast. Gingerly, the Soviets let the Communists have the abandoned Japanese arms, partly to mask and make palatable the fact that the USSR was systematically raping the industrial might of Manchuria. The Soviets also did their best to bring Red China within their fold. A number of Chinese Communists had gone to the Soviet Union at various stages of the Chinese revolution. Among them was Li Ming-jen, who at one time rivaled Mao

Tse-tung in his ambitions for power and who chose the Moscow road to achieve it. In the USSR he married a Soviet citizen and became Sovietized. For political reasons he changed his name to Li Li-san. At the end of World War II one of the prices of Soviet assistance to Mao's people was to accept Li Li-san as the political commissar of the Manchurian armies armed with the Japanese weapons. Mao accepted this but insisted that one of his generals, Chu Teh, be commander in chief of the armies and that another Yenan general, Lin Piao, be superior to Li in Manchuria. Li's influence was moderated and never rose to the level expected by Moscow. So the independence of Mao's Red China from the USSR was established immediately. That is why General Chistyakov was so leery of the Korean Volunteer Army that presented itself to him at Pyongyang in the fall of 1945 and sent the soldiers back into Manchuria. The USSR wanted no Mao-type Communists in North Korea.

The Japanese surrender, then, made of the Chinese Communists a military power. Chiang's generals were dealing with the Communists, and several of them went over to the Communist side, taking their entire armies. That action certainly indicates the political conditions and state of loyalties in China at the time. Chiang had never been able to unify and control warlord China, and this was a major factor in his undoing in the end. Had President Franklin Roosevelt lived, his political prescience might have enabled him to disengage from what was obviously a dead cause. President Truman, gifted with no feeling for foreign affairs, simply accepted a moribund China policy and carried it out. So insensitive was he to the realities of the China conflict that when the Taiwan government offered three divisions of troops to the U.N. force in Korea, President Truman was inclined to accept. Fortunately, Secretary of State Acheson pointed out to him that an action to bring Nationalist China into the Korean War would be a bludgeon that might force Peking to enter, too. "Might" was a weak word. American political and even military leaders have always had a bad habit of talking too much, and also of talking as if only their American constituency was listening. In the constant flow of bombast of American military and political leaders Peking was under no illusions about the enmity of the U.S. government or the constant threat that the U.S. posed to mainland China. If those seem to be strong words, they would be illustrated within a matter of months by Peking's strong action. In the opening days of the Korea conflict there was virtually no one left in the U.S. government to speak up against the total misreading of events in Asia; all those who opposed the shortsighted policies of the Truman administration had either been driven out or silenced by charges or hints that they were "soft on communism." The result was a growing disaster for American interests in Asia.

As far as Korea was concerned, the military and foreign-policy experts never seemed to be able to make up their minds which way to jump. General MacArthur sometimes said Korea was not a part of the American sphere of influence. At other times he said he would defend Korea as if it were California. The same sort of vacillation was endemic in the U.S. Department of State; it came to a head in that fatal speech of January 1950 by Secretary of State Acheson to the National Press Club of Washington, announcing that Korea would not be defended by the United States if it were attacked. There was the green light that Stalin wanted. Time and events were moving toward the invasion.

The vacillations of the military were more understandable than those of the politicians, for the military always is constrained to plan its defenses based on the will of Congress and the Administration. That's where the money comes from. In the late 1940s the politicians were in complete confusion as to American interests and the real threats. President Truman had adopted a policy of toughness against Soviet incursions, and he and his advisers mixed these up with anticolonialism and local left-wing (even called communist) rebellions around the world. However the truth of what was happening shows much better in hindsight than it did in the late 1940s, particularly in Washington of those days. Examine: The United States was frightened of Marshal Tito's communism in Yugoslavia, but it proved to be the first major rebellion against Moscow.

The United States devoted billions of dollars to

defeating communism in Greece; the ELAS rebellion collapsed but not because of American money; the billions were largely misspent by a venal Greek government. The tiny Communist rebellion collapsed of its own weight when Marshal Tito broke with Moscow. The United States was frightened by the Communist movement in Indonesia; it never developed into an alliance with Moscow. The United States, having had a strong hand in the beginnings of the Annamite revolution in Indo-China, chose to ignore rebel leader Ho Chi-minh at the end of the war and to support the French attempts to reinstate themselves as the colonial masters of Indo-China. Everywhere President Trumen misread the tide of freedom from outside influence that had been set flowing by Roosevelt and Churchill when they issued the Atlantic Charter. The United States chose the wrong horse in China, thus throwing the Chinese mainland into a temporary and uncomfortable alliance with the USSR, an alliance that was sustained only because of the intransigent enmity of the American government toward China. In the spring of 1950, the Chinese Nationalists on Taiwan were alternately threatening and whining, threatening to invade the China coast and whining that they were about to be invaded. American policy was hitched to a very dead horse and thus was immobile. The year 1950 was crucial. The Americans were so nervous and had their fleet so steadily poised around Taiwan that anything could have happened. The violent enmity of the American government toward the Peking government was a major factor in Peking's nervousness when the war in Korea did not turn out to be a nine-day wonder.

The American military was suffering from two sorts of malaise. The first was endemic in a military society: The war ended with two great military powers extant, the United States and the Soviet Union. Each set about building its own sphere of influence, which brought immediate conflict, as in Manchuria and Germany. The Soviets shipped the industrial plants of both areas in wholesale lots to the Soviet Union. And as for the China question, because of the virtual silencing of all the State Department's China experts in the growing anti-Communist hysteria that could not differentiate between philosophy and Soviet power, President Truman never realized that the Soviets were more worried about Red China than he was, because they already knew they could not control it. The American military foresaw only a major war against the USSR, and that is how their plans and programming were cast. Then as now the USSR and its satellite states had more military manpower and conventional weaponry than the United States and its allies. Then as now the United States depended on atomic weapons for balance. The United States pleased itself by declaring a reliance on the United Nations to defend world peace, but, at the same time it was already working out an intricate system of interlocking military alliances around the Soviet borders.

While all this was being done, American capability against nonatomic war was cut to the bone. The U.S. Army was reduced to less than six hundred thousand men, and more reductions were planned in the spring of 1950. There was not a single mobile division equipped to fight on short notice. Training in the zone of the interior (the conterminous 48 states) was so poor (eight weeks of basic training) that soldiers sent overseas had to have advanced training before they could be assigned to units. Virtually all the Army's war equipment was obsolete, and no new weapons were being produced. In 1948, for example, the Defense Department estimated that it would need $750 million for ammunition and for research and development. The military experts of the President's Bureau of the Budget cut the sum down to $275 million. Not to be outdone, the congressional military experts cut the appropriation to a final $245,532,000. It is too bad that some of those experts were not on hand north of Taegu in early September 1950 when the American troops ran out of ammunition in the face of the North Korean Naktong offensive.

Reading the foregoing chapters on the beginnings of the Korea war, one wonders why the U.S.army had so few tanks available in the first six weeks of the fighting. The Soviet T-34 tank made all the difference in the world in the speed of the North Korean advance. The South Koreans and the Americans in the beginning had absolutely no way of stopping them effectively.

In 1950 the United States had about thirty-five hundred light tanks available in the zone of interior, but only nine hundred were serviceable. The others were out of service because of lack of parts, and the parts were not being produced because there was no money to pay for them.

All this came about because of the steady decline in appropriations for the military after 1947. Following the death of Secretary of Defense James V. Forrestal in 1949, President Truman made the mistake of appointing a political crony, Louis A. Johnson, as his successor, and Johnson proved to be a total disaster as he presided happily over the dismemberment of the American military establishment. Fate might have sent Secretary Johnson on an inspection tour just in time to watch the T-34 tanks steam through Task Force Smith down by Ch'onan. But this never happened. Secretary Johnson did not believe in Korea, anyhow; on the night of June 25 he delayed the proceedings of the Truman conference for an hour while he brought up the Taiwan defense question again.

Given the desperate state of affairs in Korea and Japan that day and the complete turnabout in American military planning that had to be made, it is remarkable that any other subject than Korea could have been mentioned. On that night of June 25, at Blair House in Washington, President Truman presided over a meeting of his key defense advisers and officials. Out of that meeting, in spite of Secretary Johnson's preliminary attempts at obfuscation, came a decision that would have been regarded as impossible a few hours earlier: Korea was to be defended. The United States was not prepared, the defense was going to take an almost superhuman effort, but it was to be done. President Truman showed a strength and an appreciation of the military-political situation that had been missing earlier. Perhaps it was because for once he had a clear-cut issue. Even so, when General Omar Bradley, the Army chief of staff, summed up the results of the meeting, he referred to drawing the line against "Communist" aggression, not Soviet aggression. Washington still had not learned the lesson of Yugoslavia and the rest. Luckily in this case Soviet aggression and Communist aggression were one and the same; the North Korean government was probably just then the purest of the Soviet satellites.

The turnabout at the White House then had to be translated into fact, and that meant providing General MacArthur with the wherewithal to fight. By July 30 the U.S. Army had shipped to MacArthur every man and officer eligible for overseas assignment save a handful essential to other commands. The manpower barrel was dry, and MacArthur hadn't gotten half of what he needed just to hold the Pusan Perimeter together, to say nothing of launching an offensive. All the old evils now came to haunt the Army. The cutback from three to two battalions per regiment had produced regiments that could not do their job. But where were those third battalions to be found, and once found, how could they be integrated quickly enough into the regiments to make them useful fighting units? The answer, of course, was that new units could not be brought to old regiments in time to make much difference at Pusan, whole battalions had to be stripped from regiments and sent over, and even these could not be expected to perform with the sort of military efficiency that was needed in a combat regiments. Obviously one of the worst errors ever made in the American military establishment had been the stripdown of all regiments. Better even that the Congressmen should have cut their expense accounts and the foreign junkets on which they never seemed to learn anything about foreign and military affairs.

The generals knew what had to be done. They stripped the battalions from the general reserve, knowing that if another brushfire war developed within the next year they would be completely unable to respond.

In its way, Congress admitted its errors by granting President Truman's request that it remove all statutory personnel ceilings and by expanding the budgetary requests for appropriations to rebuild the military establishment. Suddenly all those self-proclaimed military experts in Congress became very, very quiet. That is one of the virtues of the American political system; the voters' memory is short, but it exists, and under the sort of duress that had developed that summer of 1950 Senators and

Representatives could be forced to remember this political truth in November.

There was another truth that demanded equal attention and got it because of the early events of the Korea war. This was the reevaluation of Army policy toward black Americans, and the change that came in the wake of the disgraceful failure of the 24th Infantry Regiment as a fighting unit.

At the end of World War II the leaders of the Army were strongly set against integration of the armed forces on a general basis. They simply did not trust blacks, and they based their beliefs on what they perceived as the generally low performance record of black units in all branches of the service in World War II. That, of course, was the problem. The military prejudice was self-sustaining: they put the blacks into no-win situations and then pointed at their performance to justify continued segregation. Many of the old-line military men would have been happiest to have no blacks at all in the services, except possibly for the naval officers who prized their black mess servants. Consequently in all services a black unit had two strikes against it before the table of organization ever got off the drawing board. Take the case of the 555th Parachute Infantry Battalion. In response to demands for equal opportunity for blacks in the armed forces, the battalion was formed at Camp Mackall, North Carolina, in November 1944. From the beginning it was impossible for this unit to succeed in the Army pattern. There were not enough black officers to man the battalion. There were only a handful of black paratroopers, and they were brought in reluctantly as the result of political pressures. Once the unit was established, there were new difficulties in recruiting blacks for paratroop duty. Better the evil you knew than the evil you didn't know. And yes, face it, the American educational and social system had for so long pressed blacks down that there were enormous difficulties finding men who could meet the educational requirements. When a battalion finally was hammered together, the Army used them to fight forest fires in the Pacific Northwest. Extinguishing a fire started by a Japanese fire balloon was the closest the 555th ever got to action against the enemy.

Some Army generals, such as General Lawton J. Collins, believed in integration of military units. Collins, for example, favored a system in which two blacks would be assigned to each squad of an Army regiment. If this seems to be an arbitrary manner of integration, still it had some practical virtue. It could not be denied that white soldiers generally did not trust blacks, and no amount of argument by civil-rights advocates was going to change that. Changes in attitude could come only from experience. The Collins plan would have brought that experience in short order. Unfortunately, in the cutbacks of manpower of the middle 1940s Army leaders were not willing to make that sort of commitment, so serious was their fear of black nonperformance. In a way they could not be blamed too much; the military establishment exists to perform without notice, and is not readily amenable to social experiment that might endanger its ability to act. That was the effective argument of the opponents to integration, and they had their way.

The Korean War changed all that. It brought danger and opportunity. The opportunity was for blacks to enter the service in increasing numbers. Black enlistment increased from 8 percent of the total in the spring of 1950 to 25 percent in the summer. The trouble with that increase was that the Army policy of keeping blacks in black units made those units overstrength and topheavy. And in August 1950 the Army's inspector general, Major General Lewis A. Craig, declared that the Army's social policy was unrealistic. Mixing blacks and whites in units would not be disastrous, he said; young Americans did not share the prejudices of their fathers.

Just at this time the Army became aware of the serious failure of the 24th Infantry to perform. That failure and all the difficulties it caused were proof positive of the failure of the Army's "separate but equal" policy. Meanwhile, the Tokyo command had begun solving the problem on a different level. As black soldiers came into the theater, they were assigned to various units on a basis of need, not race. The need was so desperate that the old rules were off. In August, for example, the first replacements sent to the U.S. 9th Infantry in Korea included two black officers and eighty-nine black

enlisted men. They were assigned to the previously
all-white 1st and 2nd battalions. The 3rd Battalion
was an all-black unit, but so great was the need that
before the end of summer these divisions had begun
to break down in the field, and replacements were
assigned without consideration for race. The black
soldiers assigned to the 9th Infantry performed just
as well as the whites; in fact, Army historian S.L.A.
Marshall later described one of the 1st Battalion's
units, B Company, as "one of the bravest." At the
time that company was mixed, with a black officer
in command.

The Korean War demonstrated that where blacks
were truly integrated into fighting units, they did
fine. Where black units were sent in to fight as black
units, the results were unpredictable. The performance of the 24th Infantry was the galling total failure that was needed.

Matters were not helped by two investigations of
the problems of the 24th Infantry by black leaders.
After the failures on the Pusan Perimeter, thirty-six
black soldiers were court-martialed and convicted
of extremely serious violations of the Articles of
War, particularly of misbehavior in the face of the
enemy. Families, friends, acquaintances, and the
whole black community became aroused by these
convictions. Thurgood Marshall, an attorney for
the National Association for the Advancement of
Colored People, was sent to Japan to make an
investigation. He was given carte blanche by General MacArthur. He traveled in Japan and Korea

and interviewed many people. He then concluded that military justice was unfair to the blacks and that the Army's segregation policy was responsible for it. "The men were tried in an atmosphere making justice impossible," Marshall reported, and he insisted that the NAACP had evidence that would clear most of them. However, the record indicates that the misbehavior in the face of the enemy among these troops of the 24th Infantry was far more general than the Army's selective charges would indicate. Had a white regiment performed in this fashion there would undoubtedly have been a far greater scandal in the Army and far more men would have been punished. If there is one absolute requirement of fighting units, it is that they fight and not run away, and race has nothing to do with that.

Marshall's statements may have pleased the black community, but they were the sort of ammunition that strengthened the position of segregationists. The implication was clear that the black community was willing to sacrifice the national weal to protect blacks even when they were wrong. That suspicion was given even more credence by the charges of Walter White, another black publicist, that the reports of the 24th Infantry performance were untrue and represented a conspiracy by the whites to force the blacks back into labor battalions. His charges were not only untrue, but also their widespread acceptance by many black leaders suggested an indifference to the task of really informing themselves of the facts. The Army was fair enough in giving honor to blacks in this unit who fought as they were supposed to do. The first Congressional Medal of Honor winner in the war was PFC William Thompson of the 24th Infantry's M Company. Mr. White did not talk about that. The facts in the case of the 24th Infantry were that the division commander could not trust the 24th Infantry to carry out its assigned missions, and no Army general is going to put up with any sort of unit that will not fight if it can be avoided. The performance of the 24th Infantry blackened the reputation of the entire 25th Division. At one point in the Battle of the Pusan Perimeter General Walker observed that he had no confidence in the 25th Division as a fighting unit. Army social policy was not easy to change in the midst of a campaign. Even after the failure of the 24th Infantry, and in spite of the request of the division's commander that it be taken out of action and disbanded, the course of events demanded that it be retained as a unit. The change—from segregation to integration—was to be accomplished by rotation and replacement of troops. And that is how it was done effectively in the line.

The most serious problem to be exposed by the events of the summer of 1950 was the inability of the United States to respond swiftly and powerfully to an attack on American interests. The course of the campaign just described is the proof of it. And what changes did this bring about, and when? The end of the Korean War left the United States emotionally exhausted for reasons that the American people did not quite understand. The politicians had again erred mightily in their assessment of the military problems of the post-World War II world. But that is another part of the Korean story, which will be dealt with in future volumes. It will suffice at this point to say that the events of June 1950 brought the U.S. armed forces to the realization that they must not again be caught without the ability to put a striking force into the field. And that was a major change of attitude.

Chapter Notes

1

SURPRISE ATTACK

This chapter depended on my own observations in Korea in the past, the official Korean history of the war, and Appleman. The figures about the military forces of North and South Korea are from Appleman and Schnabel. The air force figures are from Jackson. The account of the Acheson speech to the National Press club is from memory and the implication that the U.S. had definitely written off Korea, now sometimes denied in official Washington, is from my own conversations with John Davies and others, beginning in 1947. The story of the invasion is from Appleman, the official South Korean history, and from Kim Il Sung's *Yesterday Today*. The story of Captain Darrigo is from Appleman.

2
THE AMERICAN CONFUSION

The story of the air attacks is from Jackson. The story of the American air reaction is from Jackson and from conversation with General Partridge. The material about the Soviet reaction is from Schnabel, the Truman biography, and from my own conversations with the late Imri Kelen, then television director of the United Nations. The story of the North Korean battle progress is from the South Korean official history and from Appleman.

3
BATTLE FOR SURVIVAL

Again the battle material is from Appleman and the South Korean official history of the war. The material about the killing of South Korean civilians is from Riley and Schramm. The material about General Dean's 24th Division is from General Dean's memoirs, and the anecdotes are from Appleman. The observations about the "American disease" are from my own experience.

4
DELAYING ACTION

The tale of the defense of Chonan is from Appleman and from Dean. The discussion of naval matters is from Cagle and Manson. The notes about the failure of certain American weapons, particularly the small bazooka, are from my own research for *Airborne,* the story of American paratroops and glider troops. The story of the disastrous cutback of American military forces is from Appleman and Goulden and my own observations back to the days in Korea in the spring of 1946 when my friend the late Senator Ed C. Johnson of Colorado was leading the fight in the Senate, demanding that "American boys be brought home." Much of the battle material is from Appleman, some is from the South Korean official war history.

5
BOLSTERING THE DEFENSE

The story of the Collins and Vandenberg visit is from MacArthur and Schnabel, and Appleman. The material about the 24th Infantry is from Appleman and from MacGregor's study of the integration of the armed forces. The material about the air buildup is from Futrell. The story of General Dean's operations is from his memoirs.

6
THE BATTLE FOR TAEJON

Appleman and Dean are the major sources for the story of the attempt to defend Taejon. I also used the official South Korean war history here. The story of General Dean's betrayal by South Korean civilians is from his own story and from Appleman.

7
THE ROAD TO DEFEAT

The figures and estimates about the military situation are from Schnabel, MacArthur, and Appleman. The story of the Juneau raid is from Cagle and Manson. The battle tales are largely from Appleman, whose account is based on the army unit records and interviews.

8
"THERE WILL BE NO MORE RETREATING . . ."

General Walker is really the unsung hero of the Korean war. Since General MacArthur did not like him, he never got the acclaim he deserved during life, and after his untimely death in 1951 the Korea war switched status in the American public mind from holy crusade to an unpopular involvement, so there were very few heroes celebrated. It was not nearly so bad as Vietnam, but Walker was definitely given short shrift. Had he not moved inferior forces around the South Korean chessboard with the skill of a master in July and August 1950, there would never have been any Chinese involvement in the war, because Kim Il Sung's troops would have pressed on successfully to Pusan by September 1.

The battle tales are from Appleman and the official South Korean war history. "The Bugout war" is from Goulden and my own knowledge. General Walker's statement about retreating is from Appleman. The material about the marines is from Montross and Canzona.

9
BACK TO THE NAKTONG

The story of the battle is from the official South Korean history of the war and from Appleman. The higher military and political events are from Goulden, MacArthur, and Schhnabel.

10
PUSAN PERIMETER

Walker's estimates of the failings of his various units are from Appleman. The story of the marines is from Montross and Canzona's official marine history.

11
COUNTERATTACK

The story of the counterattack along the Pusan perimeter is from the South Korean war history, Appleman, and the marine history.

12
THE NAKTONG BULGE

The story of the marines is from Montross and Canzona. The story of the army troops is from Appleman.

13
THREAT IN THE EAST

The South Korean official history of the war is the basic source for the material about the battle on the east side of the peninsula, plus Appleman to put it in perspective.

14
TAEGU

MacArthur and Appleman are the basic sources here.

15
SUMMER OFFENSIVE

The South Korean official war history and Appleman were vital to this chapter. I also consulted Goulden, and Futrell.

16
DOWN THE CENTER

The South Korean official history and Appleman were basic sources. The story of Captain West's Company G is from Gugeler's study of various sorts of ground forces' actions during the war.

17
THE GREATEST THREAT

The South Korean war history was valuable for the discussion of the underwater bridges and the North

Korean forces. Again the discussion of the failures of the black 24th Infantry come from the MacGregor study of integration in the armed forces.

18
BACK TO OBONG-NI

For information about the North Korean operations the South Korean history was valuable. Battle studies are from Appleman and the marine history.

19
THE ULTIMATE EFFORT

The South Korean official history was extremely important to this chapter and so was Appleman. The story of A Battery is from the Gugeler military studies. The report on the continuing troubles of the 24th Infantry comes from Appleman and MacGregor.

20
THE PERIMETER HELD

The political discussion is my own, based on my work of the period as a Far Eastern correspondent and newspaper editor. The history is from the South Korean official war history, and from my own experience as correspondent in Korea and my acquaintance with Dr. Syngman Rhee. The figures and military material are from Schnabel, Carpenter, and the Secretary of the Army reports of the time.

Bibliography

Appleman, Roy E. *South to the Naktong, North to the Yalu*. Washington, D.C.: Office of the Chief of Military History, 1961.

Cagle, Malcolm W., and Manson, Frank A. *The Sea War in Korea*. New York: Arno Press, 1980.

Carpenter, W. M. *The Korean War: A Strategic Perspective Thirty Years Later*. Comparative Strategy. New York: Crane Russack, 1980.

Dean, William F., as told to William L. Worden. *General Dean's Story*. New York: Viking Press, 1954.

Editors, *Army Times. American Heroes of Asian Wars*. New York: Dodd Mead & Company, 1968.

Field, James A., Jr. *History of United States Naval Operations, Korea*. Washington, D.C.: U.S. Navy, 1962.

Futrell, Robert Frank. *The U.S. Air Force in Korea.* Washington, D.C.: Office of Air Force History, 1981.

Goulden, Joseph. *Korea: The Untold History of the War.* New York: Times Books, 1982.

Gugeler, Russell. *Combat Actions in Korea.* Washington, D.C.: Combat Forces Press, 1954.

Jackson, Robert. *Air War over Korea.* New York: Charles Scribner's Sons, 1973.

Kim, Chum-kon. *The Korean War.* Seoul: Kwangmyong Publishing Company, 1973.

MacArthur, Douglas. Reminiscences. New York: McGraw Hill, 1964.

MacGregor, Morris J., Jr. *Integration of the Armed Forces, 1940-65.* Washington, D.C.: U.S. Army, 1981.

Montross, Lynn, and Canzona, Nicholas A. *U.S. Marine Operations in Korea, 1950-53,* Vol. 1: *The Pusan Perimeter.* Washington, D.C.: Historical Branch, G-3, Headquarters, U.S. Marine Corps, 1954.

Paige, Glenn D. *The Korean Decision.* New York: The Free Press, 1968.

Ridgway, M. C. *The Korean War.* Garden City, N.Y.: Doubleday, 1967.

Riley, John W., and Schramm, Wilbur. *The Reds Take a City.* New Brunswick, N.J.: Rutgers University Press, 1951.

Schnabel, James F. *U.S. Army in the Korean War, Policy and Direction: The First Year.* Washington, D.C.: Office of the Chief of Military History, United States Army, 1972.

Sung, Kim-il, preface to *Yesterday, Today: U.S. Imperialism, Mastermind of Aggression in Korea*. Pyongyang: Korean People's Army Publishing House, 1977.

Index

OTHER MILITARY BOOKS FROM STEIN AND DAY